WHY
MEN
CONFESS

CHRISTIAN HERITAGE COLLEGE

CHRISTIAN
HERITAGE
COLLEGE
LIBRARY

WHY

MEN

CONFESS

By
O. John Rogge, 1903-

A DA CAPO PAPERBACK

Library of Congress Cataloging in Publication Data

Rogge, Oetje John, 1903-
  Why men confess.

  (A Da Capo Press paperback)
  Reprint of the ed. published by Nelson, New York.
  Includes bibliographical references and index.
  1. Confession—Psychology. I. Title.
  [BF634.R6 1975]   345.06'6   74-22067
  ISBN 0-306-80006-3

First Paperback Printing 1975
ISBN 0-306-80006-3

This Da Capo Press edition of
Why Men Confess
is an unabridged republication of the first edition published in 1959.
It is reprinted by special arrangement with Thomas Nelson, Inc.

Published by Da Capo Press, Inc.
A Subsidiary of Plenum Publishing Corporation
227 West 17th Street
New York, New York 10011

Manufactured in the United States of America

TO

The New York Public Library

Fifth Avenue and Forty-second Street

Author's Note

I AM INDEBTED for aid in research to my wife, Mrs. Wanda Johnston Rogge; my son, Hermann Rogge III; my daughter-in-law, Mrs. John Stern Rogge; and my law associate, Mrs. Alma Suzin Flesch; and for aid in the preparation of the manuscript to my secretary, Miss Pauline Chakonas.

O.J.R.

Contents

Introductory

1   *Brainwashing*

IN THE EARLY CENTURIES of this era many individuals in group meetings of believers made confessions of faith in a holy triune God, Father, Son and Holy Ghost, the forgiveness of sins and life everlasting. In the twentieth century many individuals in like fashion made confessions of faith in another triumvirate, Marx, Engels and Lenin, a class struggle and the victory of communism. In the early centuries of this era many individuals in group meetings of believers publicly confessed their sins. In the twentieth century many individuals in similar fashion publicly confessed their errors and deviations. In the Middle Ages many confessed to clerical inquisitors their guilt of heresies. In the 1930s and the following decades many confessed to communist inquisitors their guilt of a multitude of offenses.

Indeed the confessions to communist inquisitors reached such a point during the Korean war that afterward one of our rear admirals, Dan V. Gallery, asked, "What can we do about the communists' hellish brainwashing technique for torturing 'confessions' out of prisoners of war?" His answer was an executive order, to be publicized to the world, which would tell our men to say and sign anything. "Give the Reds anything they want for propaganda purposes and defy them to use it!"

But his solution would not have proven useful to the members of our armed forces whom the communists induced to renounce their country. There were twenty-three such, of whom eleven later changed their minds again and returned home. However, one of the eleven, Richard R. Tennyson, at a news interview in Hong Kong shortly after crossing the Chinese border, held to his belief in the germ warfare charges of the communists. At no time during the interview did he speak bitterly of his former enemies.

Nor would Admiral Gallery's solution have been of much help to such Americans as Malcolm Bersohn, Mrs. Adele Austin Rickett and her husband Walter A. Rickett, who after their release by the Chinese communists not only adhered to their confessions of spying but one of whom, Mrs. Rickett, also denied that she was a victim of brainwashing. Bersohn was a Harvard graduate and had been a student at the Peiping Union Medical College. Mrs. Rickett was a Phi Beta Kappa graduate of the University of North Carolina and had been an ensign in the Waves. Her husband had been a United States Marine Corps language officer. She and her husband had gone to China in 1948 on Fulbright fellowships, and had later lived by teaching. Although her husband was still in jail in China at the time of her release, the brainwashing tactics of the communists appeared to be so successful with Mrs. Rickett and Bersohn that they described themselves as former reactionaries who had learned morality as communist prisoners. They said they now wanted to be honest and help the people. When Mrs. Rickett was asked what sentence had been imposed upon her husband she replied: "I don't know. His crime is bigger than mine."

When her husband was released later in the year he likewise had nothing but kind words for his captors: "The Chinese government was lenient with me. They could have sentenced me to ten years but gave me only six and released me after four." The fact that he had been held for four years and two months without trial was apparently correct procedure to him. He brushed aside any comparison to individual rights under our system such as those of habeas corpus, jury trial, speedy trial, and confrontation by witnesses. He wished to return to

China in a few years to see her reconstruction and added: "I
hope I will return to China, not as a criminal but as a welcome
guest." He too believed the germ warfare charges of the communists: "I know that Chinese interrogation is very fair and
I am convinced the United States used bacteria warfare, and
the United States has never denied it."

Opposed to the view of Admiral Gallery was that of Gen.
Lemuel C. Shepherd, Jr., the commandant of the Marine
Corps. In considering the findings, opinion and recommenda-
tions of the Marine Court of Inquiry in the case of Col. Frank
H. Schwable, he concluded that the best policy was continued
adherence to the Geneva Convention, which provides that a
prisoner need furnish no information beyond name, rank,
serial number and date of birth. He observed, prefatory to
quoting from the testimony of Maj. Gen. William F. Dean:
"In general those seemed to have fared best who talked the
least although none could claim exact compliance with the
terms of the Geneva Convention." Gen. Dean testified that a
military regulation patterned after the Geneva Convention was
a practical one, but added that he himself had not been able
to live up to it.

Col. Schwable was one of half a hundred American airmen
who made confessions to their communist captors. He confessed to germ warfare. So too did his copilot, Maj. Roy H.
Bley, as well as thirty-eight Air Force fliers. The rest confessed
to such charges as espionage or crossing the Chinese border.
In Col. Schwable's case the Marine Court of Inquiry recommended against any disciplinary action. It found that the interrogation tactics of the Chinese communists inevitably led
to one of three things:

"a. The victim's will to resist is broken, and he responds as
the enemy desires.
b. The victim becomes insane.
c. The victim dies."

Although Gen. Shepherd concurred in the recommendation

that there be no disciplinary action, he took exception to some of the court's conclusions. He objected to its opinion that the inquisitional technique of the communists inevitably resulted in a broken will, insanity or death: "I seriously doubt that this extreme form of statement is fully justified. Rather, I believe a more restrained expression such as 'may result in' or 'would most often lead to' would have been more consistent both with the record and with the traditions of America's fighting men."

The secretary of the navy, Robert B. Anderson, agreed with Gen. Shepherd, and added a suggestion that the secretary of defense, Charles E. Wilson, give consideration to the appointment of a small committee of military, medical and judicial experts to study the problem and help us "develop a program of training and indoctrination which will contribute a maximum of benefit to the Armed Services and a maximum of understanding and appreciation to an enlightened and informed citizenry."

The Air Force set up a special board of five generals to study the cases of eighty-three of its repatriates. The special board sought the advice of experts in the fields of law and medicine, and of those who were familiar with the techniques of prisoner of war interrogations and with communist psychological warfare methods. One of those whom it consulted was Dr. Charles W. Mayo, United States alternate representative in the Political Committee of the United Nations General Assembly. Dr. Mayo has been of the view that brainwashing involved a perversion of the conditioned reflex technique which the Russian physiologist Pavlov developed in his experiments on dogs. Pavlov fed a dog and at the same time rang a bell. After a number of such feedings he rang a bell but gave the dog no food. The dog's saliva flowed all the same. The special board unanimously recommended that no action which would result in trial by court-martial be taken in the case of any of the eighty-three Air Force repatriates. The secretary of the Air Force, Harold E. Talbott, and its chief of staff, Gen. N. F.

Twining, concurred. The Air Force took the same stand with
reference to fourteen fliers who returned later. Few of us would
disagree with this result; but many of us would find it difficult
to accept Dr. Mayo's view, even in the limited context in
which he propounded it, that human beings can be conditioned
in the same way as Pavlov's dogs.

One may contrast the courses which the Marine Corps and
the Air Force followed with that which the Army has taken.
The Army has brought to trial before courts-martial fourteen
former prisoners of war who were subjected to brainwashing.
Eleven were convicted and three acquitted. A fifteenth was
formally charged but the charges were later dropped. Without bringing formal charges the Army has also denied prisoner
of war payments to yet others on the ground that they collaborated with the enemy.

Following Secretary Anderson's suggestion for the appointment of a small committee of experts to study the problem of
brainwashing Secretary Wilson in August 1954 appointed an
interservice committee of four generals, two from the Air
Force, one from the Army and one from the Marine Corps,
and four colonel alternates, to explore the subject and "recommend an approach for a comprehensive study of the problem,
delimiting its scope."

The interservice committee, according to press reports,
presented a split report, and in turn recommended the appointment of another committee. The Army and the Navy sided
against the Air Force, and maintained that members of our
armed forces who are taken prisoners by the communists must
give only the information required by the Geneva Convention.
The Air Force would permit them to sign false confessions
and even give some correct factual intelligence about their
own forces. Secretary Wilson said at a press conference in
March 1955 that he thought he would appoint a civilian committee to tackle the problem of brainwashed Americans. Two
months later he appointed a committee, but made up of retired
generals and admirals and Pentagon officials, to recommend

ways for preparing members of our armed forces to defend themselves against brainwashing, and to write a code of conduct for such of them as might be captured by an enemy.

After careful study this body in July 1955 suggested such a code, and presented it in an able report. The following month the president promulgated this code. In article five it urges the members of our armed forces to adhere to the terms of the Geneva Convention:

> "When questioned, should I become a prisoner of war, I am bound to give only name, rank, service number and date of birth. I will evade answering further questions to the utmost of my ability. I will make no oral or written statements disloyal to my country and its allies or harmful to their cause."

Secretary Wilson's committee felt that those prisoners of war who refused to engage in any inquisitorial tug of war with their captors came out best. Indeed they reported that an interrogator sometimes "showed contempt for the man who readily submitted to bullying. The prisoner who stood up to the bluster, threats and blows of an interrogator might be dismissed with a shrug and sent to quarters as mild as any—if any prison barracks in North Korea could be described as mild.

"All in all, the docile prisoner did not gain much by his docility—and sometimes he gained nothing. . . ."

Communist inquisitors questioned captives not only for military information but also about their home lives and educational backgrounds. They asked them to submit written biographies. Those who complied started on a losing path. "The author's mistake was in taking pen in hand."

The new code was attacked and defended. Senator Estes Kefauver of Tennessee indicated that it fell short of what should be expected of a "humane nation." He wondered how the code's principles "would serve the man exhausted by battle, hungry, cold, facing hostile interrogators and the prospect of more suffering and unknown dangers." He had his doubts "whether we as a nation are playing square with some of the boys." Dr. Albert Somit, associate professor of government at New York University and formerly with the Army psychological warfare division, called the code "unrealistic." A leading Catholic educator, the Very Rev. Francis J. Connell, dean of the School of Sacred Theology of the Catholic University of America, said it would give an enemy "an excuse for simply killing all captured Americans on the ground that they would be scheming to slay their captors." In support of the code Stephen S. Jackson, assistant general counsel of the Defense Department, made the point that those prisoners who talked least fared best.

Some attempts were made to prepare members of our armed forces for the experience of brainwashing by subjecting them to the rigors of an inquisitional interrogation as part of their training. For example, the Marine Corps had one group of Marines question another group captured in a war game. Those questioned were made to exercise to the point of near exhaustion. Their clothing was removed and they were placed in hot cages or pits that were too shallow for standing and too cramped for sitting. They were denied food, water and tobacco. This course too was debated.

The following year a psychiatrist, Dr. James Miller, chief of the Mental Health Research Institute at the University of Michigan, in an appearance before the convention of the American Psychological Association, recommended that the service men who had secret information should be given a cyanide capsule or other means of suicide in wartime to avoid their breaking under brainwashing if captured. According to him the new armed forces code was drawn up in the "T.N.T. age of brainwashing rather than the future possible atomic age." Dr. Miller's suggestion reminds one of Hermann Goering's suicide after the first Nuremberg trial and the Japanese kamikaze pilots during World War II.

Although the Chinese people coined a colorful description for the inquisitional technique of their communist rulers, the

Chinese communists did not invent this technique. Rather they borrowed it from the Russian communists. In the Moscow purge trials of 1936–38 all the defendants confessed. There were three such trials, one for each of the purge years, with sixteen, seventeen and twenty-one defendants respectively. The defendants included all the members of Lenin's Politburo who were alive and in Russia, except Stalin, and various other Russian communist leaders. Not only did all the defendants confess, but in the 1938 trial one of the defendants, Nikolai I. Bukharin, in his final plea also went on to explain that his and the other confessions in that and the other purge trials did not involve any such things as drugs or hypnotism. Nor did they involve the Dostoyevski mind or some feeling of a need for punishment. Moreover, if he had to be executed he would die a good Bolshevik. Nor did he want any help or consideration from any but the faithful. As far as he was concerned, he was kneeling before the party and the people:

"Repentance is often attributed to diverse and absolutely absurd things like Thibetan powders and the like. I must say of myself that in prison, where I was confined for over a year, I worked, studied, and retained my clarity of mind. . . .

"Hypnotism is suggested. But I conducted my own defence in Court from the legal standpoint too. . . .

"This repentance is often attributed to the Dostoyevsky mind, to the specific properties of the soul ('l'âme slave' it is called), and this can be said of types like Alyosha Karamazov, the heroes of the *Idiot* and other Dostoyevsky characters, who are prepared to stand up in the public square and cry: 'Beat me, Orthodox Christians, I am a villain!'

"But that is not the case here at all. . . .

". . . For three months I refused to say anything. Then I began to testify. Why? Because while in prison I made a revaluation of my entire past. For when you ask yourself: 'If you must die, what are you dying for?'—an absolutely black vacuity suddenly rises before you with startling vividness. There was nothing to die for, if one wanted to die unrepented. And, on the contrary, everything positive that glistens in the Soviet Union acquires new dimensions in a man's mind. This in the end disarmed me completely and led me to bend my knees before the Party and the country. . . . And, in addition, when the reverberations of the broad international struggle reach your ear, all this in its entirety does its work, and the result is the complete internal moral victory of the USSR over its kneeling opponents. . . . For in reality the whole country stand behind Stalin; he is the hope of the world; he is a creator. . . ."

". . . Counter-revolutionary banditry has now been smashed, we have been smashed, and we repent our frightful crimes.

"The point, of course, is not this repentance, or my personal repentance in particular. The Court can pass its verdict without it. The confession of the accused is not essential. The confession of the accused is a medieval principle of jurisprudence. But here we also have the internal demolition of the forces of counter-revolution. And one must be a Trotsky not to lay down one's arms.

"I may infer a priori that Trotsky and my other allies in crime, as well as the Second International . . . will endeavor to defend us, especially and particularly myself. I reject this defense, because I am kneeling before the country, before the Party, before the whole people . . ."

Some years ago Arthur Koestler in *Darkness at Noon* attempted to explain the confessions in the Moscow purge trials. It was Bukharin's plea that he had particularly in mind when he wrote the final speech for his old revolutionary.

Koestler's explanation was limited naturally to Russian communists. Today any explanation will have to be much more inclusive, for confessants to communist inquisitors have included all manner of people who were neither Russians nor communists. They have included those opposed to communism as well as those dedicated to it. They have included peasants as well as professional politicians. They have included the clergy, Catholic as well as Protestant. They have included various Americans.

On the day before the Fourth of July, 1951, William N. Oatis, an American, then head of the Prague bureau of the Associated Press, said for the benefit of his Communist accusers:

"I am sorry that I went into espionage in this country. I didn't do it because I am an enemy of the working class, I am from the working class myself. I did it only because I listened to the wrong kind of orders from abroad and came under the influence of the wrong kind of people here in Czechoslovakia. I hurt myself, I hurt my friends, I harmed the republic and helped its enemies. I harmed the cause of peace and helped the cause of war. I repeat that I am sorry for all this. . . . Your security organs have treated me with great consideration even though I didn't deserve it. Your courts have treated me courteously. I thank you for all that. I know that I did the wrong thing. I want to renounce espionage work forever. . . ."

The Korean war, a result of the large-scale, well-planned act of military aggression by the communist regime in North Korea, was a little over a year old. Mr. Oatis was on trial with three others before a five-man communist court in Prague's Prankrac prison. The charge was espionage. All gave confessions. He was making his final plea.

The next day when the court sentenced him to ten years' imprisonment he responded: "I accept the sentence of the court and ask that I be sent somewhere where I can do useful work."

At the outset of the trial he was asked, "Do you feel guilty?" "Yes, I do," he answered.

Eight months later he appeared in another trial in the same prison and testified against twelve alleged accomplices. Again he admitted his guilt.

When Mr. Oatis was released by the Czechs in May 1953, not only did he refuse to repudiate his confession but when questioned about why he gave it even responded with the enigmatic answer that psychology was used.

"Were you subjected to open terrorism or mishandled?" a reporter asked.

"No, I was not," Mr. Oatis answered firmly.

When pressed for details as to the nature of the psychology that was used on him he refused to give any. The next day he explained, referring to the Czech Communists:

"They were very efficient in their methods and preparation for my trial. It would be very difficult for me to describe what happened so that I could be understood by anyone not familiar with such proceedings or with what is done, individually.

"I think you could call it more psychological than anything else.

"If what I was heard to say or reported to have said during the trial sounded like I was reciting something, why that's the way it was."

A day later on his return to this country when it was suggested to him that some of his replies might appear puzzling and perhaps embarrassing, he gave the soft answer, "I realize I'm in an embarrassing position and I'll continue to be."

But the Russian communists did not invent the inquisitional technique either: they inherited it from the czars. The czars likewise did not invent it: they adapted it from the French; and the French in turn borrowed it from the church. The origin of the inquisitional technique goes back more than 700 years to some decretals of Innocent III, a great papal legislator and one of the ablest of popes (1198–1216). He devised it as a substitute for the older modes of proof, one of which, the ordeal, he abolished. The adoption process began in France with the Ordinance of 1260 of St. Louis. It began in Russia with the Judicial Laws of 1864 of Alexander II. Although the czars had used inquisitional torture prior to 1864—Peter the Great, for instance, used it on his son, Alexis, to such an extent that Alexis died—it was in that year that the inquisitional technique was introduced in Russia as a regular part of the procedure for the investigation of offenses. The communists, after a burst of nihilism in which they sought to destroy all the institutions of the old government, found that this technique suited their purposes. They not only went back to it: in the 1930s, especially during the purge years 1936–38 and the two or three years just preceding them, they greatly intensified it. It was the inquisitional technique made more relentless by the power of an authoritarian state that the Chinese people described as brainwashing.

By way of contrast we in this country, although we have been having our own form of political trials, have not had any guilty pleas in them, with but a single exception in only one case. Our own political cases began in 1948 with the indictment in New York City of William Z. Foster, national chairman, Eugene Dennis, general secretary, and ten other top leaders of the American Communist party. The charge was conspiracy to organize the Communist party of the United States as a group to teach and advocate the overthrow of our government by force and violence in violation of the Smith Act, passed in 1940. This case, which the communists called the case of the eleven, after Foster was severed from it because of ill health, went to trial in 1949, and after nine months resulted in a verdict of guilty as to all eleven. The United States Circuit Court of Appeals for the Second Circuit affirmed in 1950 and the Supreme Court in 1951. Since then we have had a round of indictments throughout the country, north, east, south and west, from New York to California, and in Hawaii and Puerto Rico, of other American Communist party leaders.

In addition to further indictments in New York City we have had prosecutions in Baltimore, Boston, Philadelphia, Pittsburgh, Cleveland, Detroit, Chicago, St. Louis, Denver, Seattle, Los Angeles, Honolulu, Greensboro, North Carolina, Buffalo, New York, and New Haven, Connecticut. We have prosecuted communists in groups for conspiracy, and singly for party membership. The second conspiracy indictment in

New York City included Elizabeth Gurley Flynn, a member of the party's national committee, Alexander Bittelman and Alexander Trachtenberg, two of the party's founders, and eighteen more. Of these, fifteen went to trial in 1952; thirteen were convicted and two acquitted, the latter two at the direction of the judge. The second trial in New York lasted over eight months, almost as long as the first one. In this instance the Court of Appeals affirmed in 1954 and the Supreme Court denied review, in 1955.

We have indicted over 130 American communists and convicted a hundred or more. Often the trials have been long. Yet with all these indictments and trials there have been no confessions from any of the defendants with but a single exception.

The exception was Mrs. Barbara Hartle in the Seattle conspiracy case. Ironically enough, her codefendants who stood trial and were convicted, appealed, and had their convictions reversed with a direction to enter a judgment in their favor. On February 1, 1956, Assistant Attorney General William F. Tompkins in announcing her release from prison praised her for her cooperation. He said that of all the 88 American Communist party leaders who had been convicted up to that point in Smith Act prosecutions she was the only one who had "exhibited remorse for her past activities and offered to co-operate with the Government."

There have been confessions, but they have been from ex-communists. These not only have confessed, but also, as in the cases of Harvey Matusow, Lowell Watson, Mrs. Marie Natvig, David Brown and possibly others, have confessed that their confessions were false. Indeed, Matusow's confession that his confessions were false resulted in a new trial for Trachtenberg and George Blake Charney, two of the thirteen defendants convicted in the second New York City case. However, none of the defendants except Mrs. Hartle has confessed, at least not during trial, and the chances are that none will.

This absence of confessions in contested cases is one of our characteristics. The governments of Anglo-American peoples have never dealt in confessions the way communist regimes do.

Our method in the investigation of offenses and prosecution of deviants is basically different from the inquisitional system. Referring to our method the federal Supreme Court in June 1949, on the occasion of invalidating confessions in three separate cases from three different states, South Carolina, Pennsylvania and Indiana, commented: "Ours is the accusatorial as opposed to the inquisitorial system." Under the accusatorial method there is an insistence that the investigating authorities get their case from other sources than the mouth of the accused. Under the inquisitional system the investigators try to get their case from this very source.

The Supreme Court's comment represents more than 700, and in one sense more than 1500, years of history. The accusatorial method owes its survival and growth to our grand and petit jury system. The one who laid the basis for our jury system was Henry II, a wise administrator and one of the greatest of English kings (1154–89). It would be interesting to speculate what would have been the course of history had Innocent III preceded Henry II, but of course impossible to say.

Henry II, however, did not invent the jury system; rather he fashioned it out of the inquiry of neighbors, and this institution he inherited from his Norman ancestors. They in turn borrowed it from the Frankish kings. We think of the inquiry of neighbors as a popular institution of English origin. In fact, it was neither: it was royal and it was Frankish. The great law reformer in early times was the king. In the 800s, almost 400 years before the decretals of Innocent III, the Frankish kings broke through the bounds of the old tribal customs and, where their finances were concerned, abandoned the older modes of proof. There were the customary moot hill courts with their magical, superstitious procedures. Such procedures were no longer good enough for the Frankish kings when it came to their revenues. They established a new procedure, one unknown to the old Germanic law. This procedure had the name of *inquisitio patriae,* more generally known as the *enquete du pays,* the inquiry of the country or the countryside, the inquiry of neighbors. In 829 an ordinance of Louis I, le Debonnaire, or the Pious (814–40), the third and surviving son of Charlemagne, provided that every inquiry with reference to the royal fisc was to be by the *inquisitio,* the inquiry of neighbors. This kind of *inquisitio* is to be distinguished from the later *inquisitio* of the church, the inquiry by officials. In the next century the Danes and Norwegians, Northmen, under a leader named Rollo, invaded the West Frankish kingdom; and by treaty in 911 acquired the territory which became known as Normandy. Rollo's successors as dukes of Normandy adopted and developed the Frankish *inquisitio.* One of them, William the Conqueror, with his barons invaded England, defeated Harold and the English at the battle of Hastings (1066), and on Christmas day of that year had himself crowned at Westminster. Thus the inquiry of neighbors came to England. Had it not been for the Normans and their conquest of England, this institution might long ago have become a matter of interest only to antiquaries, who might have regarded it as no more than an instrument of Frankish fiscal tyranny. Instead it developed into the jury system, and was to be regarded as an agency for the protection of the weak against the strong and of the individual against the state.

The difference between the *inquisitio* of the Frankish and English kings and the *inquisitio* of the church, between the inquiry of neighbors and inquiry by officials is subtle yet fundamental. Under the inquiry of neighbors it was the neighbors who sat in judgment; under inquiry by officials, it was some official. The inquiry of neighbors was to help in the development of a fairly independent citizenry and relatively a rather mature one, and a more or less representative form of government; inquiry by officials was not. Of course, both forms of inquiry were more rational than the old modes of proof.

Also the fact that officials questioned persons secretly need not necessarily have been an evil: after all, our grand jury proceedings are secret, too. The vice lay in a combination of circumstances: the use of secret questioning, not by a grand jury, but by a professional class, at a time when safeguards for persons who stood accused had not yet been developed. In England those safeguards did develop, and today constitute part of what we describe as the accusatorial method.

Looked at in one way the accusatorial method was centuries older even than Henry II and the sons of Charlemagne, for it may be said that primitive tribal justice already had this characteristic. It was accusatorial in the sense that the public did not prosecute, and hence officials did not question, deviants. The ones who prosecuted offenses were private persons, the parties injured or their kindred, and the modes of proof were not inquisitional but magical. In England the administration of justice remained accusatorial because of the development of the grand and petit jury system. This does not mean that the accusatorial method has to develop in connection with the jury system, but only that historically it did. Nor does it mean that other countries should adopt the jury system. However, it does mean that certain rights of the individual which developed in connection with the jury system, such as the right to counsel, bail, habeas corpus, a public trial, to be confronted with the witnesses against one, to remain silent, to have confessions obtained as a result of the inquisitional method thrown out of court, and yet others, should be accorded throughout the world.

Without such safeguards the inquisitional technique will continue to breed confessions, just as it always has. It will continue to breed them because human beings whether innocent or guilty of the offenses in question suffer from a compulsion to confess to something in any event. Why did Parson Weems' fictional story about the boy George Washington chopping down his father's cherry tree become universally popular in this country? Because it involved a confession. Why did the

Catholic church progress? One of the reasons was the practice of auricular confession, another of the tremendous changes of Innocent III. Why have a majority of the guilty as well as many of the innocent confessed to the commission of offenses? Because of the compulsion to confess. No human characteristic is more general than the compulsion to confess. There are confessions in church and out of church, in court and out of court, in life and in literature, and yet a multitude of others. There are those which are consciously given and those which are unconsciously supplied. Even the common human failing of talking too much involves the same compulsion. When to this compulsion there is added the inquisitional technique, the result will be confessions. If on both there is superimposed the power of a totalitarian state, the result will be what the whole world has come to know as brainwashing.

We have wondered that a few members of our armed forces should have changed sides; their families have found it difficult to believe. Rather we should have wondered that only the merest handful succumbed to the brainwashing tactics of the communists. We have wondered how the communists have obtained so many confessions. Rather we should have wondered that some of their victims held out and that others resisted as long as they did.

The inquisitional method, which the communists have exploited for a quarter of a century, is a throwback to the past and should be abandoned, especially in view of the growth and power of modern states. The safeguards for individuals contained in our Bills of Rights should not only be extended among ourselves but also recognized everywhere. Just as the twelfth and thirteenth centuries were the ones when the West turned from the early, irrational modes of proof to the accusatorial and the inquisitional techniques, so let us hope that the twentieth century will be the one when human beings become mature enough not only to settle their differences without a resort to war but also learn to safeguard to the individual a certain inviolate area which will be conducive to his fullest development. Just as there were added to our federal Constitution the first ten amendments, so let us hope there will be annexed to the charter of the United Nations an international covenant on human rights, and that nations which do not have a bill of rights will adopt one.

A Catalog of Confessions

2 Confessions to Clerical Inquisitors

Galileo

SOME SEVEN CENTURIES before Vyshinsky helped to set the pattern for the inquisitional system of the communists, there began the confessions to clerical inquisitors. Although Innocent III instituted the inquisitional technique, the inquisition of the Middle Ages did not commence until a number of years later. It is difficult to give a precise date, but some have suggested April 20, 1233, the day on which Gregory IX, a nephew of Innocent III, issued two bulls making the persecution of heresy the special function of the Dominicans. Later they shared this with the Franciscans. In Spain the inquisition at first played no great part. It was not until after Ferdinand and Isabella obtained from Sixtus IV a papal bull for an inquisition under royal control that it assumed serious proportions. The sovereigns asked for this bull in 1478 but did not obtain it until two years later. In order to keep royal supervision over this agency they created a new office, and one unknown to the older inquisition, an inquisitor general. They appointed to this office their confessor, Torquemada.

At first the inquisitorial office was primarily a penitential and not a penal tribunal. Its purpose was to reconcile the heretic with the Church, not to punish him. Even when the Church ordered imprisonment this was theoretically a penance rather than a punishment. Of course, if a heretic obstinately refused to abjure his heresies and seek reconciliation with the Church, the inquisitor had no choice but to withdraw the

protection of the Church from him and hand him over to the
secular arm for punishment. In medieval times the Church
and State were but different aspects of a single society—the
Christian commonwealth. Heresy was both a sin and a crime.
The inquisition could thus be used to gain a political end.
Those turned over to the secular authorities were burned at
the stake. Relapsed heretics soon came to suffer the same fate
as impenitent ones.

The inquisition pronounced its sentences at an auto-da-fé,
more correctly auto-de-fé (act of faith), a ceremony which
involved a procession, a solemn mass, an oath of obedience
to the inquisition by the king and all the lay functionaries,
a sermon by the grand inquisitor, and the reading of the sentences. A staging was erected in the center of the church,
on which the deviants were placed, surrounded by the secular
and clerical officials. The inquisitor delivered his sermon. The
king and the other lay persons bound themselves to pursue
heretics and to support the mission of the Holy Office. This
was the act of faith. The inquisitor pronounced a sweeping
anathema against all those who sought to oppose the inquisition. Then the notary read the confessions of the deviants
in the vulgar tongue, and as he finished each confession he
asked the confessant if he acknowledged it to be true, taking
care, however, to do this only when he knew the deviant to be
truly penitent and not likely to create scandal by a denial.
On his replying in the affirmative he was asked whether he
would repent, or lose body and soul by persevering in heresy;
and on his expressing a desire to abjure, the form of abjuration
was read and he repeated it, sentence by sentence. The inquisitor now absolved him from the excommunication which
he had incurred automatically by his heresy, and promised
him mercy if he behaved well under the sentence about to be
imposed. The sentence followed. The deviants were brought
forward successively, commencing with the least guilty and
proceeding to those incurring severer penalties.

Those who were to be abandoned to the secular arm were

reserved to the last. For them the ceremony was adjourned to the public square, where a platform had been constructed for the purpose, in order that the holy precincts of the church might not be polluted by a sentence leading to blood. The burning followed a day later, in order to afford the convicts time for conversion, that their souls might not pass from temporal to eternal flame, and care was enjoined not to permit them to address the people, lest they should arouse sympathy by their assertions of innocence. Bernard Guy, the first accomplished inquisitor, boasted that between 1301 and 1315 the inquisition detected more than a thousand heretics, who confessed and were publicly punished. During his sixteen years as inquisitor at Toulouse (1307–23) he convened eighteen autos-da-fé and pronounced 930 sentences. However, in all his sentences he consigned but 42 living persons to the flames. In his great auto-da-fé of April 1310 the solemnities lasted from Sunday until Thursday. After the preliminary work of mitigating the penances of some deserving penitents, twenty persons were condemned to wear crosses and perform pilgrimages, sixty-five were consigned to perpetual imprisonment, three of them in chains, and eighteen were delivered to the secular arm and duly burned. Torquemada in his fifteen years as inquisitor general (1483–1498) was said to have reconciled 90,000, condemned to be burnt in effigy 6,500, and burnt 8,800. These figures came from Llorente, who was secretary of the Holy Office (1790–92) and had access to the archives; but modern research has reduced these numbers. The only contemporary who gave figures, the secretary of Queen Isabella, placed the number of those burnt (up to 1490) at 2,000. He did not estimate the number of penitents but whosoever's figures one takes, they remain enormous.

The two most famous individuals who gave confessions to clerical inquisitors were Galileo (1564–1642) and Joan of Arc (1412–1431). Galileo at the height of his career was the mathematician extraordinary to the grand duke of Tuscany. His fame and connections were such that in 1611 both Pope

Paul V and Cardinal Barberini, the future Urban VIII, cordially received him. Both of them were later to figure in his heresy difficulties.

Galileo started as a supporter of Ptolemy, but sometime in his career turned to the Copernican theory. In 1610 he published his *Sidereus Nuncius,* which contained confirmation of this theory. The defenders of the Ptolemaic system resented the kindly reception accorded his book, even in church circles, and began a crusade against the Copernican theory on the ground that it contradicted the Scriptures. When a Florentine monk published a work attacking Galileo's views, Galileo defended his position in a letter which contained unorthodox statements:

"The Bible cannot err or deceive us; the truth of its words are absolute and unassailable. But they who explain and interpret the scriptures may be deceived in many ways, and commit fatal errors by always slavishly following the literal sense of the words. By so doing they may even teach contradictory and impious doctrines and errors, for they would be forced to ascribe to God hands, feet, eyes, etc. . . . In questions of natural science, the Bible ought to take the last place. Both nature and the Bible come from God; the one has been inspired by the Holy Spirit, while the other faithfully obeys the laws established by God. But while the Bible, accommodating itself to the average intelligence of man, often speaks, and rightly so, according to appearances, and uses terms that are not intended to express an absolute truth, nature conforms rigorously and invariably to the rules prescribed it. One, therefore, ought not to cite texts of scripture against a fact clearly proved by careful observation . . . The Holy Spirit has no intention of teaching us through the Holy Scriptures that the sun moves or that the sun does not move . . . Can anyone maintain that the Holy Spirit wishes to teach us anything which does not concern the soul's salvation?"

A copy of this letter was brought to the attention of the

Holy Office, which held the customary secret inquiry. In 1616 the theologians censured the proposition that the sun was the center of the world and was immovable as "stupid and absurd in philosophy, and formally heretical, inasmuch as it expressly contradicted many passages of the Holy Scriptures"; and the proposition that the earth was not the center of the world and that it had a diurnal motion as "erroneous in faith." Paul V, who presided at the final meeting at which the resolutions of censure were read, ordered Cardinal Bellarmine to warn Galileo to abandon his opinions. If he refused to promise "not to teach, defend or discuss his doctrine or opinion," he was to be imprisoned. Galileo offered no resistance. When Bellarmine commanded him "to relinquish altogether the said opinion that the sun is the centre of the world and immovable and that the earth moves; nor henceforth to hold, teach, or defend it in any way whatsoever, verbally or in writing; otherwise proceedings would be taken against him in the Holy Office," he readily promised to obey.

Galileo's first brush with the inquisition was in no sense a trial. While there was a denunciation, he was not formally cited but came to Rome voluntarily. He was not examined nor was any punishment prescribed. He was merely admonished. But sixteen years later he faced formal proceedings.

In the interim Cardinal Barberini, who had shown himself so friendly to him in 1611, had become Urban VIII. Bellarmine had died. The proofs of the Copernican system had accumulated. Although Galileo had not published any works openly defending this system he had maintained or assumed its truth in private letters. Whether he now relied on the character of the new pope, or on his own ever-growing fame, or whether he had not understood the scope of the promise he gave in 1616, is not certain. At any rate in 1632 he published his *Dialogues on the Two Principal Systems of the World, the Ptolemiac and the Copernican.* The work was in the form of a debate in which two interlocuters defended the Copernican theory while a third one named Simplicius argued feebly in favor of the Aristotelian school. A commission of theologians and scientists appointed to examine the book reported that Galileo had broken the injunction of 1616.

In September 1632 the pope ordered Galileo to appear before the commissary general. Galileo sought to avoid the trip. He pleaded his weakness. He spoke of his great age, his feeble health, his blindness, his contrition, his piety, his submission. It was all to no avail. The pope was inflexible: "He can come very slowly in a litter, but he must be tried here in person. May God forgive him for having been so deluded as to involve himself in these difficulties from which we had relieved him when we were Cardinal."

Once in Rome, where he arrived by litter in February 1633, he was spared all physical discomfort. Rather than inquisitorial prison, he was allotted an apartment in the mansion of a prominent friend, and a manservant was allowed to attend him. However, he was not spared a painful humiliation.

In April 1633 he appeared before the inquisition and was questioned as to his conversation with Bellarmine. He claimed that he had been allowed to write about the Copernican doctrine hypothetically and had never promised not to teach it, although he admitted that he might have been commanded not to hold or defend it. After an interval of eighteen days he was examined again. This time he was submissive. Whereas he had previously denied that he had broken any command, he now admitted his error: "My error, then, has been—and I confess it—one of vainglorious ambition, and of pure ignorance and inadvertence." He asserted that he did not hold the opinion that the condemned doctrine was true.

Despite Galileo's confession the inquisition, which was not satisfied with verbal confessions but tried to pry into the most secret recesses of the conscience in order to detect true belief, held further hearings. Galileo pleaded his great age and the passage-of sixteen years as an excuse for forgetting the injunction of 1616: "I do not hold, and have not held this opinion of Copernicus since the command was intimated to me that I must abandon it; for the rest I am here in your hands, do with me what you please." When admonished to tell the truth or he would be subjected to torture, he replied: "I am here to obey, and I have not held this opinion since the decision was pronounced, as I have stated."

The sentence and recantation were imposed in June. The sentence was that the publication of the *Dialogues* be prohibited and that Galileo be incarcerated in the inquisitional prison during pleasure. The recantation recited that Galileo had broken the injunction of 1616 and was justly suspected, and continued: "With sincere heart and unfeigned faith I abjure, curse and detest the aforesaid errors and heresies, and generally every other error and sect whatsoever contrary to the said Holy Church; and I swear that in the future I will never again say or assert, verbally or in writing, anything that might furnish occasion for a similar suspicion regarding me."

In the light of the recantation, as well as Galileo's attitude throughout the proceedings, most scholars agree that the story which has him rising from his knees after repeating the formula of abjuration, stamping on the ground, and exclaiming, *"E pur si muove!"* is entirely apocryphal. The words were said for him more than a hundred and fifty years after his death.

Joan of Arc

JOAN OF ARC AFTER INSPIRING the French and turning the tides of war in their favor was sold to the English. They found it expedient to hand her over to the inquisition. Her chief inquisitor was Pierre Cauchon, the bishop of Beauvais. She willingly told about her voices and her mission, but she refused to take the oath to answer all questions. "I do not know what you will ask me; perhaps it may be about things which I will not tell you." She agreed to reply to questions bearing on the trial. This she did with shrewdness and a touch of wit.

One of the judges, who knew of her attempt to escape while a prisoner of war, asked her whether she would now escape if she could. The question was tricky because escape from an ecclesiastical prison was a serious crime. But Joan said that she would see whether the Lord willed it. When asked whether St. Michael was naked when he appeared to her, she replied: "Do you think the Lord has not wherewith to clothe his angels?" When Cauchon got overeager in his questioning Joan warned him: "You call yourself my judge: I know not if you are, but take care not to judge me wrongfully, for you expose yourself to great danger and I warn you, so that if our Lord chastises you I shall have done my duty."

When Joan's replies proved unsatisfactory to her inquisitors she was threatened with torture and told that the executioner was on hand to administer it. To this she replied: "If you extort avowals from me by pain I will maintain that they are the result of violence." Whether for this reason or some other, torture was not used.

Joan was finally trapped on the question of her attitude toward the Church. She offered to submit to God and the Saints, rather than to the Church, for the purpose of the determination of the trial. This was unsatisfactory to the judges for it was not enough to submit to the Church Triumphant in heaven; the faithful had to bow before the Church Militant on earth. Joan finally agreed to submit to the Church if it did not demand the impossible. It could not ask her to abandon doing what the Lord commanded or to disavow the truth of her visions.

She was formally charged with sorcery, schismatism, idolatry, hereticism, attempted suicide and the wearing of male attire and hair-do; and another effort was made to persuade her to submit to the Church, but she answered that she would not give way if the fire were lit. When the sentence of relaxation was read twelve days later, however, she yielded. A formula of abjuration was read to her and she let her hand be guided in scratching the sign of the cross as her signature.

Then she was condemned to perpetual imprisonment on bread
and water. Her plea for ecclesiastical prison was denied.

In the afternoon of the same day she was given female
clothing and warned against a relapse. Nevertheless, her male
clothes were left in her cell. After a few days she put these
on again. The judges visited her cell to ascertain this fact.
Her replies to their questions were rambling and contradictory.
She first said that male dress was more suitable since she was
with men; then she stated that since the abjuration the voices
of St. Catharine and St. Margaret had told her she had incurred damnation by revoking in order to save her life, for
she had only revoked through fear of fire. She would rather
die than endure the torture of her captivity, but if the judges
wished she would again don woman's dress.

She was speedily turned over to the secular arm to the
great contentment of the English, who had never sympathized
with the inquisition's attempts to save her soul since these
would have saved her life as well. Her last word was "Jesus!"
An English soldier who witnessed the scene commented, "We
are lost. We have burnt a saint." The square at Rouen where
the deed took place remains one of the great historical land-
marks.

The Knights Templars

THE GREATEST POLITICAL TRIUMPH of the inquisition was
the prosecution of the Knights Templars. The Templars came
into existence after the First Crusade, which ended with the
capture of Jerusalem in 1099. The purpose of the brotherhood was the protection of the pilgrims journeying to Jerusalem. Its members were bound by vows of piety and poverty.
In the course of time tremendous changes occurred. The
order grew in size and wealth as pious donors all over Europe
gave it fiefs and manors. Templars became bankers and money-
changers and lived no more frugally than other men in their

station, although they were probably not more dissolute than the latter. They were, however, an international order, and as such pursued policies of their own without reference to national interests.

The reason for the Templars' downfall was their great wealth. This aroused the greed of Philip IV, the Fair, king of France (1285–1314). Philip was bankrupt. He had debased the coinage so often that he was popularly known as the counterfeiter. He was deeply in debt to the Templars but had no means to repay them. His excuse for attacking them came in the denunciations of an informer, a renegade Templar named Esquiu de Floyran, who accused the members of heresy and homosexual acts.

For some years strange stories had circulated about the secret rites which the order practiced at its midnight meetings. The time was ripe for an investigation of Floyran's charges, and Philip was ready for action. However, he first sought the cooperation of Pope Clement V, for the Templars not only were outside the reach of the civil courts but also extended beyond his domains. Clement, although in most respects servile to Philip, hesitated. But the grand inquisitor of France, William of Paris, was Philip's confessor and creature. Philip thus set the inquisition in motion against the Templars and the grand inquisitor demanded their arrest by the civil power. In October 1307 all the Templars within the French borders were arrested and questioned. Out of one batch of 138 knights examined in Paris in October and November, some of them venerable men who had been with the order many years, all but three admitted at least some of the charges. All but 15, a total of 123, confessed to spitting on or near the crucifix, an heinous crime in those days. The most damaging confession was that of the grand master himself, Jacques de Molay. With tears and protestations of contrition he publicly confessed that he had been guilty of denying Christ and spitting on the cross.

Toward the end of November the pope decided to support the king and issued the bull *Pastoralis praeeminentiae* calling on all European kings and princes to arrest all Templars everywhere. In June 1309 the Pope himself questioned about 70 Templars. They all confessed to some of the charges. With these confessions he felt that he had established a sufficient record to proceed against the order itself and a commission of inquiry was formed to take evidence and to report to a general council of the Church. The heads of inquiry drawn up were based on the confessions extorted and the original accusations. They included charges that the members of the order renounced Christ, spat upon the crucifix, worshipped a cat, did not believe in the sacrament, omitted the words "Hoc est corpus meum" from the Mass, and believed that the grand master could give them absolution. The order was also charged with encouraging homosexuality and other indecencies, and with enforcing secrecy under penalty of death.

All Templars who wished to give evidence on behalf of the order were cited to appear before the commission. It was only with difficulty, however, that a few were persuaded to volunteer for the task. The grand master, de Molay, was one of them. He retracted his confession and offered to meet any member of the commission in single combat. Gradually the Templars regained some of their courage. The following March 556 of them assembled to offer a defense of the order. They presented to the commissioners certain demands designed to give them a better opportunity for defense. They asked for the release of the order's officers from the king's charge as being subject to intimidation, for counsel, for confrontation of the witnesses against them and the subjection of such witnesses to the lex talionis, and for the exclusion of the king's officers from the court to prevent intimidation. These demands were rejected.

In May the archbishop of Lens proceeded against 54 individual Templars who had retracted their confessions, as relapsed heretics. The next day all were burned at the stake. A few days later four were burnt at Senlis, and towards the end of May nine more, at the order of the archbishop of Reims.

These events terrified not only the Templars, who abandoned all efforts to make a defense, but also the commissioners, who agreed that from then on they might sit by deputy. The evidence collected was sent to the pope, who submitted it to the council of Vienne, which met in October 1311. He proposed that the Templars be condemned. After months of vain effort to win over the council he finally prepared the bull *Vox in excelso* dissolving the order, which he caused to be published at the second session of the council in April. The council acquiesced in it.

It is interesting to compare the number of confessions obtained in France, where the inquisitional system was in effective operation, with that obtained in England, where its extension met the people's resistance. In Paris in the preliminary examination, out of 138 questioned *all* but three confessed; in England out of 229 Templars who were arrested *only* three confessed, and these three were captured fugitives. At Caen out of 13 questioned, 12 confessed. At Clermont it was 40 out of 69 and at Carcassonne 5 out of 5. Of the 231 brought before the papal commission at Paris all but 17 confessed to some charge.

The proceedings against the Templars, besides the many confessions which they produced, had two other unfortunate results: they sped on its course the inquisitional system in France; and they paved the way for the witchcraft prosecutions of the later middle ages. It was Philip IV's grandfather, St. Louis, who laid the basis for the inquisitional system in France in his Ordinance of 1260.

Savonarola and Bruno

THREE OTHER INDIVIDUALS who gave confessions to clerical inquisitors deserve mention: John XXIII, who was pope from 1410 to 1415, Savonarola (1452–98), and Giordano Bruno (1548–1600). John XXIII was deposed. Then a council of the Church tried and condemned him on 54 charges, including simony and various acts of immorality. John confessed all that was laid to his charge and submitted to the council. After a few years of imprisonment Pope Martin V rewarded him with the post of dean of the Sacred College.

Savonarola was a Dominican preacher in Florence whose voice sounded a fanatical but premature note of puritanism in a dissolute era. His austere life stood as a living indictment against the sin and debauchery of his city. He claimed direct inspiration from God as well as the power of prophecy. As his influence grew he became involved in politics. He dreamed of regenerating Florence and effecting a reform in the Church. For a time he appeared successful. Bands of young boys organized by him terrorized the city into piety and burned at a public bonfire all matter, including priceless objects of art, deemed to be immodest. His power was such that he was instrumental in bringing about the expulsion of the Medicis from Florence. His policy remained throughout his career friendly to Charles VIII of France and hostile to the Borgias. When the Borgia pope, Alexander VI, sought to bribe him by making him archbishop of Florence and cardinal, Savonarola refused with prophetic words: "I want no hat but that of martyrdom reddened with my own blood."

His downfall came when he wrote letters to the rulers of Europe urging them to convoke a general council for the reform of the church, a possibility justly dreaded by higher church authorities, including the pope. He was excommunicated and declared suspect of heresy. After the application of torture he confessed to being a conscious impostor whose sole object was personal power: his purpose in convoking a general council was either to be chosen pope or to become the most powerful man in the world; to this end he had stirred up animosities between the citizens and caused a break between Florence and the Holy See; he had also wanted to set up a government headed by a perpetual doge, on the Venetian model. Further torture brought further admissions.

In May 1497 when he was brought before papal commissioners he retracted his prior confessions as made under torture and declared himself the envoy of God. Although under inquisitorial procedure this retraction rendered him a relapsed heretic who could forthwith be burned, the pope was in need of more information and the trial continued. He was again repeatedly tortured, and information was wrung from him involving the cardinal of Naples in the plan to convoke a general council. The next day he retracted this confession. He was now condemned as a heretic and schismatic, a rebel from the Church, a sower of tares and revealer of confessions, and abandoned to the secular arm. A day later he and two of his followers were burnt at a spectacular auto-da-fé.

Bruno was an Italian philosopher. He became a Dominican at Naples but his bold and turbulent character as well as dangerous intellectual curiosity involved him in early troubles from which he never extricated himself. As a young monk he made remarks which so aroused his superiors that he was reprimanded more than once and finally denounced to the inquisition at Naples and cited to appear. Disobeying the citation Bruno fled and was condemned as being contumacious. Thenceforth he wandered from country to country. In 1591 he ventured into Venice at the urging of one of his pupils, who hoped to learn from Bruno certain secret knowledge he thought Bruno possessed. His pupil, disappointed in not obtaining from Bruno the secret knowledge he sought, denounced him the following year to the inquisition. Bruno admitted that in some of his works he had spoken "too philosophically and disingenuously, and not enough as a good Christian would" but when pressed for grave admissions he stated: "I have neither spoken nor written those things *ex professo* nor for the purpose of directly impugning the Catholic faith, but basing my arguments solely on philosophic reasoning or reciting the opinions of heretics." When questioned as to living in heretical countries, consorting with heretics and praising heretical rulers such as Queen Elizabeth he said: "I have praised many heretics, and also heretic princes, but I have not praised them as heretics, but solely for the moral virtues they possess, nor have I ever praised them as religious and pious persons."

At the end of a series of interrogations, however, Bruno's manner, which had been bold, became humble. He admitted his many offenses and asked for pardon in the following words, taken from the official account:

> Humbly beseeching pardon from the Lord God and Your Most Illustrious Lordships for all the sins I have committed, I am here ready to perform whatever shall be decided by your wisdom and shall be adjudged expedient for my soul.
>
> And furthermore I pray that you will give me a punishment severe to excess, if so be I might avoid a public exhibition which might bring disgrace on the sacred habit of the Order, which I have worn; and if by mercy of God and Your Most Illustrious Lordships my life shall be spared, I vow so notably to reform my life that the edification of my new estate may purge the scandal which I have occasioned.

From this point on, what is known of Bruno is indirect and unofficial. For some reason the court stopped its deliberations. In September 1592 the Holy Office in Rome requested that Bruno be sent to Rome to be dealt with there.

Nothing is known about his stay in Rome except that he remained in prison from 1593 until he went to the stake. All that we know, imperfect and inaccurate in some respects, comes from an account by Scioppius, a German scholar who was in Rome in 1600:

> There he was interrogated several times by the Holy Office and convicted (*convictus*) by the chief theologians. At one time he obtained forty days in which to consider his position (*quibus deliberaret*); by and by he promised to recant; then he renewed his follies (*nugas*); then he got forty other days for deliberation. But he did nothing ex-

cept to baffle the Pope and the Inquisition. After having been about two years in the custody of the Inquisitor, he was taken on February 9 to the palace of the Grand Inquisitor. In the presence of illustrious cardinals of the Holy Office (who surpass all others in age, experience, knowledge of affairs and of law and theology), in the presence of the expert Assessors and the Governor of the City, Bruno was brought into the hall of the inquisition and heard his sentence on bended knees. The sentence narrated his life, his studies, his teaching, the fraternal care which had been taken to induce him to repent and his obstinate refusal; he was then degraded, excommunicated and handed over to the secular power with the request that he should be punished as mercifully as possible and—these were the words by which death by fire was designated—'without effusion of blood.' This ceremony over, he answered with threatening air, 'Perhaps you, my judges, pronounce this sentence against me with greater fear than I receive it.' The guards of the Governor conducted him to the prison; he was left there eight days to see whether he would repent. But it was no use. So lastly he was taken to the stake. Just as he was dying a crucifix was presented to him, but he pushed it away with fierce scorn. So he was burnt and perished miserably.

3

Confessions Under the Tudors

Henry VIII's Wives and Others

THE TUDORS PROVIDED ENGLAND with a strong monarchy and many executions for constructive treason. A treason act of 1534 included within its scope not only words but even thoughts: all who did "maliciously wish, will or desire, by words or writing, or by craft imagine" any bodily harm to the king were guilty. It was as broad in its way as Article 58 of the Soviet Union's Criminal Code of 1926. Article 58 was the one which dealt with counter-revolutionary offenses.

The founder of the Tudor line was Henry VII (1485–1509). He brought the Wars of the Roses to an end and gained the crown by defeating Richard III at Bosworth Field. In the long reign of his son and successor, Henry VIII (1509–1547), came the break with Rome. Henry VIII's successors were his children Edward VI (1547–53), Mary (1553–58) and Elizabeth I (1558–1603). Under the authoritarian reigns of the Tudors a great number of the defendants in treason prosecutions confessed their guilt, if not at their trials, then at their executions. Even Anne Boleyn, the second of Henry VIII's wives, and the mother of Elizabeth I, at her beheading stated that she came to the block ready "to yield herself humbly to the will of the King." Then she besought all men "to pray for the life of the King, my sovereign lord and yours, who is one of the best princes on the face of the earth, and who hath always treated me so well that better could not be."

She was charged with having incited her own natural

brother, George Boleyn, Lord Rocheford, to incest, and with having conspired the death and destruction of the king. All those involved in her fall conceded the justice of their executions. Her brother at his execution gave the most abject confession of them all: "I was born under the law, and I die under the law, forasmuch as it is the law which hath condemned me . . . I deserve death even though I had a thousand lives —yea, even to die with far more and worse shame and dishonor than hath ever been heard of before . . . take heed not to fall into the error of my ways."

Catherine Howard, the fifth of Henry VIII's wives, and the second one of them to be beheaded, along with her accomplice, Lady Rocheford, at their execution desired "all Christian people to take regard unto their worthy and just punishment with death for their offenses against God . . . and also against the King's royal majesty." They were, they confessed, "justly condemned . . . by the laws of the realm and Parliament to die. . . ." The charge against her was adultery with her cousin Thomas Culpeper. He confessed his intentions on the point and this was enough under the Tudors. The French ambassador, de Marillac, reported that although Culpeper "had not passed beyond words" nevertheless "he confessed his intentions to do so, and his confessed conversation, being held by a subject to a Queen, deserved death."

The Duke of Buckingham on the scaffold acknowledged that "he had offended the kynges grace through negligence and lacke of grace, and desired all noblemen to beware by him, and al men to pray for him, and that he trusted to dye the kynges true man." His real trouble stemmed from the fact that he had royal blood: this made him a possible candidate for the throne should Henry VIII die without a male heir. Lord Thomas Cromwell at his execution confessed: ". . . And it is not unknown to many of you, that I have been a great travailler in this world, and being but of base degree, was called to high estate; and since the time I came thereunto I have offended my prince, for the which I ask him heartily forgiveness, and beseech you all to pray to God with me, that He will forgive me. . . . And I heartily desire you to pray for the King's grace, that he may long live with you in health and prosperity. . . ." Cromwell's difficulties arose out of Henry VIII's discarded religious and foreign policies.

Cardinal Wolsey pleaded guilty to a long series of charges against him for exercising legatine authority, and threw himself upon the king's mercy. He wrote the king: ". . . I, your poor, heavy, and wretched priest, do daily pursue, cry, and call upon your Royal Majesty for grace, mercy, remission, and pardon . . . the same only cometh of an inward and ardent desire that I have continually to declare unto your Highness, how that, next unto God I desire nor covet any thing in this world but the attaining of your gracious favour and forgiveness of my trespass. And for this cause I cannot desist nor forbear, but be a continual and most lowly suppliant to your benign grace. For surely, most gracious King, the remembrance of my folly, with the sharp sword of your Highness' displeasure, hath so penetrate my heart, that I cannot but lamentably cry . . . and say, *Sufficit; nunc contine, piissime rex, manum tuam.*" He signed an indenture by which he prayed the king to take all his temporal possessions, pensions and benefices.

Elizabeth Barton, better known as the Nun of Kent, was equally submissive. She had prophesied that Henry VIII "would not live a month after his marriage" with Anne Boleyn. She confessed and obligingly placed the blame for her prophecy upon more important persons: ". . . I have not been the onely cause of myne owne death whiche moste justly I have deserved, but also I am the cause of the death of all these persons whiche at this time here suffre: and yet to say the trueth, I am not somuche to be blamed consideryng it was well knowen unto these lerned men that I was a poore wenche without learnyng . . . but because the things which I fayned was proffitable unto them, therefore they muche praised me and bare me in hand that it was the holy ghost and not I that dyd theim, and then I beyng puft up with their praises fell into a

certain pryde and folishe phantasie with my selfe and thought
I might fayne what I would, which thing hath brought me to
this case, and for the which now I cry God and the kynges
highnes most heartely mercy. . . ."

In the next reign as a result of factional rivalry within the
council of regency established to govern the kingdom during
the minority of Edward VI, the Duke of Somerset found
himself maneuvered into a position where he could technically
be charged with felony. His real offense was his popularity
with the populace of London. Nevertheless at his execution he
said: ". . . But I am condemned by a law whereunto I am
subject, as we all [are], and therefore to show obedience I am
content to die . . ."

Lady Jane Grey, who acted as queen of England for nine
days before Mary obtained the crown, pleaded guilty to the
charge of treason. Her supporters, the Duke of Northumber-
land and his associates, avowed their crimes against God
and the crown for their vain attempt to disturb the legitimate
succession of Queen Mary. The Duke at his execution confessed: "Good people. Hither I am come this day to die, as ye
know. Indeed, I confess to you all that I have been an evil
liver, and have done wickedly all the days of my life; and, of
all, most against the Queen's Higness, [of] whom I here
openly ask forgiveness." At this he bent his knees. Then the
man who had vigorously proclaimed his Protestantism denied
his faith and blamed its advocates for his offenses: "And the
chiefest occasion hath been through false and seditious preach-
ers, that I have erred from the Catholic faith and true doctrine
of Christ." One of the Duke's supporters, Sir John Gates,
went to his execution abhorring his treasonous actions and
confessing his religious sins: "My coming here this day, good
people is to die; whereof I assure you all I am well worthy; for
I have lived as viciously and wickedly all the days of my life
as any man hath done in the world."

Lady Jane's father, who was the Duke of Suffolk, and
Thomas Wyatt condemned themselves for rebelling against

Queen Mary in 1554. Wyatt abjured his vicious life: "Good people, I am come presently here to dye, being thereunto lawfully and wourthely condemned, for I have sorely offended agaynst God and the quenes majestie, and am sorry therfore. I trust God hath forgeven and taken his mercy apon me. I besyche the quenes majesty also of forgevenes." The Duke was even more abject: "Masters, I have offended the queen and her laws, and therefore am justly condemned to die, and am willing to die, desiring all men to be obedient. And I pray God that this death may be an ensample to all men. . . ."

The Earl of Essex

PROBABLY THE MOST ABJECT of the confessants under the Tudors was Robert Devereux, the second Earl of Essex. He participated in a confused plan for a rising in London in order to regain his position with Queen Elizabeth I. At his trial, with Henry, Earl of Southhampton, for high treason, he maintained his innocence; but immediately after his conviction, and while he was yet in Westminister Hall, he hinted "that before his death he would make something known that should be acceptable to her Majesty in point of state." This he did, dragging in names the prosecution had never suggested—Sir Henry Neville, now in France as Ambassador; Lord Mountjoy, Deputy Governor of Ireland; and even Essex's own sister, the beautiful Lady Rich, who said Essex, "did continually urge me on with telling me how all my friends and followers thought me a coward and that I had lost all my valour." The Queen could never be safe while he lived. He had lied at his trial, "imagined all falsehood," and looked on himself as "the greatest, the most vilest and most unthankful traitor that ever had been in the land."

The abjectness of this recital shocked even the Privy Councilors—among them Cecil—who witnessed it. On the morning of his execution, Essex was at pains to repeat the confessions. His conduct had been sinful, he had stiffly defended an unjust

cause. He was fit to be spewed up by the commonwealth for
the foulness of an enterprise which, "like a leprosy, spread
far and wide . . . had infected many." Standing at the scaffold he again besought God's pardon: ". . . For all which I
humbly beseech my Saviour Christ to be a Mediator to the
eternal Majesty for my pardon; especially for this my last sin,
this great, this bloody, this crying, this infectious sin, whereby
so many have for love to me been drawn to offend God, to
offend their Sovereign, to offend the world. I beseech God
to forgive it us, and to forgive it me most wretched of all. I
beseech her Majesty, and the state and ministers thereof to
forgive us: and I beseech God to send her Majesty a prosperous
reign, and a long one, if it be his will. . . ." His self-abasement was so extreme that in France they said he died "more
like a silly minister than a stout warrior."

Five more individuals were put on trial for high treason
because of their involvement with Essex. They were Sir Chris-
topher Blount, Sir Charles Danvers, Sir John Davis, Sir Gilly
Merrick and Henry Cuffe. Blount, Danvers and Davis pleaded
guilty. Blount at his execution added: ". . . And although it
be true, that (as we all protested in our Examinations and Ar-
raignments) we never resolved of doing hurt to her majesty's
Person; (for in none of our Consultations was there set down
any such purpose) yet, I know, and must confess, if we had
failed of our ends, we should (rather than have been disappointed) even have drawn blood from herself. . . . And I
beseech God of his mercy to save and preserve the queen,
who hath given comfort to my soul, in that I hear she hath
forgiven me all but the sentence of the law, which I most
worthily deserved, and do most willingly embrace, and hope
that God will have mercy and compassion on me, who have
offended him as many ways as ever sinful wretch did. I have
led a life so far from his precepts as no sinner more. God
forgive it me and forgive me my wicked thoughts, my licen-
tious life, and this right arm of mine, which (I fear me) hath
drawn blood in this last action. . . ."

4 *Confessions of Witchcraft*

AFTER THE FIRST FORCE of the inquisition of the Middle Ages had spent itself, except in Spain, the prosecutions for witchcraft began and flourished for more than two centuries. A witch, according to Sir Edward Coke, "is a person that hath conference with the Devil, to consult with him, or to do some act." The inquisition had treated witchcraft along with sorcery as forms of heresy. About the sixteenth century the secular courts began to punish it. Prosecutions for it prevailed in Protestant as well as Catholic countries. A veteran inquisitor boasted that in a century and a half the Holy Office burnt at least 30,000 witches who, if they had been left unpunished, would easily have brought the whole world to destruction. Joan of Arc's death at the stake marked the time when the fear of witchcraft began to increase in intensity. It also ushered in the period when the wizard gave place to the witch. Most of the victims of the early witchcraft prosecutions were women.

With reference to the prosecutions for witchcraft in England and Scotland, William M. Best in his treatise on evidence commented: "Some of them present the extraordinary spectacle of individuals, not only freely (so far as the absence of physical torture constitutes freedom) confessing themselves guilty of these imaginary offenses, with the minutest details of time and place, but even charging themselves with having, through a demoniacal aid thus avowed, committed repeated murders and other heinous crimes. The cases in Scotland are even more monstrous than those in England."

One of the many voluntary confessants was Issobell Gowdie. The year 1662 witnessed her full confession in four installments. It was in the parish of Aulderne, about midway between Cawdor and Forres, where Shakespeare laid the scene of Macbeth's meeting with the three witches. For four days she talked. The devil, the second time she saw him, had her renounce her baptism. Putting one hand on top of her head and the other on the sole of her foot, she gave all between her hands to the devil. Then he baptized her in his name, and put a mark on her shoulder. Heaven help those who were unfortunate enough to have any birthmarks, warts or moles! She was now wholly given up to him, and her companions were employed by him in the commission of various crimes, including murder. She killed more than half a dozen people herself, and helped Janet Breadheid and others kill all the male children of the Laird of Parkis. They took away the fruit of the land in this manner: they yoked a plough of frogs, the devil holding the plough, and went about a field and up and down it praying to the devil that thistles and briars might grow there.

The women had carnal copulation with the devil. He was abler for them sexually than any man could be. His members were exceeding great and long, but he was as heavy as a sack of malt and as cold as ice. He was as cold within her as spring-well water. The youngest and lustiest women had great pleasure in their carnal copulation with him. When they went on their jaunts they put a broom or a three-legged stool in bed with their husbands. She had a little horse and would say, "Horse and Hattock, in the Devillis name," and away she would fly even as straws in a high wind. Sometimes they rode on bean stalks. They would raise and lay the wind. Her devil was in the shape of a small black hairy man. His feet were forked and cloven. Sometimes he was "lyk a dear or a roe." On one trip another devil was clothed in sea-green and two others in grass-green. She could go in the likeness of a hare or a cat or a crow. Once she traveled in the likeness of a jack daw, another witch as a hare and two others as cats. Yet another time they went in the shape of rooks.

"Alace!" she cried toward the close of her third session, "I deserw not to be sitting heir, for I haw done so manie evill deidies, especially killing of men, . . . I deserw to be reivin upon iron harrowes, and worse, if it culd be devysit." Compare this with some of the last pleas of communist leaders in the East a few centuries later who declared that they deserved execution!

Not only was Issobell Gowdie's confession a voluntary one, but what was even more remarkable, it was corroborated. Janet Breadheid confirmed Issobell's story about killing all the male children of the Laird of Parkis. They made a clay image of the first child and roasted it until the child died. Then they put the image away in a cradle until after the next child was born; "and then within half a yier efter that bairne was borne, we would tak it out of the cradle, and bak it and rost it at the fyr, until that bairn died also."

Such and similar recorded confessions occurred in various of the countries of Europe in the 1500s and 1600s. Nearly all of the confessants were women, for most of those accused of witchcraft were women. The confessions all followed more or less the same general pattern as did the confessions of communist leaders in the present century. The pattern varied a little from country to country but basically it remained the same. According to the confessants, they renounced their baptism and were baptized by the devil. They did homage to the devil by kissing his buttocks. They had carnal copulation with him. They rode through the air to their meetings, or sabbaths as they were called. The devil and they took various shapes. They committed all manner of crimes and caused all kinds of disaster. Indeed, they confessed themselves to be the authors of nearly all the disasters which overtook human beings during this period.

Scottish Prosecutions for Witchcraft

IN SCOTLAND after King James returned with his bride Queen
Anne in 1590 there were a series of prosecutions for witchcraft. The defendants were accused of causing the storm
which prevented Anne on her first venture from coming to
Scotland and of trying to bewitch and drown King James.
Three of the principal defendants were Johnne Feane, Geillis
Duncane and Agnes Sampson. All confessed. Feane repudiated
his confession, but it did him no good. He was strangled and
burned with the rest. According to Geillis and Agnes, upon
Allhallows evening 1589, they and other witches to the number of one or two hundred went to sea each one in a riddle or
sieve to the Kirk of North Berwick. Six of the witches were
men, but the rest were women. After they landed they took
hands and danced. Geillis Duncane went before them and
played the dance on a Jew's trump or harp. "These confessions made the King in a wonderfull admiration, and sent for
the saide Geillis Duncane, who upon the like trump did play
the said Daunce before the Kinges Majestie, who in respect
to the strangeness of these matters, tooke great delight to be
present at their examinations." The devil was a little black
man with a black gown and hat. Johnne Feane was always
nearest the devil at his left elbow. The devil mounted the pulpit and called the roll. He told them to do all the evil that they
could. At the close of the meeting the devil put his bare rump
over the pulpit and they all kissed it and swore true service to
him. They then returned to sea and went home again. The
king's presence at those and other examinations laid the foundation for his royal work on *Daemonologie*.

In 1630 in Scotland Alexander Hamilton confessed that he
met the devil in the likeness of a black man on a black horse.
He renounced his baptism and engaged to become the servant
of the devil, from whom he received four shillings. The devil
gave him a charm by which he killed the Lady Ormestone
and her daughter. He did this in revenge because the Lady re-

fused him the loan of a mare and called him nicknames. He had many meetings with the devil. Once the devil gave him a severe drubbing for not keeping an appointment.

In 1678 Isobel Elliot and nine other women confessed that they were baptized by the devil and had carnal copulation with him. In one case, that of Major Weir in 1670, the editor regarded the confession of such a revolting nature that he declined to publish the particulars of it. Scotland had confessions of witchcraft as late as 1697. In that year five persons confessed, implicating others, and seven were consigned to the flames.

Witchcraft Confessions in England

THE STORY WAS SIMILAR in England and in other countries, including the Massachusetts Bay Colony in the New World in 1692. In England in 1645 a number of women in Essex County confessed to witchcraft. One of these, Anne Cate, alias Maidenhead of Much Holland, admitted, among other things, to the murder of half a dozen people. "This examinant saith, that she hath four familiars, which shee had from her mother about two-and-twenty yeeres since, and that the names of the said imps are James, Prickeare, Robyn and Sparrow: and that three of these imps are like mouses, and the fourth like a sparrow, which she called Sparrow. And this examinant saith, that to whomsoever shee sent the said imp called Sparrow, it killed them presently; and that, first of all shee sent one of her three imps like mouses, to nip the knee of one Robert Freeman, of Little Clacton in the county of Essex aforesaid, whom the said imp did so lame, that the said Robert dyed on that lamenesse within half a yeare after. And this examinant saith that she sent the said imp Prickeare to kill the daughter of John Rawlins, of Much-Holland aforesaid, which died accordingly within a short time after; and that shee sent her said imp Prickeare to the house of one John Tillet, which did suddenly kill the said Tillet. And this examinant saith, that shee sent her said imp Sparrow, to kill the childe of one George Parby of Much-Holland aforesaid, which child the said imp did presently kill; and that the offence this examinant took against the said George Parby, to kill his said childe, was, because the wife of the said Parby denyed to give this examinant a pint of milke. And this examinant further saith, that she sent her said imp Sparrow to the house of Samuel Ray, which, in a very short time did kill the wife of the said Samuel; and that the cause of this examinant's malice against the said woman was, because shee refused to pay to this examinant twopence, which she challenged to be due to her; and that afterwards her said imp Sparrow killed the said child of the said Samuel Ray. And this examinant confesseth that as soon as shee had received the said four imps from her said mother, the said imps spoke to this examinant, and told her, shee must deny God and Christ; which this examinant did then assent unto."

Another, Rebecca West, confessed: "This examinant saith, that about a month since the aforesaid Anne Leech, Elizabeth Gooding, Hellen Clark, Anne West, and this examinant, met altogether at the house of the aforesaid Elizabeth Clark in Mannyntree, where they together spent some time in praying unto their familiars, and every one in order went to prayers; afterwards some of them read in a book, the book being Elizabeth Clarks; and this examinant saith, that forthwith their familiars appeared, and everyone of them made their severall propositions to those familiars, what every one of them desired to have effected: and this examinant saith, that first of all the said Elizabeth Clark desired of her spirit, that Mr. Edwards might be met withall about the middle bridge, as hee should come riding from Easberyhoult in Suffolk; that his horse might be scared, and he thrown down, and never rise again: and this examinant saith, that the said Elizabeth Gooding desired of her spirit, that she might be avenged on Robert Tayler's horse, for that the said Robert suspected the said Elizabeth

Gooding for the killing of an horse of the said Robert formerly: and this examinant saith, that the said Hellen Clark desired of her spirit, that shee might be revenged on two hogs in Misley street (being the place where the said Hellen lived) one of the hogs to die presently, and the other to be taken lame; and this examinant further saith, that Anne Leach desired of her spirit, that a cowe might be taken lame of a mans living in Mannyngtree, but the name of the man this examinant can not remember: and this examinant further saith, that the said Anne West, this examinant's mother, desired of her spirit, that shee might be freed from all her enemies and have no trouble: and this examinant saith, that shee desired of her spirit that shee might be revenged on Prudence the wife of Thomas Hart, and that the said Prudence might be taken lame on her right side. And lastly this examinant saith, that having thus done, this examinant, and the other five, did appoint the next meeting to be at the said Elizabeth Goodings house, and so departed all to their owne houses."

Elizabeth Clarke confessed that her familiars sucked upon the lower parts of her body and promised to help her get a husband as well as maintain her ever after. If a woman had a mole or a wart, especially on the unseen parts of her body, she was often induced to confess that imps sucked at these "teats." Another Essex woman confessed that her familiar "did usually suck those teats which were found about the privie parts of her body," and yet another that he "suckled it on her body."

Anne Leech's imp was gray in color, but she stated that some imps were black and yet others were white. She through her imp killed Elizabeth, the daughter of Robert Kirk, and sent him to kill the daughter of widow Raylyns of Misley. She also killed a black cow, a white one, and two horses. She and Elizabeth Gooding sent either of them an imp to destroy the child of Mr. Edwards. To Hellen Clark the devil appeared in the likeness of a white dog.

Rebecca Jones had three imps like "moules" but without

tails. One or another of them killed the wife of Thomas Bumstead, injured the child of "Mistriss Darcy," and killed a sow
of Benjamin Howes. She and Joyce Boanes each sent an imp
to kill Thomas Bumstead, and he died about three weeks later.
Joyce Boanes had two imps in the "likeness of mouses."
Through them she made ill the servant of Robert Turner,
killed ten or twelve lambs of Richard Welch, and a calf, a
sheep, and a lamb of Thomas Clynch. Rose Hollybread and
Susan Cock confessed that they also sent imps who made ill
the servant of Robert Turner. Rose's imp was in the likeness
of a small gray bird. She killed the son of Thomas Toakely.
Susan had two imps. One was in the shape of a mouse. The
other was about the bigness of a cat and of a yellow color.
She killed ten or twelve sheep of John Spalls, and six or seven
hogs of Mr. Mannock.

Johan Cooper, a widow, confessed to four murders: "This
examinant saith, That she has been a witch about twenty
years, and hath three familiars, two like mouses, and the third
like a frog; and the names of the two like mouses are Jack,
and the other Prickeare, and the name of a third, like a frog,
is Frog. And this examinant saith, that she sent one of her
said imps to kill a child of one Thomas Woodward, which
her said impe did kill a fortnight after. And this examinant
saith, that shee did send her said impe called Frog, to kill two
of John Cartwright's children, of Much-Holland in the county
of Essex aforesaid, which said imp did kill the said two children within a fortnight or three weeks after. And this examinant saith further, that at another time shee sent her said
imp Frog, to destroy the wife of one George Parby, of Much-
Holland aforesaid, which did kill her within three dayes after."

Some years earlier the devil appeared to Mary Smith in the
shape of a black man. In a low murmuring and hissing voice
he promised to revenge her upon all those to whom she wished
evil. As a result she caused bodily ailments to four people.
The report contains a description of her execution: "She in
particular maner confessed openly at the place of execution,

in the audience of multitudes of people gathered together
(as is usual at such times) to be beholders at her death . . .
And being asked, if she would be contented to have a psalme
sung, answered willingly that she desired the same, and appointed it herselfe, the Lamentation of a Sinner, whose beginning is, Lord turne not away thy face . . .'"

England had confessions of witchcraft as late as 1682. In
that year three women, Temperance Lloyd, Mary Trembles
and Susanna Edwards confessed at Devon. Temperance had
previously been accused of witchcraft and acquitted. Now she
confessed. The devil in her case was a black man about the
size of her arm; he also took the shape of a cat. She was guilty
of four murders: she pricked William Herbert of Biddiford to
death, injured Anne Fellow so that she died, and caused the
deaths of Jane Dallyn and Lydia Burman. Upon a search of
her body the authorities found in her secret parts two "teats."
She admitted that the black man often sucked them. Mary's
devil was in the shape of a lion. He lay with her, had carnal
knowledge of her body, and sucked her in her private parts. At
the execution Temperance admitted that the devil came to
her and that she hurt Grace Barnes, but she denied any murders. Susanna, as she mounted the ladder to be hanged, said:
"The Lord Jesus speed me; though my sins be as red as scarlet,
the Lord Jesus can make them as white as snow: the Lord
help my soul." In another case the confessants admitted that
they killed men, women, children, and cattle. The devil in
that case was in the shape of a chicken.

In the channel island of Guernsey three women confessed
to witchcraft before the royal court. They were Collette Du
Mont, and Marie and Isabel Becquet. Although torture was
used in this instance, the confessions were of the same order
as those voluntarily given. Collette's devil was in the form of
a dog or a cat. She had intercourse with him when he had
the form of a dog. She caused the death of the parish minister,
Mr. Dolbell, and of the wife and unborn child of his successor, Mr. Perchard. She rubbed a black ointment on her

which carried her through the air to the witches sabbath. There were fifteen or sixteen present. The devils were in the form of dogs, cats, and hares. Marie confessed that she, too, had intercourse with the devil when he was in the shape of a dog and it seemed to her as if he transformed her into a female dog. Isabel described her devil as in the form of a dog, with two great horns sticking up, and also in the form of a hare. She renounced God and worshipped him. As with the other two, the devil had intercourse with her while he was in the shape of a dog. He marked her on the upper part of her thigh. At the sabbath the devil sometimes took the shape of a goat. She never went to the sabbath except when her husband remained away all night at sea fishing. On their departure from the sabbath the devil made them kiss his butt. All three were strangled and burned.

On the Continent

THE CONFESSIONS ON THE MAINLAND of Europe were in some respects even more lurid than these. Confessants admitted not only to murder but to eating children at huge sabbaths and causing tempests, avalanches, snows, killing frosts, and the destruction of harvests. The numbers at their sabbaths ranged from 3,000 to 10,000. More than 600 women confessed to intercourse with demons. These relationships continued for periods of time running up to thirty years. One woman confessed that for twelve years she had relations with a demon to whom every six weeks she bore two "Elben" with which she bewitched people.

At Yssel in the Low Countries Marie de Sains claimed to have sacrificed hundreds of young infants at the devil's call. Where she got all of them nobody inquired or explained. Another woman confessed to killing children and causing tempests. Yet another, whose husband beat her, appealed for

help to God or the devil. A dark man appeared and promised
relief. She kissed his buttocks and gave him three of the hairs
on her head. They went to sabbaths and ate unbaptized children. A man confessed that 63 years before he had given himself to the devil body and soul. He gave his daughter to the
devil when she was six months old and the devil killed her.
By command of the devil he would beat the water of a brook,
raising destructive tempests. He would ride on a stick to the
sabbath. There they ate children. A female demon in the shape
of a twenty-year-old girl had intercourse with him. According
to another man a group of them rode on sticks and went like
the wind. Still another confessed that he took a mixture made
by a demon and threw it into a spring with the result that a
severe frost came and destroyed vineyards. A woman confessed that demons sickened men, women and beasts and destroyed harvests. Another related that the demons gave them
an ointment to sicken people. She touched the hand of a four-
year-old child with it and the child died within a fortnight.
They made a powder of the bones and intestines of children
to work evil on men and beasts. They ate the flesh of infants.
They trampled on the host. Yet another confessed that she
went to the sabbath every Saturday. There she adored the goat
and surrendered herself to him and to others. They ate the bodies of newborn children carried off at night. She killed two of
her aunts and also destroyed harvests and killed cattle.

Three women confessed that for thirty years they had carnal
relations with a demon and injured many people in body and
goods. Another admitted that for eighteen years she had intercourse with a demon who visited her twice a week. She
renounced Christ and when she took communion she retained
the host and gave it to her demon. She detailed a long list
of injuries to people. To yet another a demon promised money
and she kissed his foot. He gave her a stick eighteen inches long
and a pot of ointment. She would anoint the stick with the ointment and say, "Go in the name of the devil, go," and at once

she would be transported through the air to a sabbath. There they ate, drank, and danced. The demon changed to the shape of a black dog whom they all kissed under the tail.

The nun Jeanne Féry, of Cambrai, explained how the devil told her to do exactly the opposite of what her faith commanded: she was to stand when she had previously been taught to kneel, say the Lord's Prayer backward, spit upon the Host, and the like. Mère Jeanne des Anges, whose confessions along with those of sister nuns at Loudun sent to the stake their confessor, Urbain Grandier, told of demons and lions, the pell-mell of good and bad angels and the torment of indecent and unholy whispers in the night. A number of demons possessed her, the worst of whom called himself Isacaaron.

By comparison the stories of the Salem confessants are rather mild. Even so, they described the devil as a black man— one added a high crowned hat—and told of riding through the air on a pole or a stick. One related that she was carried through the air on a pole with three others to Five-mile Pond and baptized by the devil, who dipped her face in the water and made her renounce her former baptism.

5 Confessions of the Innocent, 1580-1958

FROM THE TIME of the witchcraft prosecutions onward, and even before, there were many other confessions of the innocent. Moreover, such confessions were free and voluntary. Whenever a particularly atrocious act was committed innocent people often came forward and on their own initiative confessed themselves to be the authors of it. Indeed the more heinous and sensational the offense the greater were the number of innocent confessants. More than 200 innocent people confessed to the kidnapping and murder of the Lindbergh baby. At least seventeen innocent persons confessed to the highly publicized sex murder of Elizabeth Short, who was known as "the Black Dahlia" because of the sheer black clothing she wore. Various innocent persons at various times claimed responsibility for the death of Joseph B. Elwell, the bridge expert, who was mysteriously slain in 1920 in his home in New York City. More than one innocent person claimed responsibility for the Wall Street explosion of the same year.

The centuries recorded a string of similar confessions. Numbers of early Christians falsely claimed to have committed offenses against the state. Indeed, so many of them at Antioch wilfully sought martyrdom by such claims as well as actually by outraging pagan temples or insulting the magistrates that the proconsul Antonius amazedly asked whether they had not ropes or precipices to kill themselves.

In November 1580 a man was convicted and executed on his own confession for the murder, near Paris, of a widow who was missing at the time. Two years later she returned to her home. In 1660 arose the case of the Perrys in England. John Perry gave a detailed confession how he, his brother Richard, and his mother Joan had murdered and robbed their master William Harrison. Richard, so John said, strangled Harrison while he and his mother stood by, took a bag of money out of his pocket, and threw it in their mother's lap. They were all three executed. Some years later Harrison returned, with a story of being kidnapped and sold to the Turks. One may not believe Harrison's story, but certainly John's was false. Six years later, the year of the great London fire, came Hubert's case. Hubert, a young Frenchman, gave a detailed account how he and three others were hired in Paris to set London on fire and how he had done it. He related so many circumstances that he was tried and executed. The account, however, related the doubts of those who heard the story: "Yet neither the judges nor any present at the trial did believe him guilty, but that he was a poor distracted wretch weary of his life, and chose to part with it this way."

John Bunyan told of the case of old Tod, who was hanged with his wife at Hartford about the same time that Hubert was hanged in London. While the judge was on the bench at a summer assize at Hartford, old Tod came into court clothed in a green suit, with a leathern girdle in his hand, his bosom open, and all in a dung sweat as if he had run for his life, and confessed: "My lord, here is the veryest rogue that breathes upon the face of the earth; I have been a thief from a child; when I was but a little one I gave myself to rob orchards, and to do such other like wicked things, and I have continued a thief ever since. My lord, there has not been a robbery committed this many years, within so many miles of this place, but I have either been at it or privy to it." The judge thought him mad, but after conferring with some of his brother judges let him and his wife be indicted of several felonious actions. He heartily confessed to all the charges.

In September 1797 the crew of the *Hermione,* an English frigate, mutinied, murdered the captain (a harsh man by the name of Pigot) and a number of the officers under circumstances of extreme barbarity, and took the ship into an enemy port. One midshipman escaped. He later identified many of the offenders. This incident became the basis for the confessions of numerous innocent English sailors. An admiralty official later stated: "In my own experience I have known, on separate occasions, more than six sailors who voluntarily confessed to having struck the first blow at Captain Pigot. These men detailed all the horrid circumstances of the mutiny with extreme minuteness and perfect accuracy. Nevertheless, not one of them *had ever been in the ship* nor *had so much as seen Captain Pigot in their lives*. They had obtained by tradition, from their messmates, the particulars of the story. When long on a foreign station, hungering and thirsting for home, their minds became enfeebled; at length they actually believed themselves guilty of the crime over which they had so long brooded, and submitted with a gloomy pleasure to being sent to England in irons for judgment. At the Admiralty we were always able to detect and establish their innocence, in defiance of their own solemn asseverations."

Sir Samuel Romilly told of another such English sailor whose case did not end so happily. This one confessed: "At the time the mutiny took place, I was a boy in my fourteenth year. Drove by the torrent of mutiny, I took the oath administered to me on the occasion. The examples of death which were before my eyes drove me for shelter amongst the mutineers, dreading a similar fate with those that fell, if I sided with or showed the smallest inclination for mercy . . ." He was executed. But he was innocent. At the time of the mutiny and murders on the *Hermione* he was at Portsmouth on board the *Marlborough*.

A sensational murder was committed in Edinburgh, Scotland in 1806: a bank porter with four or five thousand pounds of banknotes was struck dead by a single stab and robbed. A number of innocent people charged themselves with the offense. Lord Henry Cockburn later commented: "According to a strange craze or ambition not unusual in such cases, several charged themselves with the crime who to an absolute certainty had nothing to do with it."

In 1819 there occurred in Manchester, Vermont, a much-discussed case in this country, that of the Boorns, Stephen and Jesse, brothers. Stephen and Jesse's sister Sarah was married to Russell Colvin. In May 1812 Russell disappeared. Some years went by. In 1819 a neighbor had a dream which set investigation afoot. A boy walking near the Boorns' hovels came across a hollow stump partly filled with bones. The tidings ran. Murder will find a tongue: Manchester found hundreds. Jesse was taken into custody. He said Stephen did it. Stephen was extradited from New York, and confessed. They were tried, convicted, and sentenced to be executed. Then a reward was offered for the discovery of the missing man. He was located in New Jersey and returned home in time to prevent the executions. The bones were those of an animal. Years later, in 1860, Jesse Boorn was arrested in Cleveland, Ohio, for forgery. In custody he confessed that forty years before he was concerned in a murder and escaped by a false impersonation of the deceased. Both confessions were false.

In 1888–89 the Jack the Ripper murders took place in Whitechapel: again and again the bodies of women, murdered and mutilated, were found in the East End of London. These murders produced a round of innocent confessants, and furnished the basis for this observation by a subsequent editor of Best's work on evidence: ". . . murders of a specially horrible kind—as, for instance, the Whitechapel murders of prostitutes in 1888 and 1889—are followed by a series of false confessions."

A man named Shellenberger confessed that he and another murdered a husband and wife near Omaha, Nebraska. The facts showed that he was innocent. Later he gave a detailed account how in June 1899 he murdered Julian Bahuaud. There was corroboration but the indications were that he was innocent of this murder as well. The Supreme Court of

Nebraska pointed out: "There are numerous cases upon record where men have voluntarily confessed themselves to be guilty of atrocious crimes, where investigation has proved their innocence, and the confession could only be attributed to a defective or abnormal mentality. . . . Even in this state in recent years, unfounded confessions of murder have been made, and the confessing party acquitted when all the facts were disclosed."

In 1904 in Stepney, England, Emily Farmer was murdered. After the conviction of the real murderers, two in number, an innocent man came forward and made a full detailed confession of the crime. Frederick P. Wensley, who related the case in his book *Detective Days,* added: "He was just one of those half-wits who, for some queer reason, turn up not infrequently to confess to crimes that have attracted public attention." At another point in his book he stated: ". . . I thought it was one of the usual bogus confessions that are not uncommon in murder cases."

An interesting case, which reflected great credit on the prosecutor, involved the murder in 1924 of Father Hubert Dahme of the St. Joseph's Church of Bridgeport, Connecticut. Someone shot Father Dahme in the back of the head. An innocent person, Harold Israel, confessed to the murder. The prosecutor in the case was Homer S. Cummings, later Attorney General of the United States under President Franklin D. Roosevelt. His investigation developed the man's innocence and the case was dropped.

In Essex, England, a village constable named Gutteridge was brutally murdered on night patrol in September 1927. Two shots were fired into his head at close range and after he fell a shot was fired at each eye. A false confession was soon forthcoming. The confessant had given himself up earlier in another sensational case, a trunk murder committed the same year. This confession, too, was false. J. F. Moylan, who narrated the case in his book *Scotland Yard,* commented: "Bogus confessions by notoriety hunters or persons of unbalanced mind are common in murder cases, and one was soon forth-coming in this."

A French girl, Adele Bernard, was accused of murdering her newborn child. She confessed. But in prison she gave birth to a child in less than three months after the alleged birth of the child to whose murder she confessed. There are other instances where women have accused themselves of the murder of infants whom they never bore or who died naturally. One such described the whole scene with touching minuteness, the wailing of the young child, its piteous look, its burial in a little grave at the foot of a pine tree. And none of it was true.

The Chicago newspapers headlined the brutal killing of a pregnant woman whose body was found in a snowbank. William Kiss, a factory worker, turned himself in. Feeling immediately ran high against him because of the nature of the crime. Fortunately for him, a 19-year-old sailor at the Great Lakes Naval Station also came forward and confessed. This confession turned out to be true.

In 1953 Francis R. Noble, a 39-year-old counterman, confessed that he had strangled his common-law wife, whose nude body was found dead in bed beside him. He told the police: "I loved her so much, I had to do it." Actually the woman died of a heart attack.

In 1958 a New York seaman, Leo Turck, told the police that he had killed Serge Rubinstein, the financier who got into many legal difficulties, criminal as well as civil. But the seaman was innocent.

There are many, many more examples. In fact, there have been such a steady stream of them that various authorities, judges, prosecutors, detectives and legal scholars, have commented at different times on the frequency of the confessions of the innocent. Some of these comments we have seen. There are others. Johann Heineccius, a German lawyer, wrote in the first part of the 1700s: "Confession is sometimes the voice of conscience. Experience, however, teaches us that it is frequently far otherwise. There sometimes lurks, under the shadow of an apparent tranquility an insanity, which impels men readily to accuse themselves of all kinds of iniquity. Some, deluded by their imaginations, suspect themselves of crimes which they have never committed. A melancholy temperament, the tedium vitae, and an unaccountable propensity to their own destruction, urges some to the most false confessions."

Francis Wharton, an American scholar, in an excellent work for its time observed: "Delusion, a morbid desire to attract attention, a sort of epidemic which strikes down whole classes with a passionate impulse to insist upon some bloodstain on the conscience, something like hypochondriac epidemic impulse which insists upon some personal abnormality, weariness of life, a propensity to self-destruction through a channel which from its very tortuousness possesses its own fascination, a Lara-like desire to appear mysterious and dark, though in this case the propensity exudes in vague intimations of participation in nameless deeds of guilt rather than in confession of specific offences . . . So the publication of a conspicuous homicide is apt to generate a series of pretenders to the deed." In a treatise on criminal law Wharton remarked: "There is a species of morbid vanity which sometimes leads innocent persons to declare themselves guilty of crimes to which public attention is particularly drawn."

6 *Stalin and Vyshinsky*

A Burst of Nihilism

TWO KEY FIGURES in the exploitation of the inquisitional technique by the Communists were Stalin and Vyshinsky. Their predecessors in the preceding years and centuries by their excesses in government prepared the ground for them. In the immediate past such excesses were those of the Communists themselves.

When the Bolsheviks first came to power in Russia they sought in a burst of nihilism to destroy all existing legal and political institutions. As Vyshinsky explained twenty years later on the first page of *The Law of the Soviet State:* "The violent seizure of authority by the proletariat, the demolition of the exploiting society's machinery of state, and the organization (in lieu of the old state machinery, now reduced to fragments) of a new state is the most important thesis of the Marxist-Leninist doctrine of proletarian revolution." The nihilism of the Bolsheviks included the courts, the office of the procurator, or czar's attorney, and the legal profession itself. The first decree on the courts of November/December 1917 abolished them all (the czarist secret political police, the Ochrana, had already been abolished in February). For the old system of courts the communists substituted people's courts, with instructions that they were to be guided by the "revolutionary conscience and revolutionary concept of law." As for the procuracy, nothing specifically was at first put in its place. According to Krylenko, who was at one time people's commissar of justice, the picture of the feared and hated czarist procuracy

74

"was so fresh in the minds of the toiling masses that the mere thought of reviving the office was deemed a reactionary move." The legal profession was opened to "all honest persons of either sex who enjoy civil rights." Any unblemished citizen could appear in court as prosecutor or defender.

The first period of the communist revolution in Russia many have called militant or war communism (1917–21). There followed that of the New Economic Policy, or NEP (1921–28). Then came the five-year plans. During the period of war communism the regular courts functioned very little. Most of the new government's decrees relating to offenses were carried out administratively by the Cheka (Extraordinary Commission for Combating Counterrevolution, Sabotage, and Breach of Duty by Officials), set up in December 1917, and by special revolutionary tribunals. Cheka is a coined word from the beginning letters of the Russian equivalent for extraordinary commission. The Cheka, in the words of Lenin, was the "unsheathed punishing sword of the revolution." It had power to try and execute on its own authority. It and the special revolutionary tribunals were without judicial procedure and enforced what the regime itself called the Red Terror. This was the period when the communists drummed the theme of the expropriation of the expropriators and the liquidation of the bourgeoisie. The special revolutionary tribunals, by a decree of April 1919, were to be guided "exclusively by the circumstances of the case and by revolutionary conscience."

The regular courts not only did little business; they were also at first subjected to almost constant change. By the end of 1918 there had been no fewer than five decrees on the judiciary, three of which were not even enforced. A decree of February/March 1918 substituted for "revolutionary concept of law" the words "socialist concept of law" and "concept of law of the toiling masses." A decree of November 1918 on the people's courts provided that if there was no decree of the new government directly in point the "socialist concept of law" was to prevail. A note to this provision forbade the citation of any prerevolutionary law: "Any citation of the laws of the over-thrown government in a court decision or sentence is pro-hibited."

In theory nihilism continued to flourish for some years. A decree of December 1919 on the basic principles of criminal law announced that when communism finally arrived, the proletariat would "destroy the state as an agency of coercion, and law as a function of the state." There were to be no classes, no state, and no law. In the 1920s the leading Soviet jurists regarded law as an opiate like religion, a bourgeois fetish. With the triumph of collectivism, law, like the state, was bound to wither away. Stuchka, one of the first commissars of justice and president of the supreme court, wrote in 1927 that communism meant "not the victory of socialist law, but the victory of socialism over any law, since with the abolition of classes with their antagonistic interests, law will disappear al-together." High officials of the People's Commissariat of Justice told an English visitor in 1930 that all litigation, civil as well as criminal, would disappear within the next six or seven years, and those who disagreed with this prediction found it only much too short.

Eugene Pashukanis, the leading Soviet legal philosopher, in the decade before his disappearance in 1937 expounded these ideas. According to him, once capitalism was abolished there would be no more law, but only technical regulation: "The withering away of bourgeois Law can under no circumstances mean its replacement by some new categories of Proletarian Law, but only the withering away of Law in general, i.e., the gradual disappearance of the judicial element from human relations." Or again, ". . . morality, law, and state are forms of bourgeois society . . . They have no adequate capacity to hold a socialist content and are bound to die out to the extent that it is brought into being."

Retreat

NIHILISM DID NOT WORK and was soon abandoned in practice. One of the first parts of the old social structure to make a comeback was the legal profession itself. The decree on the courts of February/March 1918 admitted to the practice of law for remuneration members only of a special body of legal representatives embracing prosecutors and defense counsel, appointed by the local soviets. The decree of November 1918 put all members of this body on a straight salary basis and ordered the fee for an attorney's services to be collected by the state treasury. But the attempt to eliminate legal fees failed as dismally as the attempt to eliminate lawyers. Krylenko admitted the failure: "The result of this experiment was that whenever a person threatened by a penalty appeared before the court and wished to make his defense attorney defend him in the best way, he offered the attorney a fee. To eliminate this is beyond our power; it would be necessary to remake human nature." The old laws, too, continued to be applied, although in a somewhat lay fashion in the form of the ideas of lay associate judges, or people's assessors as they were called, as to how a case should be decided. "We only imagined," said Stuchka, "that we abolished the law. . . . The old law was quite persistent in the form of customary law. . . . The workers from the factories, when they were appointed as judges and came in contact with civil cases, and therefore with private law, became jurists; 'juridical logic' overtakes them."

In 1921 came what many called a strategic retreat, a bourgeois restoration, the NEP, which made certain concessions to the very ideas which the communists had denounced, such as the individual ownership of the means of production, individual profit from such ownership, individual employment of labor, and private trade for individual profit. The communists explained, however, that by means of the large socialist sector which remained the proletarian state controlled the commanding economic heights. During the NEP period the Soviet Union took shape. In 1922 and again in 1926 new criminal codes were promulgated. The 1922 Code was amended in 1923 and the 1926 Code in 1927, but Soviet lawyers continued to refer to them as the 1922 and 1926 Codes. The 1926 Code contained the sweeping Article 58 relating to counter-revolutionary offenses. In 1922 and 1923 there also appeared a Judiciary Act, a Civil Code, a Code of Civil Procedure, a Land Code, and a new Labor Code. In December 1922 the Russian Soviet Federated Socialist Republic (RSFSR) joined with some of its sister republics to form the Union of Soviet Socialist Republics (USSR), and a new constitution, which sealed the act of union, came into force in 1924.

The biggest retreat was in the case of the procuracy. Here the communists went back not only to czarist but to pre-1864 czarist Russia, when there was no separation of judicial and administrative functions. The RSFSR reestablished government attorneys in May 1922. Under Stalin the procuracy emerged as a centralized agency completely independent of provincial executive control.

Theory began to catch up with practice. This started even with Lenin. Although he deemed Soviet Russia to be living in a sea of illegality, he never ceased to demand revolutionary legality. He wanted to combine two opposites: nihilism on the one hand and orderly procedure on the other. He wanted terrorism to continue, and was reported on one occasion to have said that every Bolshevik should make himself a chekist; and yet he wanted to try to legalize it. In arguing for the definition of counter-revolutionary crimes in the 1922 Code he stated: "Justice ought not to remove the terror; to promise this would be to deceive either ourselves or others. It ought to establish and legalize it by principles, clearly and honestly."

Lenin also laid the basis for interpreting into obsolescence Engels' idea of the withering away of the state. In his *State and Revolution* he explained: "The bourgeois State does not 'wither away' according to Engels but will be 'abolished' by the proletariat in the course of revolution. It is the proletarian State or rather semi-State which will gradually wither away after this revolution."

Master and Servant

UPON THIS SCENE after Lenin's death in January 1924 arose Stalin. During the last year of Lenin's life the Politburo consisted of seven. In addition to Lenin, there were Trotsky, Stalin, G. E. Zinoviev, L. B. Kamenev, Nikolai I. Bukharin and M. P. Tomsky. In this period Stalin joined with Zinoviev and Kamenev to form a triumvirate within the Politburo in order to prevent Trotsky from becoming Lenin's successor. Trotsky had come to be commonly so regarded. The members of this triumvirate had an uninterrupted association with Bolshevism dating back to the split at the meeting of Russian socialists in London in 1903, which resulted in the two factions of Bolsheviks and Mensheviks. In the last days of the meeting, when it came to electing the leading bodies of the party, Lenin and his followers, the revolutionaries, obtained an unexpected victory over the moderates—some of the moderates had already departed. From then on, the former were called the men of the majority, Bolsheviki, and the latter the men of the minority, Mensheviki. In spite of their name, the Mensheviks were actually in the majority, certainly after the meeting in Stockholm in 1906. However, they were not as well organized as the Bolsheviks, and it was the Bolsheviks who picked up power in Russia in 1917 and carried out the October-November coup d'état.

In 1923 Zinoviev was chairman of the soviet of Petrograd, formerly St. Petersburg, soon to be renamed Leningrad, and also head of the Communist International, the Comintern. Kamenev presided over the Moscow soviet, and acted as Lenin's deputy in various capacities. Bukharin was in charge of press and propaganda. Lenin in his testament described him as "a most valuable and most eminent Party theoretician." Tomsky was president of the All-Union Central Committee of Trade Unions, and an advocate of trade union independence.

Stalin's first combination accomplished its purpose. In January 1925 Trotsky resigned from his post of people's commissar of war. In October 1926 came his removal from the Politburo, in November 1927 his expulsion from the party, two months later his exile to Alma-Ata in Central Asia, and in January 1929, an order for his deportation. He then went to the Turkish island of Prinkipo.

With Trotsky out of the running, Stalin in 1925 formed a new combination, this time with Bukharin, Alexey I. Rykov and Tomsky, in order to dispose of Zinoviev and Kamenev. Rykov had been the first people's commissar of the interior, but had resigned from the Central Executive Committee when that body decided in November 1917 to restrict the freedom of the press. He had also been opposed to the October-November revolution. After Lenin's death he rejoined the Politburo and became chairman of the council of people's commissars, the Soviet premier, succeeding Lenin.

Stalin's second combination also achieved its objective. At the fourteenth congress of the Bolsheviks, in December 1925, he managed to discredit his ex-partners. Then he sent Sergei M. Kirov, one of the old Bolsheviks from the Caucasus, to replace Zinoviev as chairman of the Leningrad Soviet. Zinoviev's position as head of the Comintern went to Bukharin. In November 1927, the party expelled Zinoviev along with Trotsky. The next month, at the fifteenth party congress, Kamenev and many others met the same fate. Zinoviev, Kamenev and others with them issued a statement in which they abased themselves and renounced their views. However, the congress refused to accept their capitulation and left the question of their readmission up to Stalin. He thus won an even more complete victory over them than he had over Trotsky. In June 1928, he allowed them to be readmitted to the party.

After the fourteenth congress, V. M. Molotov, K. Voroshilov and Michael Kalinin, often called "Papa," joined the Politburo; and after the fifteenth congress V. Kuibyshev and I. Rudzutak did so. Having demoted Zinoviev and Kamenev, Stalin now used the votes of the newcomers to undermine Bukharin, Rykov and Tomsky. Bukharin was removed from the leadership of the Comintern, Rykov from the premiership of the government and Tomsky from the leadership of the trade unions.

There were issues over which these men fought, although one has the feeling that a power struggle overshadowed any such issues. In Lenin's time there were no clear-cut lines of division on policy. Individuals moved from one position to another. Zinoviev and Kamenev, who later came to lead the left, had voted against the October-November revolution and had resigned with Rykov from the Central Executive Committee when that body in November 1917 decided to restrict the freedom of the press. Bukharin, who with Rykov and Tomsky later came to head the right, had headed the left during much of Lenin's time.

In the years after and just before Lenin's death the country was in its NEP period. Three of the principal issues at this time were: the building of socialism to completion in one country; the rate of industrialization; and the treatment of the farmers. On the issue of the building of socialism in one country there were some who said that this could not successfully be brought to completion unless the whole world was becoming socialistic. According to them, communism could not succeed in one country so long as capitalist states surrounded that country. Communism could not prevail if it remained but an island in a sea of capitalism. There were others who said that socialism could be built to completion successfully in one country.

On this and the other two issues Stalin at first took one position and then another. On the building of socialism in one country he first took the stand, early in 1924, that it could not be done. Later in the same year, in order to prove that Trotsky was not a good Leninist, he took just the opposite point of view. Scrutinizing Trotsky's past he and the other triumvirs came upon Trotsky's theory of permanent revolution, which Trotsky had announced back in 1905. They framed an argument against it. The result was the idea that socialism could be brought to completion in one country. This became Stalin's thesis. Bukharin later supplied the arguments for Stalin's position, and may fairly be said to be the co-author of the doctrine. Stalin and Trotsky thus had an issue.

During the time of the triumvirate, Zinoviev and Kamenev let Stalin go ahead with this thesis. However, at the fourteenth congress they denounced it as a substitution of national- communism for old-time bolshevism. Bukharin, Rykov and Tomsky, and the congress accepted Stalin's position.

On the other two issues, Stalin at first straddled. Bukharin, Rykov and Tomsky urged an almost Fabian gradualism. They were willing to have industrialization proceed at its own pace and they wanted to encourage the farmers to work hard and become prosperous. The more prosperous peasants, those who employed others, were the ones whom the communists called kulaks. The word kulak is not Russian but Estonian and literally means fist. Before the revolution it was applied to a usurer, especially in the village. The Russian word for peasant is muzhik. In 1928, when Russia resumed its socialist offensive and embarked upon the first of its five-year plans, Stalin denounced the kulaks. The following year he came out for rapid industrialization. These steps were the beginning of the end for Bukharin, Rykov and Tomsky.

By the end of 1929 Stalin had eliminated all his rivals. His dominance in the party was complete. In December Moscow celebrated his fiftieth birthday with more acclaim and propaganda than Russia had ever seen. Messages came to him from every part of the country. He was hailed as the "Lenin of today." The Russian masses would be taught to revere "our own dear father, Stalin," just as their predecessors had revered the czar as their "Little Father."

Stalin completed the return, which began under Lenin, to the autocracy of the czars. In his speech to the sixteenth party congress in 1930 he put the finishing touch on the elimination of Engels' idea about the withering away of the state, and white became black: "We are for the withering away of the state, while at the same time we stand for strengthening the dictatorship of the proletariat which represents the most potent and mighty authority of all the state authorities that have existed down to this time. The highest development of state authority to the end of making ready the conditions *for* the withering away of state authority: there you have the Marxist formula. Is this 'contradictory'? Yes, it is 'contradictory.' But it is a living, vital contradiction and it completely reflects Marxist dialectics." The following year Stuchka in the second edition of his *Course of Soviet Civil Law* in contrasting the general attitude toward law during the period of war communism with that of the NEP dealt with the former under the subtitle of "Down with the Law" and the latter of "Return to Law."

It was when Stalin was on the point of consolidating his position that the communist mass confession show trials began their development. The best known of these are the three Moscow purge trials of 1936–38, but there were four earlier ones which deserve mention: the trial of 50 engineers from the Shakhty mining area in the Donetz basin in 1928 for economic counter-revolution; the trial of Professor Leonid Ramzin, an expert in thermodynamics, and seven other Russian experts in November and December 1930 for economic sabotage; that of W. G. Groman, a statistician who had pressed for lower estimates of production in the first five-year plan, N. N. Sukhanov (whose real name was Himmer) and twelve other professors and state officials, and allegedly former Mensheviks, three months later on a charge of counter-revolutionary conspiracy; and the *Metropolitan Vickers* case in 1933.

The 50 engineers were accused of seeking to destroy coal mines and pave the way for the intervention of France and Poland on behalf of the expropriated Russian bourgeoisie.

Ramzin and his co-defendants were charged with the organization of a secret political party, a so-called Industrial Party, and a conspiracy with an organization of White Russians in France to induce a French invasion of Russia. Groman, Sukhanov and their co-defendants were alleged to be in a conspiracy with Mensheviks at home and abroad. All the defendants in these three cases confessed. Joel Carmichael, an editor, abridger and translator of Sukhanov's seven-volume *Notes on the Revolution,* wrote of the so-called Menshevik trial:

"At this late date it would doubtless be pointless to attempt an analysis of the evidence at this trial: it is interesting primarily for the exactitude with which it foreshadows the later trials. Sukhanov distinguished himself by a sort of inverted honesty: he gave a perfectly persuasive description of his views on a variety of political themes, and then, having perhaps enjoyed his favorite pastime of political exposition and analysis, he simply leaped over the hurdle between theory and action, and ended by blandly saying, more or less, that since he had had such and such opinions in the past about, for instance, the pernicious absurdities of 'War Communism,' and had once been sympathetic to Menshèvism, *therefore* he began actively plotting to promote armed intervention on the part of the 'bourgeois democracies,' etc."

The *Metropolitan Vickers* case involved eleven Russian and six British defendants. They were charged with industrial sabotage, espionage, and counter-revolutionary acts in the course of construction work at certain power stations. All of the Russians and one of the Englishmen, W. L. MacDonald, pleaded guilty. Another English defendant, L. C. Thornton, during the course of the pre-trial questioning, signed a statement containing damaging admissions, but at the trial he pleaded not guilty and repudiated the statement he had signed.

Such trials became a part of Stalin's technique of ruling. After a period of the excesses involved in them there would be some lessening of the regime's severity. This too was part of the pattern. When the drastic courses which the government

took under Stalin tended to get out of hand he went on record
from time to time to ask for a little moderation. After a breath-
ing spell the excesses would begin again, often enough because
he asked for them. He engineered the liquidation of the independent farmers. When this program was approaching catas-
trophe in 1930 he came out with an article in which he accused his followers of being "dizzy with success" and told them
to stop compulsory collectivization. After the confession trials
of the experts in 1930–31 he called for greater consideration
for them and a truce with the intellectuals.

This was in June 1931. Then in January 1933 he made a
speech in which he reviewed the alleged accomplishments of
the first five-year plan and concluded with a call for greater
vigilance against counter-revolutionary elements which he
claimed were still in their midst: "We must bear in mind that
the growth of the power of the Soviet State will increase the
resistance of the last remnants of the dying classes. It is precisely because they are dying and living their last days that
they will pass from one form of attack to another: to sharper
forms of attack. . . . That is why revolutionary vigilance is
the quality the Bolsheviks particularly require at the present
time." A few months later came the *Metropolitan Vickers* case.

However, one has the impression that up to this point the
communists had not yet refined their use of the inquisitional
technique. Of the six English defendants only one pleaded
guilty, and even he stated at the trial: "According to the testimony given by myself, I plead guilty; in actual fact, not guilty."
Another of the English defendants, Allan Monkhouse, who
later wrote a book about his experiences in Russia, during the
course of the trial, after hearing the performance of one of the
Russian defendants, commented: ". . . it is perfectly clear
to me that this case is a frame-up against the Metro-Vickers,
based on the evidence of terrorized prisoners."

Nevertheless the basic pattern in the case was confessional,
and the confessions that were given in this and the other trials
betoken their future nature. The first of the defendants in the

Metropolitan Vickers case to make a final plea, Gussev, began with this: "Citizen Judges, I have related to you the crimes I have committed. Here in this Court I once again keenly live through the heinousness of those crimes. . . ." The next one, Sokolov, started out in a similar fashion: "I have fully admitted the seriousness of all the crimes I have committed. Both at the preliminary examination and at this trial I have again lived through the horror of it. . . ." The various counsel for the defendants helped them out in their self-castigations as well as their denunciations of others.

A comparison of the records in these earlier cases with those in the three Moscow purge trials of 1936–38 indicates that it was in the three-year period between the *Metropolitan Vickers* case and the first Moscow purge trial that the communists increased the severity of the inquisitional system which they inherited from the czars. One of those who had a leading hand in this process, and who participated as well in all but one of the four earlier cases, was an ex-Menshevist lawyer, Andrei Y. Vyshinsky. He was the president of the court, the presiding judge, at the Shakhty trial and that of the experts, and the prosecutor in the *Metropolitan Vickers* case.

He joined the Social Democratic movement in 1902, and was associated with its Menshevist wing until after the October/November revolution. In 1920 he jumped on the Bolshevik bandwagon. He was a prosecutor of the RSFSR and a professor of law at Moscow University. In 1933 he became a prosecutor of the USSR and in 1935 chief prosecutor. He was the prosecutor in all three of the Moscow purge trials of 1936–38. He sat on the commission which formulated the 1936 constitution. Bukharin and Radek, whom he was to prosecute, were also members of this commission. Stalin chaired it. Vyshinsky became the chief authority on soviet law and the spokesman for the supremacy of Stalin's police state, a status which he retained until after Stalin's death in 1953. From 1949–1953 he was foreign minister, both succeeding and preceding Molotov in this post. Immediately after Stalin's death he was reduced to deputy foreign minister and permanent representative to the United Nations.

An incident occurred which furnished the circumstances for the expansion of Vyshinsky's role as inquisitor and the demonstration of his talents for invective. This was the assassination of Kirov, Stalin's lieutenant at Leningrad on December 1, 1934. He was killed in his office in the Smolny Institute by a young communist, L. V. Nikolayev. Whether some other incident could have served as the fuse for the great purge of 1936–38 one cannot say: this one seems to have done so. However, more than a year elapsed before the purge began in all its violence, and in the meantime the government took various unnecessarily drastic steps to deal with the situation.

On the day of the assassination the Central Executive Committee purportedly issued a decree applicable to cases involving "terrorist organizations and terrorist acts" which provided:

> 3. The cases must be heard without the participation of counsel.
> 4. Appeal against the sentences and also petitions for pardon are not to be admitted.
> 5. Sentence to the highest degree of punishment [death] must be carried out immediately after the passing of the sentence.

Russian lawyers know this decree as the Kirov Law.

Stalin sped to Leningrad and, as had the czars before him, himself engaged in questioning the author of the act. Nikolayev and his associates, and many others, were tried secretly and executed—104 in all, at Leningrad, Moscow, Kiev and Minsk. In addition, Zinoviev, Kamenev and eleven others were brought to trial, also in secret, in January 1935, before a military collegium of the Supreme Court of the U.S.S.R. at Leningrad. They were charged with forming an underground counter-revolutionary terrorist group which looked for armed assistance from foreign powers. Zinoviev got ten years and Kamenev five.

But Stalin was apparently still in fear lest Zinoviev and Kamenev become martyrs. After all they were old Bolsheviks. He proposed a deal to them in which he would publicly state that they had no connection with Kirov's assassins and they would admit that they had aimed at the restoration of capitalism. Zinoviev would not go this far. However, he was finally persuaded to give a statement in which he shouldered part of the responsibility for encouraging Nikolayev and those alleged to be involved in the Kirov incident: "The former activity of the former opposition could not, by the force of objective circumstances, but stimulate the degeneration of those criminals."

Yet Stalin's misgivings continued. In the spring he put some 40 of his own bodyguards through a secret trial. Two were executed and the rest sentenced to various prison terms. At Leningrad, Andrei Zhdanov, whom Stalin designated to replace Kirov, caused tens of thousands to be deported to Siberia. Many from other cities suffered the same fate. Stalin confessed his own involvement in these deportations: ". . . we were obliged to handle some of these comrades roughly. But that cannot be helped. I must confess that I too had a hand in this." The Russian people referred to these trainloads of deportees from various parts of Russia as "Kirov's assassins." Then in 1936, as if the pressure under the surface had been mounting all the time, the purge began and continued for three years.

Each purge year had its mass confession trial. In 1936 it was the trial of the sixteen, headed by Zinoviev and Kamenev. In 1937 it was the trial of the seventeen, headed by Y. L. Pyatakov and Karl B. Radek. In 1938 it was the trial of the twenty-one, headed by Bukharin, Rykov and H. G. Yagoda. Pyatakov had been chairman of the state bank, and assistant commissar of heavy industry, of which he was the real organizer. He and Bukharin were "the young members of the Central Committee" about whom Lenin wished to say a few words in his testament. Lenin appraised him as "a man of undoubtedly outstanding will and outstanding ability, but too much given

to administration." Radek had been the chief journalistic inter-
preter of the Politburo's foreign policy. Yagoda had helped to
prepare the 1936 case. He had been head of the political
police for two years, from September 1934, when he had succeeded V. R. Menzhinsky, until September 1936, when in turn
he had been replaced by Nikolai I. Yezhof. The defendants
in the three trials included all the members of Lenin's Politburo
except Stalin, Trotsky, who was abroad, and Tomsky, who shot
himself in July 1936, in order to avoid arrest. They included
an ex-premier, several ex-vice-premiers, two ex-heads of the
Comintern, most of those who had been Soviet ambassadors
in Europe and Asia, and an ex-chief of the political police.
The 1936 case was called that of the Trotskyite-Zinovievite
terrorist centre, the 1937 case that of the anti-Soviet Trotskyite centre, and the 1938 case that of the anti-Soviet bloc of
Rights and Trotskyites. The charges included treasonable negotiations with foreign powers, espionage, industrial sabotage,
and conspiracy to assassinate various members of the Politburo, including Stalin, and to restore capitalism. All the defendants confessed. As the cases progressed, the defendants
became more submissive and their self-accusations more revil-
ing. In the 1937 and 1938 cases the defendants condemned
themselves in language which was even more abusive of themselves than that of the prosecutor, Vyshinsky; and his theme
song was "that dogs gone mad should be shot—every one of
them!"

After the 1938 case the great purge gradually ground to a
close, and in the manner characteristic of Stalin's method of
ruling: he had some subordinate officials charged with exceeding their authority. In December 1938 there took place
before a military court at Tiraspol in the Moldavian republic
in the southwest corner of Russia a public trial of a Captain
Shiroky, head of the political police in Moldavia, and four
of his assistants. They were accused of arresting innocent
people and forcing them to give false confessions. Shiroky and
his co-defendants in turn gave confessions. They confessed

that they had extracted false confessions from others. He was sentenced to be shot. Earlier in the same month Yezhov, who had succeeded Yagoda in 1936 and helped to prepare the 1937 and 1938 cases, started on the road of his predecessor. He was removed from his post. His successor was one of Stalin's Georgian fellow countrymen, Lavrenti P. Beria. A few months later Yezhov was dead under mysterious circumstances. According to one report he hung himself.

At the eighteenth party congress in March 1939, convened after an interval of more than five years, Stalin announced that the great purge was at an end and promised his followers that there would be no more: "Undoubtedly, we shall have no further need of resorting to the method of mass purges." But at the time of his death in 1953 his old associates were living in fear that another purge was in the making. The charges against fifteen so-called "terrorist" doctors, nine of whom were publicly accused in January of that year and alleged to have given confessions, accentuated this fear. Nikita S. Khrushchev, the Russian communist party boss, in his secret speech of February 1956 declared:

> "This ignominious 'case' [of the doctors] was set up by Stalin; he did not, however, have the time in which to bring it to an end (as he conceived that end), and for this reason the doctors are still alive. . . .
> "Let us consider the first Central Committee Plenum after the Nineteenth Party Congress when Stalin, in his talk at the plenum, characterized Vyacheslav Mikhailovich Molotov and Anastas Ivanovich Mikoyan and suggested that these old workers of our party were guilty of some baseless charges. It is not excluded that had Stalin remained at the helm for another several months, Comrades Molotov and Mikoyan would probably have not delivered any speeches at this congress.
> "Stalin evidently had plans to finish off the old members of the Political Bureau. He often stated that Political Bureau members should be replaced by new ones."

Some have speculated whether Stalin's associates hastened his death in order to eliminate the danger of a new purge.

One of Stalin's greatest weapons was a centralized procuracy. He established this agency formally in the constitution which he caused to be ratified in December 1936. This was a few months after the 1936 case. The communists were to call this document the Stalin Constitution and hail it as the most democratic in the world. It announced in Article 113: "Supreme supervisory power to ensure the strict observance of the law by all Ministries and institutions subordinated to them, as well as by officials and citizens of the U.S.S.R. generally, is vested in the Procurator-General of the U.S.S.R." Then article 117 provided: "The organs of the Procurator's Office perform their functions independently of any local organs whatsoever, being subordinate solely to the Procurator-General of the U.S.S.R." The procurator general was appointed by and responsible to the Supreme Soviet alone. He was independent even of the council of ministers, and his term was the lengthy one of seven years. He in turn appointed the procurators of republics, territories and regions. Procurators had the power to order the arrest of those suspected of crime, and to appoint the examining magistrates who conducted the pretrial investigations of criminal cases. They were the prosecutors in criminal trials. Beyond all this, the procurator general was the eye of the state, just as in the days of Peter the Great. He had not only the powers which he had under the Judicial Laws of 1864, but also those which he had before.

Under the impact of Stalin's call for an all-powerful state and the drafting of the 1936 Constitution, Pashukanis and Krylenko in true Russian fashion had to confess the error of their ways—Stuchka died in 1932. In March 1936 Pashukanis wrote: "All talk about the withering away of law under socialism is just opportunistic nonsense, like the allegation that the governmental power begins to wither away the next day after the bourgeoisie is overthrown."

In November, Stalin in his report on the 1936 Constitution

stated: "And we need stability of laws now more than ever."
The following January *Izvestia* began a campaign demanding
a purge of the legal front. One of its editorials in March explained, echoing Stalin, that soviet citizens had to be sure of
the firmness of soviet law. Vyshinsky then led the attack. In
true bolshevist fashion he tried to harmonize opposites. He
praised the nihilistic destruction involved in the October/No-
vember 1917 communist coup d'état, but then demanded an
all-powerful communist state and denounced Pashukanis and
those whom he identified with him for their nihilistic approach to soviet law: "They preached anti-Party subversive
'theories' of withering away of the State and law . . . To the
students, the growing *cadres,* a nihilistic attitude toward the
soviet law was suggested." Indeed, Vyshinsky's very manner
of attack was nihilistic, for he did not try to persuade an op-
ponent, or others, by any kind of reasoned analysis; rather
he sought to annihilate him by vituperation. Labels took the
place of ideas. Pashukanis and Krylenko disappeared, not to
be heard from again after the early months of 1937. Recently
they were, as the expression goes, rehabilitated—posthumously.
Vyshinsky in *The Law of the Soviet State,* which came out in
1938, on one page asserted that Pashukanis had been "un-
masked as a spy and wrecker" and on the next referred in
scurrilous fashion to "the rotten theory of the wrecker Pashukanis." In yet another piece he called him a traitor along with
Krylenko and others.

The return by the communists, often in the name of patriotism, to the ways of czarist Russia, some have described as the
great betrayal and others as the great retreat. Whether one
calls it either of these or something else, the fact remains
that in the treatment accorded deviants in Russia, especially
those of a political nature, one can say as truly as one can
ever say it that the more things changed, the more they remained the same. It was this system which the communists
extended to other countries in which they seized power.

Lack of Independent Counsel

UNDER THE INQUISITIONAL SYSTEM of the communists, as Stalin and Vyshinsky helped to shape it, one of the great lacks of an accused, especially in a political case, was independent counsel. If the case was a political one, no matter what the procedure or what the court, an accused really had no one to be his advocate. Almost any trial that has occurred under a communist regime will illustrate the ineffectiveness of counsel for an accused. This will be true whether the trial took place in the 1930s, when publicized confession cases began their development, or in the 1950s. The only difference will be that as time went on, the pattern, just as in the case of the confessions themselves, became more pronounced. In the *Metropolitan Vickers* case in 1933 the counsel for one of the British defendants, Allan Monkhouse, in his argument for him admitted that he was guilty of bribery, although this was contrary to his client's position and wishes. Monkhouse on his return to England wrote a book about Russia in which he included a fairly dispassionate account of his trial. On the role of defense counsel he had these observations: "Subsequent developments, in my own case anyhow, show that these lawyers were only able to defend their clients in so far as it suited the prosecution that they should do so. My own counsel, Kommodov, actually pleaded 'Guilty,' on my behalf, to the charge of bribery, although I myself had pleaded 'Not Guilty.' He did this against my instructions and my wishes. His reason for his action and for the relatively poor defense which he made out of good material he had available can only be explained in one way, i.e., undue influence from the Prosecution. It must be remembered that in another trial where foreigners were involved, a Moscow lawyer who did too well for its [sic] clients was afterwards found guilty of some small technical offence, and banished from the city of Moscow for some years."

The best known of the defense counsel in the case was I. D. Braude. He represented another English defendant, L. C. Thornton. He, too, admitted that his client was guilty of one of the charges against him, although his client insisted on his innocence. In this instance the charge was espionage. Another lawyer, Kaznacheyev, who represented three Russian defendants, Oleinik, Gussev and Sokolov, by his questioning led Oleinik to characterize his own conduct thus: "There could be nothing more despicable, of course." In what was regarded as an argument on their behalf he stated: "Comrade Judges, it is difficult to detect anything abnormal in the fact that the Court is trying, must try, to punish the grave crimes, the ghastly picture of which has been unfolded before our eyes during the last few days! . . . The crimes committed by Gussev, Oleinik and Sokolov are immeasurably grave. They came here to answer for these crimes. They now appreciate the gravity of their crimes, appreciate it to the full. And Oleinik, in giving evidence here, found the proper words with which to appraise them; he frankly said: 'Nothing could be more vile.' . . . Under these circumstances, Comrade Judges, the plea that I can make for the mitigation of the punishment of the accused is very limited."

Yet another lawyer, who said that he was lucky because his clients chose the right method of self-defense in that they confessed with such repentant fullness, began his argument with this: "Comrade Judges, I can quite understand the indignation against the accused in the dock, and the agitation which moved the Public Prosecutor during his speech yesterday and at this morning's session—it is quite natural and follows from the essence and nature of the present trial. Indeed, not only is every lawyer who has taken part in the present proceedings agitated by the circumstances of this case; every honest rank-and-file Soviet citizen finds it difficult to maintain his equanimity in the face of crimes such as those with which the accused are charged; I say difficult, because these crimes were directed against the main branch of Soviet economy, I say more, directed against socialist construction."

And yet another who based his efforts on the submissive nature of the confessions of his clients stated near the outset of his argument: "Public opinion in the whole Soviet Union is unanimous in its feeling of great indignation evoked by the grave crimes which those who sit behind us in the dock have committed."

Braude, Kommodov and Kaznacheyev each represented a defendant in the 1937 Moscow purge trial. Braude and Kommodov were also in the 1938 case. In these cases most of the defendants did not have counsel. In the 1936 cases none of them had counsel. Vyshinsky, the prosecutor, conducted himself in his usual vituperative fashion. He demanded that all of them be shot like dogs. In the 1936 case he characterized them as "dogs gone mad," and in the 1938 case as "dirty dogs." After his demand of the death penalty in the 1937 case, Braude began: "Comrade Judges, I will not conceal from you the exceptionally difficult, the unprecedentedly difficult position in which the defence finds itself in this case. First of all, Comrade Judges, the Counsel for Defense is a son of his country. He, too, is a citizen of the great Soviet Union, and the great indignation, anger and horror which is now felt by the whole population of our country, old and young, the feeling which the Prosecutor so strikingly expressed in his speech, cannot but be shared by Counsel." Kaznacheyev followed Braude: "Comrade Judges, monstrous was the picture of treason and treachery which was unfolded before you in the course of these few days. The guilt of the accused in the dock is immeasurable in its gravity. The wrath of the people of the Soviet Union is understandable. The essence of the work of the Trotskyite organizations and the methods these organizations used to enlist those who it would appear had no connection with these organizations in the past, have been exposed here in the court with utmost clarity and cogency . . . the mere fact of being

a member of these organizations is a most heinous crime."
Then came Kommodov: ". . . Comrade Vyshinsky was pro-
foundly right when he described the struggle as a struggle
between two systems . . . the last stage of the struggle—
I hope that it really will be the last stage—was the most cynical
and most shameless. Here, as in a focal point, converged all
the forms of struggle which had spread in these nineteen years.
Diversive acts and wrecking, espionage and terrorist acts,
agreements with foreign interventionists and the partition of
Russia are here tied into one knot." In the 1938 case Kommodov began: "I think Comrade Judges, that there is no need
for me to tell you how difficult is the task of Defense Counsel
in the present case. This difficulty is rendered greater by the
stern demand of the State Prosecutor, which has met with
universal endorsement by Soviet public opinion."

The subservient note of defense counsel in political cases
in communist countries has continued to the present time.
Z. F. Stypulkowski, a prominent Polish lawyer and one of
the Polish leaders in the underground fight against the Nazis,
in his book, *Invitation to Moscow,* described what happened
in 1945 in the Moscow trial of himself and fifteen other underground Polish leaders:

> "The Moscow counsel, however, approached their 'de-
> fence' duties differently. The most eminent among them,
> Braude, was acting for two ministers of the underground
> Government, and his case was that both of his clients
> had made 'a full and sincere confession' of their guilt
> and had repented. Therefore he pleaded for the maxi-
> mum leniency.
>
> "He then added these remarks: 'As a Soviet citizen
> and as a barrister there is one other thing I must say
> . . . A feeling of the profoundest indignation fills the
> Soviet people when they hear of crimes committed
> against the Red Army—against the Soviet Union—by
> those sitting there in the dock, on the instructions of a
> handful of politicians and the Polish *emigré* government.

This handful of politicians, of bankrupt jobbers, is not
to be identified with the Polish people . . ."

On this speech, by as able counsel as the defendants could
get, Stypulkowski commented: "After listening to this speech
I was more than glad that I had not briefed any of the Soviet counsel. I don't know whether he would have helped much
in my defence, but I do know that he would have done all he
could degrade me, in accordance with instructions, or perhaps from an instinctive servility."

When Traicho Kostov, formerly deputy chairman of the
council of ministers of Bulgaria and secretary of the Bulgarian
communist party, who went to trial with ten others in Sofia
in December 1949 for being too independent to suit the tastes
of the Soviet Union, repudiated his confession at the trial
and admitted ideological errors only, his counsel rebuked him
and apologized for defending him. The audience hooted Kostov. When it came time for final arguments his lawyer, according to the official account, began by saying that he himself
had a confession to make: "Comrade Supreme Judges! I must
make a confession before you. My task at this trial as Counsel
for Traicho Kostov, the central figure in the trial, is a rather
hard one. But hard as the task of the Defence may be, it is
obliged to fulfil its professional duty." However, he explained
how in a socialist state there was no division of duty between
the court, the prosecutor, and defense counsel. All were seeking the real and actual truth, of course. He showed how completely the prosecution had made out its case, during the
course of which he declared: "At these disclosures one's hair
stands on end. This was my feeling. I trust that it was the feeling of every honest person, following the trial." He depreciated
confessions, for his client had repudiated his, but then in closing subtly implored him to return to it: "His fate is in his own
hands. If from his last words you feel and understand . . .
that a completely sincere repentance has taken place in him,
that he is wholly admitting his guilt, . . . this fact, which he

is able to bring you with the sincerity of his repentance, is such that the Court would have to take, is bound to take, into consideration. Such was also the warning of the comrade President." Note the use of the word "warning."

But Kostov did not yield to the warning either of the presiding judge or of his own counsel. He was sentenced to death —he would have been in any event. Two days later he was hanged. The next day the Sofia press carried the text of a new alleged confession.

Oatis reported on his trial: "Judge Novak [the presiding judge] said a lawyer had been assigned me. 'The function of a lawyer,' he said, 'is not to help the defendant escape sentence. It is to help him get a lighter sentence.' (This seemed to mean that I stood convicted even before I went to trial. And it was the presiding judge that was giving me the news.)"

In the biggest show trial since those of 1936–38, that of Rudolf Slansky, the secretary general of the Czech communist party, and thirteen other leading Czech communists in Prague in 1952, the five defense lawyers admitted that the prosecution had proven its case but suggested that the complete confessions of their clients were a ground for clemency.

Yet more recently Lieut. Roland W. Parks, one of the fifty American airmen who gave confessions to communist Chinese inquisitors, and who went on trial before the Chinese communists with three other American airmen, wrote: "Then my defense counsel made his 'plea.' You could imagine my surprise when my lawyer opened up by saying that he couldn't help being indignant at the 'crimes' that I had committed, and that the evidence against me was 'irrefutable.' He sounded more like a prosecutor than a defense attorney. But finally he got around to asking for clemency on the ground that I was only 22 when I committed these 'crimes' and that I was only 'acting on the orders of superiors.' He also emphasized that I had fully repented of my 'crimes.'"

7

Confessions to Communist Inquisitors

THE FIRST PEAK in the confessions to communist inquisitors occurred in the Moscow purge trials of 1936–38. An excerpt from the report of the 1936 case, which contains a bit of Vyshinsky's examination of Kamenev interspersed with a couple of questions to Zinoviev, and some editorializing, will show how the defendants put on sackcloth and ashes and proclaimed their sins:

> *Vyshinsky:* What appraisal should be given of the articles and statements you wrote in 1933, in which you expressed loyalty to the party? Deception?
> *Kamenev:* No, worse than deception.
> *Vyshinsky:* Perfidy?
> *Kamenev:* Worse.
> *Vyshinsky:* Worse than deception, worse than perfidy —find the word. Treason?
> *Kamenev:* You have found it.
> *Vyshinsky:* Accused Zinoviev, do you confirm this?
> *Zinoviev:* Yes.

Proceeding to explain the motives of his conduct, the accused Kamenev declares:

> "I can admit only one thing: that having set ourselves the monstrously criminal aim of disorganizing the government of the land of socialism, we resorted to methods of struggle which in our opinion suited this aim and which are as low and vile as the aim which we set before ourselves . . .

> *Vyshinsky:* Consequently, your struggle against the leaders of the Party and the government was guided by motives of a personal base character—by the thirst for personal power?
>
> *Kamenev:* Yes, by the thirst for power of our group.
>
> *Vyshinsky:* Don't you think that this has nothing in common with social ideals?
>
> *Kamenev:* It has as much in common as revolution has with counter-revolution.
>
> *Vyshinsky:* That is, you are on the side of counter-revolution?
>
> *Kamenev:* Yes.
>
> *Vyshinsky:* Consequently, you clearly perceive that you are fighting against socialism?
>
> *Kamenev:* We clearly perceive that we are fighting against the leaders of the Party and of the government who are leading the country to socialism.
>
> *Vyshinsky:* Thereby you are fighting socialism as well, aren't you?
>
> *Kamenev:* You are drawing the conclusion of an historian and prosecutor.

All but one of the defendants, I. N. Smirnov, were completely submissive, and he was virtually so. He admitted that he was "a member of the Trotskyite-Zinovievite centre" and that "the centre was organized on the basis of terrorism against the leaders of the Party and the government"; but he denied "responsibility for the crimes committed by the Trotskyite-Zinovievite centre after his arrest." Smirnov was one of the leaders for the Bolsheviks in the civil war which followed the October/November revolution.

The defendants, again with the possible exception of Smirnov, in their last pleas, which followed Vyshinsky's demand that they all be shot like "dogs gone mad," showed their acceptances of the prosecutor's version of the case. The first to speak, S. V. Mrachkovsky, ended with this: "I depart as a traitor to my party, as a traitor who should be shot. All I ask is that

I be believed when I say that during the investigation I spat out all this vomit."

Others followed in a similar vein. G. E. Evdokimov: "I don't consider it possible to plead for clemency. Our crimes against the proletarian state and against the international revolutionary movement are too great to make it possible for us to expect clemency."

E. A. Dreitzer: "I, at any rate, am one of those who have no right to expect nor to ask for mercy."

I. I. Reingold: ". . . The representative of the State prosecution, speaking with the voice of 170,000,000 Soviet people, demanded that we be shot like mad dogs. I knew where I was going and what I was going for. I and the whole of the terrorist Trotskyite-Zinovievite organization sitting here have been exposed by this trial as the shock troop, as a white-guard, fascist shock troop, of the international counter-revolutionary bourgeoisie . . . I fully admitted my guilt. It is not for me to plead for mercy."

I. P. Bakayev: ". . . We Trotskyites and Zinovievites not only worked for the benefit of the international counter-revolutionary bourgeoisie, we also worked hand in hand with the agents of the most bitter enemy of the working class, fascism."

R. V. Pickel: "Only one conclusion can be drawn. We represented a most brutal gang of criminals who are nothing more nor less than a detachment of international fascism. Trotsky, Zinoviev and Kamenev were our banner. To this banner were drawn not only we, the dregs of the land of the Soviet, but also spies, and agents of foreign states and those sent here for diversive activities.

"The last eight years of my life have been years of baseness, years of terrible, nightmarish deeds. I must bear deserved punishment."

So ended that evening's session. The next morning the statements continued. Kamenev: "Thus we served fascism, thus we organized counter-revolution against socialism, prepared, paved the way for the interventionists. Such was the path we took, and such was the pit of contemptible treachery and all that is loathsome into which we have fallen."

Zinoviev: "My defective Bolshevism became transformed into anti-Bolshevism, and through Trotskyism I arrived at fascism. . . ."

K. B. Berman-Yurin: "Yesterday, in his speech for the prosecution, the citizen State Prosecutor drew the complete picture of my crimes. And the proletarian state will deal with me as I deserve. It is too late for contrition."

E. S. Holtzman: "Here in the dock beside me, is a gang of murderers, not only murderers, but fascist murderers. I do not ask for mercy."

None of them got it. They were all sentenced to be shot.

The 1937–38 Purge Trials

THE 1937 AND 1938 TRIALS showed that Vyshinsky had tightened the screws of the inquisitional system yet a little more. Some of the defendants in condemning themselves in their final pleas used language which was even more abusive than his. One defendant, Pyatakov, wanted the judges to assure him that by his self-humiliation he had found favor in their eyes. Another, Radek, insisted that it was not he who had been tormented but that on the contrary it was he who had tormented his inquisitors—by not confessing sooner. He also urged, as did still another defendant, N. I. Muralov, the Bolshevik giant and a famous fighter, that henceforth there be the strictest adherence to the communist party line. To this Muralov added the formulation that he did not want to become a symbol, or banner as he put it, for counter-revolutionary forces. Yet another, A. A. Shestov, declared that the court must not and could not spare his life. With his blood he wanted to wash away the stains of his treason.

Pyatakov: "For the most painful thing for me, Citizen Judges, is not the just sentence which you will pass. It is the realization . . . that as a result of the whole preceding criminal underground struggle I have landed in the very heart, in the very centre of the counter-revolution—counter-revolution of the most vile, loathsome, fascist type, Trotskyite counter-revolution. . . .

"In a few hours you will pass your sentence, and here I stand before you in filth, crushed by my own crimes, bereft of everything through my own fault, a man who has lost his Party, who has no friends, who has lost his family, who has lost his very self.

"Do not deprive me of one thing, Citizen Judges. Do not deprive me of the right to feel that in your eyes, too, I have found strength in myself, albeit too late, to break with my criminal past."

Radek: ". . . I have admitted my guilt and I have given full testimony concerning it, not from the simple necessity of repentance . . . not from love of the truth in general . . . but I must admit my guilt from motives of the general benefit that this truth must bring . . . We must convince, firstly, the diffused wandering Trotskyite elements in the country . . . And we must also tell the world that what Lenin—I tremble to mention his name from this dock—said in the letter, in the directions he gave to the delegation that was about to leave for The Hague, about the secret of war. . . .

". . . For two and a half months I tormented the examining official. The question has been raised here whether we were tormented while under investigation. I must say that it was not I who was tormented, but I who tormented the examining officials and compelled them to perform a lot of useless work. For two and a half months I compelled the examining official by interrogating me and by confronting me with the testimony of other accused, to open up all the cards to me, so that I could see who had confessed, who had not confessed, and what each had confessed.

"This lasted two and a half months. And one day the chief examining official came to me and said: 'You are now the last. Why are you wasting time and temporizing? Why don't you say what you have to say?' And I answered: 'Yes, tomorrow I shall begin my testimony.' . . .

"And finally, we must say to the whole world, to all who are struggling for peace: Trotskyism is the instrument of the warmongers . . . We cannot, nor can I, ask for clemency, we have no right to it. . . ."

Muralov: ". . . I did not want to remain a fool. I did not want to remain a criminal, for had I refused to give testimony I would have been the banner for those counter-revolutionary elements that unfortunately still remain on the territory of the Soviet Republic. I did not want to be the root from which poisonous shoots would sprout. . . ."

He was led to give this formulation earlier during Vyshinsky's examination of him at the trial on the reason why he finally began to confess after holding out for eight months: "And I said to myself, almost after eight months, that I must submit to the interests of the state for which I had fought for twenty-three years, for which I had fought actively in three revolutions, when my life hung by a thread dozens of times.

"Was I to remain and continue to aggravate the affair? My name would serve as a banner to those who were still in the ranks of counter-revolution. . . ."

Shestov: ". . . I am not asking for mercy. I do not want clemency. The proletarian Court must not and cannot spare my life. Here before you, in the face of the whole working people, in the face of those oppressed by capitalism in all countries, to the best of my ability I shot to pieces the ideology that held me captive for thirteen years. And now I have only one desire, to stand with calmness on the place of execution and with my blood to wash away the stain of a traitor to my country."

M. S. Boguslavsky: "The trial has disclosed a hideous picture of crime, treachery, blood and treason . . . I stand before you today as a state offender, a betrayer, a traitor."

Y. N. Drobnis: "Yesterday the State Prosecutor gave a complete and exhaustive summary of all my heinous crimes . . .

"All of this happened because for years I continued to live in the stuffy, stinking, foul, evil-smelling Trotskyite underworld. . . .

"Arrest and imprisonment were the purgatory which enabled me completely to sweep away, to rid myself of, all that filth. I did this with complete determination, with complete firmness and consistency."

I. A. Knyazev: ". . . Yes, I will say more than was said by the State Prosecutor. I worked to prepare for war. To put it simply I worked for the approach of war, in order to clear the path, to pave the way for the carrying to power of the scoundrel Trotsky. . . ."

Shestov got this wish. He was sentenced to be shot. So, with the exception of Radek and three others, were the rest.

In the 1938 case the most independent of the defendants, Christian G. Rakovsky, successively premier of the Ukraine, Soviet ambassador at London and then at Paris, who for a time had refused to return to Moscow but finally had gone back after all, denied that the communist revolution in Russia ended by devouring its own children:

"Like a galley-slave fettered to his galley, I am fettered to the 'bloc of Rights and Trotskyites' with the heavy chain of my crimes . . . People are satisfied with the trite and bourgeois explanation, according to which all revolutions finish by devouring their own children. The October Revolution, they say, did not escape this general law of historical fatalism.

"It is a ridiculous, groundless analogy . . . bourgeois revolutions did indeed finish by devouring their own children. . . ." But not, to be sure, the communist one. His reference, without naming the author, was to Vergniaud's statement: "The revolution, like Saturn, successively devours its children."

Another defendant, S. A. Bessanov, went Radek in the 1937 case one better. He did not stop at saying that he had tormented his inquisitors but rather called his resistance to them a crime, and an additional one to those which Vyshinsky had already enumerated: "But apart from the crimes spoken of in the Indictment and in the speech of Citizen the State Prosecutor, I must admit yet another crime against proletarian justice, which has not been spoken of at the trial." The "crime" was his refusal for ten months to confess.

As had Radek and Muralov in the 1937 case, so Bukharin and Yagoda in the 1938 case stressed the importance of blind obedience to the communist party line. So in one form or another did a number of others, Rykov, V. F. Sharangovich, A. P. Rosengoltz, I. A. Zelensky, and yet others. Rykov: "In my last plea I confirm the admission of my monstrous crimes which I made during the trial. I have betrayed my country . . .

". . . And so I want, to this end, firstly, that my former supporters should know that I have given away—as we say in the underground movement—exposed all of them whom I could remember.

"I would like those who have not yet been exposed and who have not yet laid down their arms to do so immediately and openly. . . .

"Salvation lies only in laying down their arms. . . ."

Sharangovich: "Citizen Judges, I do not intend to say anything in my defence. I have committed loathsome, vile and heinous crimes against the country and the people, and I perfectly realize that I must fully answer for them before the proletarian Court. I have betrayed my country, and as a traitor I deserve no mercy. . . .

"I have come to understand the full horror of the treasonable and treacherous crimes I have committed against the Soviet people and the Soviet country . . . I desire only one thing, namely, that my crimes, which I have frankly recounted, may serve as a warning to those who are still trying to carry on, or who are carrying on treasonable activity against the Soviet Union and against the Soviet people. . . ."

Rosengoltz: "Trotskyism is not a political current but an unscrupulous dirty gang of murderers, spies, provocateurs and poisoners, it is a dirty gang of henchmen of capitalism. . . .

"The lesson and the conclusion which must be drawn from this trial by the vast masses of the Soviet Union consists, in the first place, in the fact that the general line of the Bolshevik Party must be kept undeviatingly pure. Woe and misfortune will betide him who strays even to the smallest extent from the general line of the Bolshevik Party. . . ."

Zelensky: "Citizen Judges, I must say that the sum total of our crimes, our vile and treacherous activities, is horrifying . . . This only honest thing open to us was relentlessly and thoroughly to expose to the country, to the revolution, to the revolutionary people, all our vile actions and crimes, all our accomplices and confederates, all the monstrous criminal activity of the 'bloc of Rights and Trotskyites.' . . ."

M. A. Chernov asserted that his crimes were so heinous that no punishment would be adequate: "Citizen Judges, I am taking advantage of my right to the accused's last plea not in order to defend or exculpate myself. The heinous crimes which I committed against the great Soviet country can neither be exculpated nor defended.

"I am a traitor to the Socialist fatherland. I was selling the interests of the fatherland to fascism, the enemy of the working class and of the whole of humanity. . . .

"The crimes which I committed, I repeat, can be neither defended nor exculpated. They merit the most severe punishment. . . .

"My crimes are great and monstrous. Any punishment which the Court deems necessary to mete out to me would be inadequate as against these crimes."

P. T. Zubarev affirmed that for his crimes no punishment

would be too great: ". . . I realize the profound depths to which I have fallen and the full gravity of the crimes I have committed. I also realize the utter gravity of my responsibility before the proletarian Court. I fully and entirely agree with the speech of the State Prosecutor, with the description he gave of my criminal activities, and with his demand for the supreme penalty. The penalty he demands would be a merited punishment for the gravity of those crimes I have committed. And there is no punishment which the gravity of these crimes does not warrant."

V. I. Ivanov could find nothing to lessen his guilt: "In order to give a clear idea of my state of mind by the time of my arrest I would like to say a few words about the poisonous, asphyxiating atmosphere that prevailed in our counter-revolutionary underground organization. . . .

"It is especially painful for me to stand before the people, the broad masses, as a betrayer of my country, as a traitor. But I must say that I have now made a clean breast of my crimes to the Court. When I began to analyze my crimes and wish to find mitigating circumstances, I cannot, amidst my dastardly crimes, find anything to mitigate them. . . .

". . . It is hard to go on living when you have been through a black and stinking cesspool. When I pondered whether there was anything to lessen my guilt, whether there was any crime about which I could say that I had not committed it, I could find nothing."

And woe to those such as Rakovsky, who in reliance on the party's pledges about the independence of the outlying republics had stood up to Great-Russian chauvinism. A whole section of the 1938 case was given over to plots in the Ukraine, Uzbekistan, White Russia and Kirgizia for separation from the Union. Excerpts from two final pleas, those of C. F. Grinko of the Ukraine and A. Ikramov of Uzbekistan, are enough to show what Moscow demanded.

Grinko: ". . . I have no right to a mitigation of the sentence. I am wholly and completely in agreement with the qualification and political estimation, both of our crimes in general and of my crimes in particular, as given in the speech of the Procurator of the USSR. . . .

". . . as one of the organizers of the Ukrainian national fascist organization, I operated particularly in the Ukraine. . . .

"The Procurator of the USSR was right when he said that under the leadership of the Bolshevik Party and the Soviet government, the Ukrainian people, advancing along the road of the national policy of Lenin and Stalin, have been raised to such a high level as never before in all its previous history . . . this Ukrainian national fascist organization, which it is my sad lot to represent before the Court, was, by resorting to bogus slogans of national 'independence,' leading the Ukrainian people to the yoke of German fascists and Polish gentry. . . .

"And to all this I replied by betrayal, by darkest betrayal, of the Party, the fatherland and Stalin.

". . . In my testimony I did not spare myself, did not spare any of my confederates. I named all the facts and all the plotters known to me. I must confess that I did not do this at once . . . In a word, could I at once lay bare my soul, the soul of a traitor, the like of which the world has never seen? But I have done this to the very end. . . .

"I will accept the most severe verdict—the supreme penalty —as deserved. . . ."

Ikramov: ". . . We have been quite rightly called enemies of the people, traitors to the fatherland, spies and assassins. . . .

"Fully admitting all the crimes committed by me and by the nationalist organization in Uzbekistan which I directed, admitting my crimes as a participant in the 'bloc of Rights and Trotskyites,' I have told all I knew, named all the accomplices in the crimes, and have laid down my arms. And so, if there is anything that can be said in my favor when asking for mercy, for clemency, it is that I, a beast in man's shape, stand absolutely naked. I have told everything I know. I have lanced the ulcer within me. And I now feel greatly relieved. . . .

"I do not say all this so as to save my vile skin. I say this so that every citizen of the Soviet Union may know what criminals we are, what the nationalists were making for, and whither they would have led the peoples of Uzbekistan. Our path was the path of oppression, the path of enslavement of the peoples of Uzbekistan."

The last to speak was V. A. Maximov-Dikovsky: ". . . In the light of the picture of the crimes which was unfolded here in Court I cannot but add my voice to the estimation which was given here by the State Prosecutor: a gang of traitors and spies, of diversionists and betrayers, provocateurs and murderers. These are grave, sinister words, but the criminal deeds committed by us are even more grave, the people who committed these deeds are even more despicable. . . ."

All save three, Rakovsky, Bessanov and D. D. Pletnev, were sentenced to be shot.

With the 1938 case the confession show trials were at an end for a time, but the pattern for their preparation and conduct had become fairly well set. Such trials could now be used at will. There were two in Russia during the war and there have been many since in all parts of the communist world. In December 1943 the Russians tried three Germans and a Russian for atrocities committed during the German occupation of Kharkov. They were: Captain Wilhelm P. Langheld, age 52, a Nazi counter-espionage officer; Reinhard Retslau, age 36, a member of the German secret police; Lieutenant Hans Ritz, age 24, an assistant commander of an SS company; and Mikhail Bulanov. All confessed in the usual fashion. All were hanged.

In 1945, when the Soviet Union was engaged in circumventing Great Britain and the United States in order to put into effect its own scheme for the new government of Poland, it carried off to Lubianka prison and placed on trial in Moscow sixteen Polish leaders in the underground fight against the

Nazis. They were tried before the Military Collegium of the Supreme Court of the U.S.S.R. in the same room where the 1936–1938 trials took place. The charges included espionage, planning military action with Germany against the U.S.S.R., and acts of sabotage against the Red Army. Among the defendants were General L. B. Okulicki, Commander-in-Chief of the Polish Underground Home Army, Jan S. F. Jankowski, deputy prime minister, Kazimierz S. Baginski and Stanislaw F. Mierzwa, leaders in Stanislaw Mikolajczyk's peasant party, Kazimierz W. Puzak, general secretary of the Polish socialist party, and Z. F. Stypulkowski, a prominent Polish lawyer and one of the leaders of the National Democratic party. None of the defendants was a communist. All of them had suffered much for five years in order to help defeat the Nazis. Yet all save one, Stypulkowski, gave a confession. Stypulkowski later managed to get to England. Here he gave a convincing account of his interrogations in his book *Invitation to Moscow*. The ruse which the Russians used to get custody of the sixteen Polish leaders in order to take them to Moscow was an invitation to lunch with Marshal Zhukov. This proceeding allowed Great Britain and the United States to lull themselves sufficiently so that Russia could proceed with its Lublin Committee and ultimately a communist government for Poland.

Post var Trials

AFTER THE WAR the communists took over not only in Poland but in Hungary, Rumania, Bulgaria, Yugoslavia, Albania and Czechoslovakia as well. They found the farmers in these countries as independent and difficult as the Russian communists had found the Russian peasants. Accordingly in 1947 and 1948 various peasant leaders in a number of these countries were put through confession trials: Nikola D. Petkov, secretary of the agrarian union in Bulgaria, and four others;

Zygmunt Augustynski, editor-in-chief of the leading daily paper of the peasant party in Poland and two others, and subsequently Mierzwa, one of the sixteen Polish leaders tried in Moscow in 1945, and others; Dr. Iuliu Maniu, president, and Ion Mihalache, vice-president, of the national peasant party of Rumania, and others, and later fifty-six additional members of this party. Petkov himself did not plead guilty, but his associates did, and he was alleged to have written a statement after his sentence admitting guilt.

In 1948 the Soviet Union and its Communist Information Bureau, the Cominform, broke with Yugoslavia. This resulted, beginning in 1949, in numerous trials in the countries which were the associates of Russia in Eastern Europe of persons who were too friendly with Tito, too independent, or otherwise unsuitable to the Soviet Union: Lieut. Gen. Koci Xoxe, vice premier, minister of the interior, and organizational secretary of the communist party of Albania, and four other leading Albanian communists; Laszlo Rajk, formerly minister of the interior and then minister of foreign affairs of Hungary, and seven others; Traicho Kostov, formerly deputy chairman of the council of ministers of Bulgaria and secretary of the Bulgarian communist party, and ten others; and many more.

In August 1951 Poland and Rumania each concluded such trials at the same time. The trial in Poland involved nine persons and the one in Rumania eight. Those in Poland were former army officers, four of them generals. Those in Rumania included Maj. Gen. Mihail Romanescu, formerly a top air force general, and Alexander Liciu, formerly president of the Bucharest court of appeals. The respective prosecutors made their speeches on the same day, each asking for severe punishment, and three days later the respective courts both passed sentence. One of the witnesses in the Polish case was Marjan Spychalski, a former general as well as vice minister of defense. He confessed to his fellow-communists that he had suffered from a Tito-like nationalism. Kostov was the one who at his trial insisted on repudiating his confession in spite of hoots from the audience and rebukes by his own counsel, and admitted ideological errors only. According to the report of the case put out by Bulgaria he admitted having had an incorrect attitude toward the Soviet Union, but he refused to "plead guilty to having capitulated before the fascist police, nor to having been recruited for service in the British Intelligence, nor to conspirative activities with Tito and his clique," and would not confirm his deposition. The correspondent for the Associated Press at this trial was later to give his own confession—in Prague. He was William N. Oatis.

Confession cases have involved clergymen, Catholic as well as Protestant: Joseph, Cardinal Mindszenty and six others in Hungary in 1949, and Archbishop Joseph Grosz and three co-defendants in 1951; fifteen Protestant pastors in Bulgaria in 1949; and two Catholic bishops and eight others in Rumania in 1951. Their confessions have not been much different from the rest. Mindszenty said he was sorry he had violated the laws; if his actions had in any way harmed the people of Hungary or the Roman Catholic Church, he wanted to be forgiven for this. Archbishop Grosz stated: "Honorable County Court! Availing myself of the right to the last plea I wish to declare that I regret and I am sorry about my offences against the Hungarian People's Republic. . . .

". . . In the loneliness of the cell I pondered and meditated much and I have realized . . . that my acts have damaged and harmed the Hungarian working people. But the words of the Gospel encourage me . . . God has no contempt for a humble and contrite heart . . . I hope that my fellow priests, believers and friends, learning from my example will not travel the road which I trod and will refrain from harmful acts, disadvantageous even for the Church, which I committed."

Csellar, one of Grosz's co-defendants acknowledged: "Honorable Court! I have committed grave crimes. These originated in the bottomless morass of immorality that surrounded me in the Order of St. Paul and which I had not the strength to get rid of. . . .

". . . Honorable Court! I have committed infamous and sinful deeds against both God and men. I only realized the profundity and gravity of my crimes when in the course of the investigations I surveyed my life. Then the real gravity of my crimes and offenses unfolded before me. I have confessed everything. I have to atone for my criminal deeds, I shall have to suffer punishment for them. . . ."

The year 1949 witnessed not only numerous confession show trials in Russia's satellites, those of Cardinal Mindszenty and Laszlo Rajk in Hungary, of fifteen Protestant pastors and Traicho Kostov in Bulgaria, and that of Koci Xoxe in Albania; but also one in eastern Siberia, that of Gen. Otozo Yamada, formerly commander-in-chief of the Japanese Kwantung army, and eleven of his subordinates. This trial took place in Khabarovsk at the end of December. The charges were the preparation and use of germ warfare weapons. All the defendants confessed. The story the communists presented at the trial was that in 1935 and 1936 the Japanese general staff and war ministry, acting upon secret instructions from Emperor Hirohito, formed two top-secret units for engaging in germ warfare. The germs, so the story went, were tested on Chinese and Russian prisoners, and used in the Nimpo and Changteh areas in China and on the borders of Russia; and would have been used on a much wider scale had it not been for the swift advance of the Russian army into Manchuria and its destruction of the Kwantung army. The defendants told of planes equipped with special receptacles for carrying and dropping "plague-infected fleas," which were supposed to have caused plagues in the Nimpo area. Gen. Yamada, under the leading questions of his own counsel, concluded his examination this way:

> *Question:* What is now your attitude towards the deeds of which you have confessed yourself guilty, and for which you have been brought to trial?
> *Answer:* I must say that I consider all that I did an

evil thing—I want to correct myself: I consider it a very evil thing.

Question: May I, your counsel, understand your reply to mean that you repent of your deeds?

Answer: Yes, I want it to be understood that way.

In his final plea he said:

"As for the monstrous crimes that were committed for the sake of preparing to conduct bacteriological warfare, I realize that responsibility for this rests upon the chiefs of detachments 731 and 100 and upon all the Commanders-in-Chief of the Kwantung Army, ending with myself. . . .

"I realize the whole gravity of my guilt. I realize the whole weight of my crimes and I give no thought to the question as to whether the penalty will be severe or light for me."

The other defendants followed suit. The first one to make his last plea was Kiyoshi Kawashima, a major general in the medical service. He told the court:

"I fully realize that the crime I committed was a very heinous crime against humanity.

"This is not the first time I think so, these thoughts are not new to me, but here, in this court, I became particularly strengthened in these thoughts and feelings.

"I am ready to accept the severest sentence the Court may pronounce."

Yet another, Yuji Kurushima, a laboratory orderly, stated: "I am filled with infinite hatred for the militarists who dragged me into this wicked business—participation in preparations to conduct bacteriological warfare. From childhood I was brought up in a false environment, brought up on the principles of a decayed ideology. But, as my counsel for defence said, I am not the same Kurushima that I was four years ago.

"In conclusion, I express thanks for the kind way in which I and the other prisoners of war here have been treated."

All of the defendants were of course found guilty and all but two of them drew sentences of from fifteen to twenty-five years. In February 1950 the Russians presented Secretary of State Dean Acheson with a twenty-two-page note in which they demanded that Emperor Hirohito be tried for germ warfare. A few months later the communists invaded South Korea.

The first American to confess was Vogeler. He went on trial with six others in Budapest in February 1950, a few months before the Korean war broke out. According to the report of the case issued by Hungary his final plea included: ". . . I am sincerely sorry for the subversive activities that I carried on against the People's Democracy of Hungary. Especially as I was sent here from a big country, America, to Hungary, a small country, to interfere and undermine its efforts in rebuilding and rehabilitating itself from the effects of war. I wish to avail myself of the privilege of the last word to state that I gave testimony freely and openly, without coercion or maltreatment, as to my knowledge has been claimed in such cases. But I would like to state that I have been treated correctly and fairly throughout the investigation and my trial. I hope that my testimony will serve in some small measure to show the remorse I feel at my guilt. . . ."

After much negotiating between the United States and Hungary Vogeler was finally released in April 1951, but five days before this occurred Oatis was arrested in Czechoslovakia.

Vogeler, after his return to this country, reported that one of his chief inquisitors said to him: ". . . If Mindszenty told me what I wanted him to tell me, so will you. Make no mistake about it. Even if Jesus Christ were sitting in your chair, He'd tell me everything I wanted Him to." One wonders if the inquisitor was familiar with Ivan's story about the Grand Inquisitor in Dostoevski's *The Brothers Karamazov*. Ivan did have Jesus return to the earth, to Seville, Spain, the day after the Grand Inquisitor had burnt almost a hundred heretics at an enormous auto-da-fé.

To Oatis' confession in 1951 communist inquisitors added

the first reported confessions from members of our armed forces. In November four American fliers, Captains David H. Henderson and John J. Swift and Sergeants Jess A. Duff and James A. Elam, on a flight from Erding Air Base, near Munich, to Belgrade, Yugoslavia, with supplies for the American Embassy there, got lost, were forced down in Hungary, and taken into custody. The following month they were put on trial and, according to an official Hungarian announcement, admitted that they had deliberately flown over Hungary by daylight in good weather with their navigation equipment at all times working. In a later account Captain Swift told how he had finally signed a statement in which he had admitted that they had crossed the Hungarian Border.

Each year brought its new crop of reports of confessions and confession trials. In 1952 the Chinese communists procured the confessions of two American pilots, Lieutenants Kenneth L. Enoch and John S. Quinn, that they had dropped germ bombs on North Korean cities. Rumania and Bulgaria each had a mass trial of ten. The charge in the Rumanian case was sabotage on the work of the Danube-Black Sea canal and in the Bulgarian case espionage. Bulgaria also tried various leaders of the Catholic church in a series of cases. A returning American lawyer, Robert T. Bryan, Jr., who had been a captive of the Chinese communists, admitted that he had given them a confession, but asserted that his captors had tortured him and injected a drug into his spinal column. On the other hand a released American missionary, the Rev. Francis Olin Stockwell, related in Hong Kong how his captors had gotten him to give a detailed wire-recorded confession to charges of espionage without any physical maltreatment: "In the beginning I defended my own viewpoint. Then I decided that I would be in jail until I died unless I interpreted myself as they interpreted me . . . I admitted to six code messages and also manufactured a story that I kept a rifle. This helped convince them I was sincere."

At the time of the Rev. Francis Olin Stockwell's release the communists were staging the biggest show trial since those of 1936–38. They were putting it on in Prague. The defendants were fourteen leading Czech communists who had all held important posts: Rudolf Slansky, the secretary general of the Czech communist party, an ardent Moscow-trained Muscovite who returned to Czechoslovakia in 1944 with the Soviet army and was the mainspring of the communist coup in 1948; Bedrich Geminder, chief of the international section of the Czech communist party; Ludvik Frejka, head of the economic department in the office of the president, author of Czechoslovakia's two- and five-year plans; Josef Frank, Slansky's deputy; Dr. Vladimir Clementis, minister of foreign affairs; Bedrich Reicin, deputy minister of national defense; Karel Svab, deputy minister of national security; Arthur London and Vavro Hajdu, deputy ministers of foreign affairs; Evzen Loebl and Rudolf Margolius, deputy ministers of foreign affairs; Otto Fischl, deputy minister of finance; Otto Sling, district party secretary in Brno; and André Simone, editor of the communist central organ, *Rude Pravo*. According to Dr. Edith Bone, Simone twenty years earlier was Otto Katz, and was in Paris editing the *Brown Book on Nazi Atrocities*. Before his arrest Clementis was in the United States representing his country at the United Nations. Like Rakovsky before him he hesitated for a time about going back, but finally, like a good communist, he returned. Part of the case against Oatis consisted of a request to him to check on the reported disappearance of Clementis. The trial took place before a five-man People's Court in Pankrac prison, where Oatis was tried.

Eleven of the fourteen, all except Clementis, Frank and Svab, were Jews, and the indictment described each of the eleven as "of Jewish origin." The charges included participation in a worldwide "Jewish nationalist Zionist imperialist" conspiracy to overthrow the government, high treason, espionage, sabotage, murder, and planning to kill the Czech president, Klement Gottwald. None of the defendants gave any aid to Zionism. Indeed, Slansky, being a Jew, may well have made sure that he gave less consideration to Jews than to others. Ehud Avriel, Israel's first minister to Czechoslovakia, quoted Slansky as saying to him in 1948: "When it comes to Jewish affairs, I must think twice to check my anti-Jewish feelings." Yet all confessed. Slansky confessed to high treason, espionage, betrayal of military secrets, sabotage, murder, and planned murder. He related that he had allowed wealthy Jews to flee Czechoslovakia with excessive quantities of valuable properties to the detriment of Czech finances. He described how he had protected "nationalist bourgeois Zionist" organizations: "I deliberately shielded them by perverting the campaign against so-called anti-Semitism. By proposing that a big campaign be waged against anti-Semitism, by magnifying the danger of anti-Semitism, and by proposing various measures against anti-Semitism—such as the writing of articles, the holding of lectures, and so forth—I criminally prevented the waging of a campaign against Zionism and the revelation of the hostile character of Zionist ideology."

Simone, the editor, outdid them all in turning the truth upside down and in self-vilification. He belonged, he said, on the gallows. "Which are the countries where fierce anti-Semitism is on the increase? The United States and Great Britain. I have joined the spies of those states. Which country has a law against racialism and anti-Semitism? The U.S.S.R. I have joined U.S., British, and French anti-Semites against the Soviet Union. Therein lies my crime.

"I am a writer, supposedly an architect of the soul. What sort of architect have I been—I who have poisoned people's souls? Such an architect of the soul belongs to the gallows. The only service I can still render is to warn all who by origin or character are in danger of following the same path to hell. The sterner the punishment . . ."

Margolius and Loebl confessed to economic sabotage by means of a one-sided trade agreement favorable to the "bourgeois" state of Israel and the misuse of foreign trade to the advantage of Zionist organizations at home and abroad. They added that they had supported an agreement with Great Britain for the repayment of a 1938 credit as a sort of compensation for the Munich decision to let Hitler take over Czechoslovakia! To round off the story, they said that a part of the repayment was earmarked for the support of Czechoslovak and other emigrants to Palestine. Frejka confessed that he had helped wreck the Czechoslovakian economy so that there was still rationing of food and electricity.

The anti-Semitic character of the trial was emphasized in this bit of the prosecutor's examination, deliberately designed to bring out that Geminder as a child spoke Yiddish:

> *Prosecutor:* You never learned to speak decent Czech?
> *Geminder:* That's right.
> *Prosecutor:* What language do you speak usually?
> *Geminder:* German.
> *Prosecutor:* Can you really speak a decent German?
> *Geminder:* I didn't speak German for a long time but I know the German language.
> *Prosecutor:* As well as you know Czech?
> *Geminder:* Yes.
> *Prosecutor:* That means you speak no language decently. A typical cosmopolitan!
> *Geminder:* Yes.

In his closing argument the prosecutor declared: "It is no accident that of the fourteen accused eleven are the product of Zionist organizations. The danger of Zionism has increased with the foundation of the state of Israel by the Americans. Zionism and Jewish bourgeois nationalism are two sides of the same coin which was minted in Wall Street." The defendants, he further asserted, had weakened the army, and planned to establish a fascist regime which would turn the country into a base for war against the Soviet Union.

Eleven of the defendants, eight of whom were Jews, including Simone, were sentenced to be hanged. The other three—London, Hajdu and Loebl—got life imprisonment.

After the sentencing the defendants announced that they would not appeal. Simone, and ten more, went where he said he belonged. During the trial London's wife, Lisa, wrote to the court that her two older children, when she told them what their father had done, had promised her that they would remain good communists all their lives. She demanded a just verdict against her husband.

In January 1953 came the announcement from Moscow of the arrest of nine "terrorist" doctors, the majority of whom were Jews, on charges of murdering two top Soviet leaders, Andrei A. Zhdanov, a member of the politburo, who died in 1948, and his brother-in-law, Alexander S. Scherbakov, head of the political administration of the Soviet army, who died in 1945, and plotting to kill others at the instance of "international Jewish bourgeois-nationalist" organizations alleged to be acting in concert with American and British intelligence forces. The doctors were reported to have confessed to the two alleged murders. In the same month Bulgaria had a trial of ten and Poland of seven, four of whom were Catholic priests. The charge in the one case was espionage and in the other they were espionage and black market activities. The next month twenty-three more Rumanians confessed to high treason and espionage. In the same month the Chinese communists claimed to have the confessions of two more American officers, Col. Frank H. Schwable and Maj. Roy H. Bley, about the use of germ warfare.

Inquisition in Korea

WITH ALL THESE confessions our authorities began to show their concern about the results which communist inquisitors might obtain from American prisoners in the Korean war. In April at the time of Little Switch, which consisted of the exchange of sick and wounded war prisoners, Allen W. Dulles, the director of our Central Intelligence Agency, made a speech to a group of Princeton University alumni in which he said: "The Communists are now applying the brainwashing techniques to American prisoners in Korea and it is not beyond the range of possibility that considerable numbers of our own boys there might be so indoctrinated as to be induced, temporarily at least, to renounce country and family." Later the same month our Defense Department announced that it was flying to this country some exchanged American soldiers for special medical and mental treatment. These soldiers had shown indications of "having succumbed to communist indoctrination."

The worst fears of our authorities were to be realized. The twenty-three soldiers who changed sides and the more than fifty airmen, including two Marine fliers, who gave confessions, forty of them to germ warfare charges, were but part of the story. According to Dr. Julius Segal of George Washington University, who conducted a research project for the Army on its repatriated prisoners of war, 70 per cent of them "made at least one contribution to the enemy's propaganda effort." Thirty-nine per cent signed propaganda petitions. Twenty-two per cent made propaganda records. Eleven per cent wrote articles for enemy newspapers. Five per cent wrote propaganda petitions. Five per cent circulated them. Sixteen per cent held full-time propaganda jobs. These percentages total more than 70 per cent because a number of prisoners made more than one propaganda contribution.

Ten per cent of the returning Army prisoners of war reported having heard bacteriological warfare lectures by Air Force personnel. Ten per cent informed on a fellow prisoner at least once during their internment. Twelve per cent accepted at least a little of the ideology of their captors: one per cent became converts; four per cent gave evidence of an acceptance of a moderate amount of communist propaganda; and seven per cent yielded to a little of it.

The British experience in one respect was even grimmer than our own: according to the Ministry of Defence about one-third of the junior N.C.O.s and other ranks absorbed sufficient indoctrination to be classed as communist sympathizers. Forty individuals returned home convinced communists, but some had such leanings or affiliations before they went to Korea. One stayed. However, officers and senior N.C.O.s remained unaffected.

Meanwhile the confession cases in the various communist countries continued. In August 1953 the communist regime in North Korea had its own mass purge trial. The defendants were twelve in number, headed by Lee Sung Yop, former minister of justice. All twelve confessed. Ten were sentenced to be shot. The next month Poland tried a bishop, three priests and a nun for espionage. All confessed. The bishop, speaking of his codefendants, said: "I led them astray and I repent for it." Rumania had a confession spy trial of sixteen, of whom it executed thirteen. Russia, beginning with Beria and his aides, had a treason trial a year of police officials. The second trial was headed by Viktor S. Abakumov, minister of state security under Beria; and the third one involved five Georgian police officials. In 1956 Russia similarly tried M. D. Bagirov, former leader of Soviet Azerbaijan, and five other officials. All were alleged to have confessed and all save two were executed. In the same year China had a series of four trials involving a total of forty-five Japanese on war crimes charges, and Hungary had a trial of seventeen on charges of trying to overthrow the government by force. As usual all were said to have confessed. Even in the Poznan cases all but two of the first twenty-four defendants to come to trial pleaded guilty to some of the charges—these two were the only ones in these first cases to be acquitted.

The later responses of those who experienced a communist inquisition ran the gamut from continued acceptance of the views of their inquisitors to complete rejection of such views. A group of 335 Japanese repatriates whom the Chinese communists released in the summer of 1956 continued, like the Ricketts, to accept the views of their captors. A correspondent for the Kyodo news service, who made the round trip on the repatriation ship, said all those with whom he had talked had told him they were fully guilty of all the charges against them and felt that the charges of the communists against them were fair. One of these was a woman who had confessed that she had helped to prepare for germ warfare. Gen. Yamada, whom the Russians released two weeks earlier, refused to comment on the germ warfare charges against him. On the other hand Dr. Harold G. Wolff and Dr. Lawrence E. Hinkle, Jr., medical consultants to the Defense Department, reported that the effects of brainwashing could soon wear off and that the practice often backfired, generating an intense hatred of communism: "When they [the confessants] have felt safe to acknowledge their resentment, they have expressed extreme feelings of hostility toward those responsible for their bad prison experiences, and they have nearly always rejected Communism and all of those connected with it." When William A. Cowart, Otho G. Bell and Lewis W. Griggs, three of the twenty-three soldiers who became converts to communism, returned to this country after again changing their minds about changing sides they declared: "Death is better than communism."

The Recent Past

The year 1957 produced another confessant to Chinese communists who appeared to be almost as thoroughly brainwashed as the Ricketts. He was the Rev. Paul J. Mackensen, Jr., of Baltimore, the last missionary of the United Lutheran Church in America remaining in Communist China. He told William Worthy, who interviewed him in prison there, that he was grateful to the Chinese government for its help to him in remolding his thoughts. The Chinese government's "reasonableness, kindness and consideration" were constantly recurring themes in his statements. In 1956 the Chinese communists had taken him and some other prisoners on a month-long train trip "to see the New China." He told Worthy that he was greatly impressed with the improvement in the people's condition and the popular support for the regime. He used the orthodox communist time of demarcation—pre-liberation and post-liberation. Some of his other comments were. "I believe religion in China is stronger than ever before . . . I myself will be happy if I am released when my sentence is up March 7 . . . The Chinese have helped me to see the changes in their country, but there has been no pressure to change my beliefs. The British charge d'affairs in Peking notified me of the Geneva agreement on prisoners, but I have not asked to see him since there is no reason." He was uncertain whether he would return home to his father, also a Lutheran minister, pastor of St. Paul's Evangelical Lutheran Church in Baltimore, and his mother, both in their 70s. On March 7 the Peiping radio announced his release and also that he wished to remain in China.

A few months later a Roman Catholic priest, the Rev. Fulgence Gross of Omaha, who had also been a prisoner of the Chinese communists, defended American turncoats and collaborators in the Korean war. He told the Senate Internal Security Subcommittee: "Let me only remark that those who too readily condemn our American soldiers who found their way into Communist prisons and even made confessions or who even might have revealed secrets committed to them, should themselves pass just one month in a Communist prison and court. Let these armchair tacticians and judges understand that Communist methods are diabolic."

Earlier in the year Hungary put on public trial twelve of the rebels in the unsuccessful Hungarian revolt in the fall of 1956. One of the defendants, Miss Ilona Toth, 25 years old, held the spotlight before a microphone for three and a half hours. She told how she disabled a Soviet tank with a hand grenade on November 4, 1956, the day of the big Soviet attack. She gave the details of the killing of a member of the security police. "I felt I had to kill him," she said in a tearful voice. She related that one of the accused had stood on the policeman's neck and she had stabbed him.

In 1958 the Chinese communists released the last two American Roman Catholic priests they held prisoner: the Rev. Cyril P. Wagner, a Franciscan missionary of Pittsburgh and St. Louis, and the Rev. Joseph P. McCormack of the Maryknoll Seminary in Ossining, New York. The Rev. Cyril Wagner did not deny to reporters the charges of black market dealings and economic sabotage which the Communists made against him. At this the other asserted: "He's raving—he's talking through his hat."

In the same year Hungary ran through a secret trial former Premier Imre Nagy, his defense minister, Gen. Pal Maleter, who led the Hungarian revolt of 1956, and seven others on charges of organizing a plot to overthrow the "people's democratic state order" in Hungary. According to the government, six of the defendants "showed repentance at the trial and fully confessed their guilt"; and even the remaining three, who were Mr. Nagy, Gen. Maleter and Jozsef Szilagy, "made partial confessions concerning the facts of their crimes." One of the confessing defendants, Zoltan Tildy, after a showing at the trial of a film of the Hungarian uprising of 1956, is alleged to have said:

"The film has had a staggering effect. I am sorry that my name is linked with these things."

Another, Ferenc Donath, and one of those who along with Mr. Nagy took asylum in the Yugoslav embassy in Budapest for a time:

"The news of the white terror reached Parliament. It is possible to explain the fact that we still upheld the standpoint of the government, but it cannot be extenuated . . . I believe it to be a duty of conscience to apologize to the memory of the communists, the Hungarian and Soviet soldiers who lost their lives during the counter-revolution."

And yet a third, Sandor Kopacsi:

"I am guilty and ashamed that my name has been completely

and rightfully dishonored in the eyes of my friends. I saw now this documentary, showing how people were murdered. I feel that I am indirectly responsible for this, too. I saw Soviet soldiers who were taken out of the tank dead; and their commanders wept, saying that they would have been demobilized the next day and now they were dead . . . I am sorry for what I did and now I have qualms of conscience."

Such are the results of the inquisitional system. Four—the three who made only partial confessions, and one of the others—were executed; the remaining five received sentences of from five years to life.

Archbishop Groesz, who along with Cardinal Mindszenty and others was released in Hungary in 1956, the following year formed an organization called Opus Pacis (Work of Peace) to cooperate with the communist sponsored peace movement. In 1958 he was pictured at a reception in Budapest exchanging smiles and a handshake with Soviet Premier Khrushchev. Referring to this picture the Vatican newspaper, *L'Osservatore Romano,* said that in Hungary Catholics "virtually are prisoners of the bureaucratic and police machine, even when they seem to enjoy apparent personal freedom."

8 *"Criticism and Self-Criticism"*

COMPARABLE TO THE EARLY Christian practice of confessing one's sins publicly in group meetings of believers, is the communist practice which goes by the name of "criticism and self-criticism." Although in form the call is for self-criticism, in substance it is for confession and conformity. Periodically numbers of communist leaders in various fields have to get up, beat their breasts, and, as at revival meetings, publicly confess the errors of their ways. This practice of course is not new with the communists: it is an old human and an old Russian custom. Ivan IV, the Terrible, got up before the first Zemsky Sobor or National Assembly in 1550 and made a public confession of the sins of his youth. He called upon his boyars to do likewise. Stalin gave a new prominence to this Russian custom. He was quoted by communists as writing to Gorki: "We cannot get along without self-criticism. We positively cannot, Alexei Maximovich." In 1928 he said: "Is it not clear, comrades, that self-criticism must be one of the most important forces promoting our development?" And in 1929: ". . . we cannot push forward the business of socialist construction or curb bourgeois wrecking unless we develop criticism and self-criticism to the full . . ." So-called criticism and self-criticism became a slogan of the communist party. A later writer called for a "business-like revolutionary criticism and self-criticism." The draft text of the new statute for the communist party in Russia issued in 1952 provided in section 3(g) that party members were "to develop self-criticism and criticism from below."

This so-called criticism and self-criticism has come in intermittent volumes, following periods that were more or less mild.

There was, for instance, a relatively calm period from 1933 to 1936. Then came a major round of "criticism and self-criticism" in the purge years, 1936–38. During this period Pashukanis, the leading Soviet legal theorist, and Krylenko, at one time people's commissar of justice, confessed the errors of their ways. Pashukanis had earlier, in 1930, asserted: ". . . we must now develop properly our scientific self-criticism." Then confessing a series of errors, he called parts of his former reasoning variously "a crude methodological mistake," "all a muddle from beginning to end," and "a manifest spewing out of the notorious mechanistic theory of equilibrium." In 1936 he described his former reasoning about the withering away of the state as "just opportunistic nonsense." Others who became self-criticizers in this period included Rubinshtein, a psychologist, and Sergei M. Eisenstein, the greatest movie director whom the Russians have produced.

World War II during its cooperative phase brought with it a widening range of permitted thought, so much so that in 1945 a Soviet physicist, Kapitza, could assert that "there is really no such thing as Soviet science, or British science: there is only one science, devoted to the betterment of human welfare. Science must, therefore, be international." Then came Stalin's pre-election speech of February 1946, followed by a series of decrees known collectively as the ideological decrees, and a number of Andrei A. Zhdanov's admonitions from 1946 to 1948. Zhdanov was a Politburo member. He was also one of those whom the nine Moscow doctors confessed that they had murdered. The result of the "ideological decrees" and Zhdanov's castigations was another major round of so-called self-criticism, even bigger than the last. The "ideological decrees" defined the role of the theatre, literature, movies and music in ideological education. There was to be no more art for art's sake. Partisanship was to be the keynote. Zhdanov followed in September with a speech to the Moscow Union of Writers. Soviet writers were kowtowing before petty-bourgeois foreign literature. In May 1947 came an attack on economists, with Eugene Varga as the chief target. The next month Zhdanov flayed 90 assembled philosophers. This time the one who had to bear the brunt of the attack was Georgi F. Aleksandrov, whose one-volume *History of Western European Philosophy* had received a Stalin prize the year before. In January and February 1948 Zhdanov and the Central Committee censured Shostakovich, Prokofieff, Khachaturian and others. Soviet art had to free itself of all foreign influences. Cosmopolitanism and formalism became the deadly sins. After Zhdanov purged the arts Lysenko purged the sciences. The so-called unmasking of cosmopolites extended to such unlikely areas as sports and circuses. In sports circles a Professor A. Bernstein was described as a slavelike sycophant of the West.

Zhdanov and the Politburo's insistence on the supremacy of the Soviet state and the Communist party and their emphasis on isolationism and Russian nationalism produced self-criticizers in every field of soviet life, from athletics to philosophy, from humor to statistics, in literature, music, the stage and screen, biology, medicine, physics, sociology, history, economics, literary criticism, and teaching. Over the years those who made public confession of errors ran the gamut from the satirist Zoshchenko to the old bolshevik Molotov. In October 1946 leading movie directors, including Eisenstein, abjectly admitted that the party was right and they were wrong. It was the second occasion for Eisenstein. In 1947 Alexander Fadayev, whose novel *Young Guard* received acclaim in the party press, and K. Simonov in public statements admitted their shortcomings and acknowledged the correctness of party criticism. In 1948 there were a whole series of confessions in art and science both. Among the confessants in music were Shostakovich, Prokofieff, Khachaturian and Muradeli. Shostakovich confessed: "I know that the party is right, that the party wishes me well, and that I must search for and find creative paths which lead me to Soviet realistic popular art . . . I must and want to find paths to the heart of the Soviet people." Prokofieff confessed twice. In February he wrote: "However hard it is for me to realize that I was among those who expressed a formalistic trend, I am convinced that the Soviet people and the musical public will help me to overcome this trend in my work, and that my future creations will be worthy of my people and my great country." He promised in his new opera to draw upon Russian folk melodies. Toward the end of the year he was accused of remaining formalistic in spite of a directive against decadent, apolitical compositions showing servility to the bourgeois West. In December he issued another confession and said he was sorry that he had failed to eliminate "bourgeois formalism" from his music. Khachaturian confessed: ". . . I followed a path alien to the Soviet artists." He promised to reform and thanked the party for its concern. Muradeli appeared in the auditorium of the House of Composers and fully agreed publicly that his latest opera *Great Friendship* was a chaotic, dissonant collection of noises completely alien to the normal human ear. He described his work as a creative defeat caused by striving for innovations which led him into the false road of musical invention and formalism alien to the understanding of the people. "I realize my responsibility for all my mistakes and I will strive with all my heart to amend them."

In August 1948 Lysenko had his hour of triumph. It was at a session of the All-Union Agricultural Academy. The issue was whether acquired characteristics were passed by inheritance. Lysenko said they did. According to the theories of Gregor Mendel and Thomas Hunt Morgan what passed depended on what was in the genes. Lysenko took the position that these theories were a bourgeois fraud, and, what was even more important, the party supported him. Now scientist after scientist, in one field after another, beat his breast, confessed his errors, and submitted to the party line. Professor Anton R. Zhebrak, an internationally known geneticist, wrote: "I as a party member, do not consider it possible for me to retain the views which have been recognized as erroneous by the

Central Committee of our party." During the following week hardly an issue of *Pravda* appeared which did not contain a renunciation of a lifetime of work by some leading Soviet scientist. "As a communist, I cannot and must not pit my personal views and understandings against the course of development in biological sciences . . ." "You must understand that this [foreign] rottenness has influenced some Soviet scientists, and it is necessary to eradicate it to the end. I will work for Lysenko." The All-Union Academy of Medical Sciences gave this pledge to Stalin: "We promise you, our beloved Leader, to correct in the shortest time the errors we have permitted, to reconstruct the whole of our scientific work . . . to struggle for Bolshevik partyness in medicine, to root out the enemy, bourgeois ideology and blind servility before foreignness in our midst . . ." One editorial in a scientific journal acknowledged with a flagellant satisfaction that the discussions at the meetings of the All-Union Agricultural Academy revealed a series of errors committed by Soviet biologists. These errors, it asserted, delayed the development of biological sciences. "All of us failed to appreciate fully the reactionary essence of idealistic tendencies in the theories of inheritance . . ."

Sometimes individuals confessed without waiting for an attack. For instance, in February 1948 N. Rubinstein, an historian, was the first to denounce his own book. He deplored his having become a victim of a "formal," "objective," and "academic" approach instead of adopting the only admissible "militant party outlook" in dealing with scientific problems. In March he was attacked anyway. He was accused of impartiality, unpolitical attitudes, abstract realism, shallow liberalism, and servility to the bourgeois West. He agreed, and did not even ask for revision of his own work. Instead he suggested an entirely new book to be prepared collectively by the whole body of Soviet historians.

The most pathetic case was that of Professor Boris Kedrov, a prominent Soviet philosopher. He had taken the position that it made no difference who had invented something: the important thing was that human beings had the benefit of it. Also he did not show a proper respect for the new party line in biology. But the Russians were claiming to have invented almost everything, from the steam engine to the airplane, from the wireless to the electric light, from penicillin to the psychological theory of natural child birth. They were the originators of armored cruisers, submarines, naval torpedoes, icebreakers, trawlers, steam turbines, helicopters, tractors, radios, twenty kinds of strawberries, fourteen kinds of cherries, electric harvester combines, ascents in a balloon, and even the game of baseball. The czars had concealed the facts of various of these inventions, such as the steam engine and the steam turbine, in order to please foreign capitalists.

The attack on Kedrov began early in 1949. Aleksandrov, who himself had been criticized in June 1947 for his un-Marxist treatment of philosophy, accused Kedrov of anti-Marxist and cosmopolitan viewpoints. Kedrov had to bow down. In a letter published in *Culture and Life* he wrote: "I consider it my party duty to state that I fully agree with the criticism and definitely denounce the sermon of alien cosmopolitan viewpoints that I permitted myself to carry out. The danger of such viewpoints becomes especially obvious now, when all along the ideological front our party and entire Soviet nation are engaged in a determined struggle against corrupt bourgeois ideology and against bourgeois cosmopolitanism as the ideological weapon of American imperialism; in this condition the slightest advocacy of cosmopolitan viewpoints is direct treason to the course of communism." He had been wrong in failing to support Russian claims of priority: "Any mistake of a cosmopolitan character is not only theoretical but also political, inasmuch as it inflicts direct harm on the cause of educating our people in Soviet patriotism. Of such character were the mistakes I made, and above all the anti-Marxist thesis I advanced when I said that questions of priority were not essential for the history of science." He also confessed that he made one of the worst mistakes when, in a pamphlet prepared the preceding October, he neglected to report the results of the August 1948 session of the All-Union Agricultural Academy in which Lysenko laid down the line in biology.

The bulk of this batch of confessions came in 1948. However, additional ones appeared from time to time thereafter. Kedrov gave his in March 1949. Varga and Aleksandrov gave theirs in the same year. In a lecture in Moscow Aleksandrov explained that the mistakes in his work *A History of Western European Philosophy,* which had been assailed in 1947, were "precisely those concessions to bourgeois philosophy which followed the route of bourgeois objectivism." These mistakes had to be corrected by carrying out the directions of Lenin and Stalin. Any concessions to bourgeois philosophy would be a betrayal of the interests of the proletariat. In January 1950 V. Katayev, a writer, confessed in *Pravda:* "I agree with the just and principled criticism of my new novel *For the Power of the Soviets* given in the article of M. Bukenov in *Pravda.* I promise my readers that I shall make a fundamental revision of the novel. I consider this a matter of honor as a writer." In the same year I. Y. Pisarev, one of the chief statisticians in the Soviet Union, had to recant. He was charged at a conference of statisticians in Moscow in February with considering statistics to be "a universal science for the study of nature and society based ultimately on the mathematical law of large numbers and not on Marxist-Leninist theory." This was wrong, dead wrong, he was told. Statistics like everything and everyone else had to be class conscious and party conscious. In July 1951 A. Prokofiev, a Leningrad poet, apologized in *Pravda* for a "gross political mistake" and promised to amend his attitude.

Soviet psychiatrists came under repeated attacks in 1950–51. They apologized, but not with sufficient fullness, and as happens in such instances, their cases remained open. At a joint meeting of the Soviet Academy of Medicine and the All-

Union Society for Neuropathology and Psychiatry in October 1951, a drive was launched to eliminate the final remnants of support for such Western concepts as Freudian psychology, American behaviorism, and psychosomatics. Professor Mikhail Gurevich, a worker in the field of brain pathology, and Professor A. S. Shmaryan gave explanations, but their explanations by no means satisfied the session for they "stubbornly" did not want to acknowledge the "complete rottenness" of their previous theory, which was described as being ideologically similar to bourgeois psychology.

In January 1953 Soviet economists had to go through another confessional, arising out of these circumstances. During the years 1947–48 they praised a book by Nikolai A. Voznesensky, *War Economy of the USSR in the Patriotic War* (World War II), published in 1947. During those years of course everyone was praising the work. Voznesensky was a Politburo member and head of the State Planning Commission. But early in 1949 Voznesensky disappeared from the scene. A few months later the Central Committee removed the editor-in-chief, P. Fedoseyev, and two members of the editorial board, Georgi F. Alexandrov and T. Ivochuk, of the magazine *Bolshevik* (known since the nineteenth party congress as *Communist*), for praising Voznesensky's book. After several years Fedoseyev, back in some favor, published a couple of articles in *Izvestia* about Stalin's new economic theses, but he naturally said nothing about having been previously corrected. For this he was seriously taken to task. Mikhail A. Suslov, secretary of the Central Committee, in an article in *Pravda* in December 1952 rebuked Fedoseyov for not using the occasion of his articles for some self-criticism, and suggested that he might be playing sly: "Why did he not take advantage of such a suitable opportunity for self-criticism?" Early in January *Pravda* published a letter in which Fedoseyev apologized for his shortcomings: "I displayed a non-self-critical attitude toward my own errors on questions of the political economy of socialism." He promised to "derive the requisite lessons from the criticism in *Pravda* and bend every effort to rectify and overcome errors that I have made." Six days later nearly a thousand Soviet economists met in Moscow and publicly recanted en masse for once praising Voznesensky's book. K. V. Ostrovityanov, a leading Russian economist and head of the Economic Institute of the Soviet Academy of Sciences, set the tone of the meeting. He said he was "subjecting to criticism my own mistakes and the mistakes of other economists who propagandized and praised the faulty, anti-Marxist booklet by Voznesensky on the military economy of the USSR in the period of the Fatherland war." He also called the attention of the audience to certain economists present who "conveniently forgot" to mention their own mistakes in connection with Voznesensky's book. The following week the Society for the Dissemination of Political and Scientific Knowledge held a meeting and put on the same kind of performance. I. Laptev, the society's deputy chairman, acknowledged his mistake in publishing a laudatory review of Voznesensky's book. He also admitted that in his work for the society he had set forth a number of "subjectivist idealistic propositions."

In 1955 two of the top leaders, Georgi M. Malenkov, then premier of the Soviet Union, and Molotov, had to make public confessions of error. Malenkov confessed to mistakes in the handling of agriculture. Molotov wrote to the party journal *Communist* and admitted that in his report to a session of the Supreme Soviet of the U.S.S.R. earlier in the year he had made an ideological error. In his report he had said: "Together with the Soviet Union, where the foundations of a Socialist Society have already been built. . . ." Since this statement was susceptible to the interpretation that *only* the foundations for socialism had been established, he confessed that his formulation was "theoretically mistaken and politically harmful."

Public confession of errors and adherence to the official creed has been a frequent theme in recent Russian writing, for the young and old alike. In a play for youth, *The Certificate of Maturity,* the climax is a confession. The principal character

is a boy who is too gifted and too individual. The result is
that he is expelled from the Komsomol. Why, some of his
comrades ask, does he not confess his wrongdoing and promise to improve. Of course he does just this. In a play for children, *Our Daily Bread*, by Nikolai Virta, which received a
Stalin prize, error purifies itself through confession. Sergei
Mikhalkov's play *Ilya Golovin* is based on the theme of a com-
poser (Shostakovich) who confesses the "modernistic deviations" in his music. In V. Kurochkin's *Brigade of the Smart* a
person's individualism brings about an explosion in a furnace
he is attending. He repents being too individualistic and makes
a public confession of error to his associates: "I, fellows, am
not going to lie to you. What is there, is there. I am here in
front of you as at confession. I cannot feel my hands and feet,
I feel so good . . ."

After Stalin's death in 1953 scientists and artists began to
function a little more freely, but not for long. When this freedom produced such a work as Ilya Ehrenburg's novel, *The
Thaw*, in which he referred to a whole series of subjects which
had long been on Stalin's index—the horrible effects of the
purges of the 1930s, the spreading terror of the so-called
Moscow doctors' plot, squalid housing conditions of workers,
shortages of consumer goods, cynicism among artists and
writers, toadyism and careerism, and the use of slander and
smear—the state made itself felt again. Those who spoke out
for freedom were condemned and some of them were dismissed from their posts. Alexander T. Tvardovsky, renowned
Russian poet, lost his job as editor-in-chief of *New World*, one
of the Soviet Union's leading literary magazines. The philosopher Georgi F. Aleksandrov, one of Zhdanov's victims, who
had been appointed Minister of Culture, was dismissed from
his post.

Again there were confessions of faith. Khachaturian denied
that he rejected the basic principles of "communist realism."
Soviet composers generally maintained that Zhdanov's speech
on music laid down the only ideal for composers. Khachaturian

had criticized only bureaucratic interference and mistakes in the Composers' Union. At the Second All-Union Congress of Soviet Writers, which assembled at the end of 1954, all agreed that the method of "socialist realism" which the party prescribed for all writers offered ample scope for diversity of form and content.

Then came Khrushchev's secret speech of February 1956, followed by somewhat greater freedom and stirrings of it among the people. But when this resulted in such works as Vladimir Dudintsev's *Not by Bread Alone* and Boris Pasternak's *Doctor Zhivago,* which is still not available in Russia in its original text, the state again stepped in. At a special meeting of the Communist party unit of the Moscow Writers Union in June 1957 Mme. Ekaterina Furtseva laid down the line. A resolution was passed that in effect gave nonconforming writers a choice between surrendering or being expelled from the party and maybe even worse. A few days later two of the outstanding Soviet writers, Miss Margarita Aliger, a Stalin prize winner, and Emanuel Kazakevich recanted their "errors" in public. She declared that after long periods of depression and passivity, she was again able to accept "every party document as something wholly and boundlessly my own, as unquestionable." She promised to remember that "any work of a Soviet writer is a political work and that it is possible to carry it out honorably only by unswervingly following the party line and party discipline." Khrushchev himself lent a hand. He singled out for condemnation Dudintsev and Aliger. Finally Dudintsev gave a qualified confession of error.

Another leading Russian who in 1957 confessed the error of his ways was Marshal Georgi K. Zhukov, the Russian hero of World War II. At the Central Committee meeting at which he was expelled from the party leadership he was reported to have admitted his "mistakes." He told his party comrades that he accepted their criticism of him as being "in the main correct." He was also said to have accepted the attack on his leadership of the armed forces as being of "comradely party

assistance to me personally and to other military workers." He
was charged with promoting his own "cult of personality" in
the army. This is the phrase which came into use among communists to describe Stalin's one-man rule, after the Twentieth
Congress of the Communist party in Russia in 1956 strongly
condemned it.

The practice of so-called criticism and self-criticism resulted in a creed which defined what was "orthodox in biology,
literature, medicine, textile manufacture and the shade of a lip-
stick, in economics and the effect of brush strokes on canvas,
in the treatment of children and the care of plants, in astron-
omy, lyric poetry, and the striking of a musical chord." Of
course, whenever the party line changed more than once one
might be in the position, if one had previously made a confession of errors, of having to confess that one's previous confession was itself an error. In order to see that this thought is
not far-fetched one has but to consider what has happened
up to this point to Lysenko and to run down the list of those
whom Russia and its associate countries have rehabilitated.

In 1958 Pasternak himself, after winning and accepting the
Nobel Prize for literature, rejected it and wrote to *Pravda:*

> "I accepted the award of the Nobel Prize as a literary
> distinction. I rejoiced at it and I expressed this in the
> telegram addressed to the secretary of the Swedish Acad-
> emy.
> "But I was wrong. I had reason to make such a mis-
> take because I had already been nominated as candi-
> date for it approximately five years ago, i.e., before my
> novel existed.
>
> *   *   *
>
> "The editorial office of *Novy Mir* warned me that the
> novel might be understood by readers as a work directed
> against the October Revolution and the foundations of
> the Soviet system. I did not realize this and I now regret
> it.
> "Indeed, if one were to take into consideration the

conclusions emanating from a critical appraisal of the novel, it would appear that in my novel I am allegedly maintaining the following erroneous principles. I am supposed to have alleged that any revolution is a historical illegal phenomenon, that the October Revolution was such, and that it brought unhappiness to Russia and the downfall of the Russian intelligentsia.

"It is clear to me that I cannot endorse such clumsy allegations. At the same time, my work, which has received the Nobel Prize, gave cause to this regrettable interpretation, and this is the reason why I finally gave up the prize.

"If the publication of the book had not been undertaken, as I had asked my publisher in Italy—its publication in other countries was made without my authority— I should perhaps have been able to have corrected it at least in part. But the book has been printed and it is too late to discuss this.

"During this stormy week I have not been persecuted. My life has not been endangered, nor has my freedom been imperiled.

"I want to stress once again that all my actions have been entirely voluntary. . . .

*   *   *

"I firmly believe that I shall find the strength to redeem my good name and restore the confidence of my comrades."

Indeed when Soviet composers Shostakovich and Khachaturian obtained from the Communist party's Central Committee a declaration in 1958 that the party's accusation of them and others in 1948 of "formalistic perversion" was unjust, it would seem that this involved an admission by these composers that their 1948 confessions of errors were false.

Members of communist parties everywhere indulge in the practice of so-called self-criticism. The Chinese communist party's eighth congress in 1956 had so much of it which was uttered with such conviction that the congress sounded at times like a revival meeting. Li Li-san, a 60-year-old member of the central committee, confessed that he had been making mistakes since 1930, and that he would continue to make them if the party did not watch him carefully: "If I do not thoroughly rid myself of cocksureness, conceit and self-complacency, and if I do not receive constant supervision from the party, it is very likely I shall make mistakes again. . . . Subjectivism—the damned idealistic way of thinking—cannot be got rid of by cursing and swearing, or by issuing orders and writing magic formulae. When you have not got the help of a good doctor to inject enough anti-pox into your body, and when your understanding of Marxism-Leninism has not yet reached a sufficiently high level, this subjectivism will creep up again whenever conditions permit it to do so."

In China non-communists as well as communists engage in such self-condemnations. Four such in 1957 were Chang Po-chun, Minister of Communications, Dr. Lo Lung-chi, Minister of the Timber Industry, Prof. Fei Hsiao-tung, and Gen. Lung Yun, former governor of Yunnan Province. They apparently took Mao Tse-tung at his word when he said: "Let a hundred flowers bloom, let a hundred schools of thought contend." Mr. Chang and Dr. Lo made abject and sweeping confessions of anti-communist activity at the closing session of the Chinese National People's Congress (Parliament). Mr. Chang stated that he had sought "to replace the proletarian dictatorship and the National People's Congress with bourgeois democracy." He said this "anti-constitutional attitude would inevitably have led to a capitalist comeback against the Communist party and the people." He explained that he had a landlord-feudal-bourgeois background and had always adopted a "two-sided attitude" toward the Communist party. He asked for help to return to orthodoxy. Dr. Lo in addition to confessing at the meeting also circulated a statement in which he said that he had cooperated with Mr. Chang to distort Mao Tse-tung's "let-a-hundred-flowers-bloom" policy of free criticism, using the distortion "to attack the Communist party and leadership." He recited that he came from a family of predominantly feudal and bourgeois outlook, and at schools abroad had absorbed an Anglo-American bourgeois education. The next year the Peiping radio announced that these two had been branded as Rightists for criticizing the Communist regime and that they had admitted their crimes.

Confessions
of Ex-Communists

NOT ONLY HAVE communists confessed in communist countries and self-criticized themselves all over the world; but also ex-communists, including defecting Russians, have confessed in noncommunist countries. In this country probably the great majority of them have done so. However, most of such confessants we have not become aware of, for we have not heard about them. They have usually acquired a status of confidential informants and secret witnesses—there are many types of determinations today, such as those relating to loyalty and security questions, the status of aliens, draft classifications, the blacklisting of organizations, and applications for passports, in which one is not yet entitled to face one's accusers. Nevertheless, some of the ex-communists have appeared as witnesses in public hearings of legislative committees or been used as witnesses against their former associates in criminal cases, and these individuals we do know about. Those who were the most publicized were Louis F. Budenz, Elizabeth T. Bentley, Whittaker Chambers, Harvey Matusow, Paul Crouch, Manning Johnson and John Lautner. Budenz, Bentley, and Chambers beat their breasts, confessed to espionage, betrayals, lying, and illicit sexual relations, and named many former associates.

A number of ex-communists also produced autobiographical confessions, indeed, to such an extent that they became a genre. The most significant of these was *Witness* (1952) by Chambers. Others were *False Witness* (1955) by Matusow; *I Confess* (1939) and *The Whole of Their Lives* (1948) by Benjamin Gitlow; *This Is My Story* (1947) by Budenz; *Out of Bondage* (1951) by Bentley; *This Deception* (1951) by

143

Hede Massing, formerly Gerhart Eisler's wife; *In Stalin's Secret Service* (1939) by Gen. Walter G. Krivitsky; *Out of the Night* (1941) by Richard J. H. Krebs under the pseudonym Jan Valtin; *Memoirs of a Soviet Diplomat* (1938), and *One Who Survived* (1945) by Alexander Barmine; a piece by Arthur Koestler in *The God that Failed* (1949); and *I Chose Freedom* (1946) by Victor Kravchenko.

Chambers, Budenz, and Bentley surrendered unconditionally. They exchanged one communion of saints for another. Chambers became a Quaker. Budenz returned to Catholicism, a faith which Bentley also accepted. *Witness* and *This Is My Story* were not only confessions of sins but also confessions of faith. In *Witness* Chambers in a "Foreword in the Form of a Letter to My Children" wrote: ". . . I am writing a book. In it I am speaking to you. But I am also speaking to the world. To both I owe an accounting . . . Much more than Alger Hiss or Whittaker Chambers was on trial in the trials of Alger Hiss. Two faiths were on trial . . . I was a witness. I do not mean a witness for the Government or against Alger Hiss and the others . . . A man is not primarily a witness *against* something. That is only incidental to the fact that he is a witness *for* something. A witness, in the sense that I am using the word, is a man whose life and faith are so completely one that when the challenge comes to step out and testify for his faith, he does so, disregarding all risks, accepting all consequences."

He urged other ex-communists to make the same absolute change that he had. Otherwise they would be "self-divided, paralyzed, powerless to act against" communism. ". . . to the challenge: *God or Man?* they continue to give the answer: *Man* . . . Not grasping the source of the evil they sincerely hate, such ex-communists in general make ineffectual witnesses against it. They are witnesses against something; they have ceased to be witnesses for anything." For the Western world "the only possible answer to the Communist challenge: Faith in God or Faith in Man? is the challenge: Faith in God."

His foreword closes with the cross: ". . . But, in the end, if I have led you aright, you will make out three crosses, from two of which hang thieves. I will have brought you to Golgotha —the place of skulls . . . You will know that life is pain, that each of us hangs upon the cross of himself. And when you know that this is true of every man, woman and child on earth, you will be wise."

A good ex-communist, according to Chambers, had to be an informer and betray old associates: ". . . For, in the end, the choice for the ex-Communist is between shielding a small number of people who still actively further what he now sees to be evil, or of helping to shield millions from that evil which threatens even their souls. Those who do not inform are still conniving at that evil. That is the crux of the moral choice which an ex-Communist must make in recognizing that the logic of his position makes him an informer." Accordingly, as Ignazio Silone said to Palmiro Togliatti: "The final conflict will be between the Communists and the ex-Communists." Silone was head of the underground section of the Italian communist party until he broke with communism in the 1930s. Togliatti, once Silone's close friend, is secretary of the Italian communist party. For the ex-communist, informing was a public duty.

At the end of the first Hiss trial a newsman asked Chambers: "What do you think that you're doing?" He answered slowly: "I am a man who, reluctantly, grudgingly, step by step, is destroying himself that this country and the faith by which it lives may continue to exist." Toward the close of his book he explained that the kind of witness he was bearing "required only that a man testify to every crime, every sin, every evil, that he had committed or that had beset his life, without reserve."

Krebs confessed to participation in murder, mayhem, insurrection, espionage, betrayals, and sex orgies. Massing confessed to espionage and various sexual sins. She also narrated the sexual escapades of her father. Kravchenko detailed his sexual affairs. One of these was with the wife of a high-ranking government official. He further confessed a theft he once committed. Confessions of espionage, betrayals, and sexual offenses are frequent in these autobiographical efforts.

Massing traced the beginning of the end of her espionage days to a copy of a letter to Stalin which she and her third husband received from Ignace Reiss, better known as Ludwig Lore. Reiss was a former member of the GPU and was probably murdered by its agents. He wrote his letter shortly before this happened. In it he said:

"The letter which I am addressing to you today I should have written a long time ago, on the day when the Sixteen [the defendants in the Moscow purge trial of 1936] were murdered in the cellars of the Lubyanka at the command of the Father of Nations [Stalin]. I kept silent then. I raised no voice of protest at the subsequent murders, and for this I bear a large responsibility. My guilt is great, but I shall try to make up for it, to make up for it quickly, and to ease my conscience.

"Up to now I have followed you. From now on, not a step further. Our ways part! He who keeps silent at this hour becomes an accomplice of Stalin, and a traitor to the cause of the working class and of Socialism."

The confessions of ex-communists give one the impression that as time went on their stories sometimes grew. Take, for example, Budenz. In his book *This Is My Story* he did not refer to Harold Roland Christoffel at all. Christoffel was a labor leader in Milwaukee, Wisconsin, against whom Budenz subsequently testified on three separate occasions: in 1947 before the House Committee on Education and Labor, in 1948 in a perjury case, and in 1950 in a retrial of the same case. By the time of the first perjury trial he had made Christoffel into one of the key revolutionaries in this country and party to a plot to overthrow our government by force and violence. At the second trial he added still more details to those he had given at the first one. While it is true that in his book he did not purport to tell about communist infiltration into labor unions and political organizations, nevertheless one would expect to find at least a mention of Christoffel. But it is not there. Now of course a witness may actually have his recollection refreshed. However, one cannot help but wonder in such cases as that of Budenz how much of his last story he actually remembered.

We not only have ex-communists who confessed, but we also have those who confessed and then confessed that their confessions were false. Examples were Harvey Matusow, Mrs. Marie Natwig, Lowell Watson, and David Brown. Matusow and Mrs. Natwig were convicted of perjury.

10

Confessions in Court and Church

NOT ONLY HAVE the innocent often confessed to acts which they have not committed, but the guilty have usually confessed to the acts which they have committed. They have done this both in court and out of court. They have done it both in church and out of church. They have done it both directly in the form of confessions, and indirectly in various forms of self-betrayal. They have done it by talking too much.

It may come as a surprise to many, but the majority of defendants in criminal cases have entered pleas of guilty or comparable pleas. In the 86 United States District Courts having purely federal jurisdiction the number of defendants in such cases during the seven-year period ending June 30, 1954 who pleaded either guilty or nolo contendere amounted to the surprising figure of 224,920 out of a total of 268,620. Of the remainder 23,274 were dismissed, 6,988 were acquitted, and 13,438 were convicted. Reduced to percentages this means, if one excludes the defendants who were dismissed, the astounding figure of 91.67% for those who pleaded either guilty or nolo contendere. If one includes the defendants who were dismissed the figure becomes 83.70%. These figures exclude those charged as juvenile delinquents but include immigration cases. The immigration cases were almost entirely confined to the five federal districts touching the Mexican border and the pleas of guilty of defendants in these cases amounted to almost 98%. If immigration cases are omitted the figure becomes 87.67%, if one excludes the defendants who were dismissed, and 77.16%, if one includes them.

The story in our state courts cannot be far different, although here one is handicapped by a lack of statistics. Some of the best state court statistics are now being kept by the Administrative Office of the Courts of New Jersey, but even these are not yet as good as the federal statistics. According to the New Jersey statistics it would appear that in the three-year period ending August 31, 1954 the number of defendants who pleaded either guilty or non vult exceeded by more than two and a half times the number who went to trial.

In Church

THE GUILTY CONFESS not only under lay but also clerical auspices. The practice of confessing one's sins has a continuous history from the kings of the Hittites, centuries before Christ, to the present. Customarily in the ancient East a king practiced confession and penitence whenever his country was stricken by a calamity. King Mursilis II (1334–1306 B.C.) of the Hittites confessed not only his own sins but also those of his father. Ideas of the transmission of sins from father to son as well as from a ruler to his country and people were common in the ancient oriental mind. A group of Theban inscriptions (c. 1300 B.C.) of the 19th dynasty show that confessions of sins were long practiced in Egypt. In China, too, the emperor engaged in confession if a drought or some other calamity overtook his country.

In India confessions of sins probably went back, as in the Near East, to the pre-Aryan substratum. Manu, in a later period in his authoritative Hindu law book, said: "In proportion as a man who has done wrong himself confesses it, even so far is he freed from guilt, as a snake from its slough." The Buddhist Samgha was a confraternity of monks who at stated intervals made confessions to one another according to a set formula.

The Old Testament contains many references to confessions

of sins: Leviticus 5:5,6: ". . . he shall confess that he hath sinned in that thing: And he shall bring his trespass offering unto the Lord for his sin which he hath sinned, a female from the flock, a lamb or a kid of the goats, for a sin offering; and the priest shall make an atonement for him concerning his sin." Leviticus 16:21: "And Aaron shall lay both his hands upon the live goat, and confess over him all the iniquities of the children of Israel, and all their transgressions in all their sins . . ." Numbers 5:5–7: "And the Lord spoke unto Moses, saying, Speak unto the children of Israel, When a man or woman shall commit any sin that men commit, to do a trespass against the Lord, and that person be guilty; Then they shall confess their sin which they have done . . ." Joshua 7:19: "And Joshua said unto Achan, My son, give, I pray thee, glory to the Lord God of Israel and make confession unto him, and tell me now what thou hast done; hide it not from me." Psalm 32:5: "I acknowledged my sin unto thee, and mine iniquity have I not hid. I said, I will confess my transgressions unto the Lord; and thou forgavest the iniquity of my sin." Proverbs 28:13: "He that covereth his sins shall not prosper: but whoso confesseth and forsaketh them shall have mercy." Daniel 9:4: "And I prayed unto the Lord my God, and made my confession . . ." Nehemiah 1:6: ". . . and confess the sins of the children of Israel." Nehemiah 9:1–3: ". . . the children of Israel were assembled with fasting, and with sackclothes, and earth upon them . . . and stood and confessed their sins and the inquities of their fathers. And they stood up in their place, and read in the book of the law of the Lord their God one fourth part of the day; and another fourth part they confessed, . . ." Daniel 9:20: "And whiles I was speaking, and praying, and confessing my sin and the sin of my people of Israel . . ." The Jews developed the yearly practice of beating their breasts and confessing their sins at the time of the Day of Atonement.

Ovid (43 B.C.–17 A.D.) mentioned the confession of sins

in the religion of Isis at Rome. The sins involved were largely
sexual. Isis was originally an Egyptian goddess. Juvenal
(c. 60–c. 140 A.D.) indirectly referred to the same thing in a
passage of the sixth satire deriding Roman matrons for their
devotion to oriental divinities. Ovid further related how King
Midas raised his arms to heaven, confessed his sin, invoked
pardon from the offended god, and the god, merciful to the
confessing sinner, pardoned him and told him what he had
to do: he had to follow the river Pactolus to its source and
there immerse himself in its frothy waters.

The New Testament, as does the Old, contains various references to confessions. Paul in his epistle to the Romans said,
14:11: "For it is written, As I live, saith the Lord, every knee
shall bow to me, and every tongue shall confess to God."
James and John dwelt on the redeeming character of mutual
confessions of sins and the power of intercessory prayer:
James 5:16: "Confess your faults one to another, and pray one
for another, that ye may be healed"; 1 John 1:9: "If we confess our sins he is faithful and just to forgive us our sins, and
to cleanse us from all unrighteousness."

The early Christians made their confessions to each other
in group meetings of believers. Confessions were both public
and voluntary. Later they came to be made to religious leaders.
Innocent III by a canon of the great Fourth Lateran Council
of 1215–16 made confession obligatory as well as secret.
This canon ordered "that every one of the faithful of both
sexes, after coming to years of discretion, shall confess all
his sins alone, at least once a year, to his own priest, and be
careful to perform the penance enjoined upon him with all his
strength, reverently receiving the sacrament of the Eucharist
at least at Easter . . ." Priests were enjoined to be careful
not to betray a sinner in any manner. Thus both Jews and
Catholics confessed yearly, the Jews at the time of the Day
of Atonement, and the Catholics at Easter.

The Lateran Council was silent as to age. In 1227 the

Council of Narbonne fixed the age at fourteen years. Later it came to be seven years. In 1907 Pope Pius X advised weekly confessions.

If one were to list the main reasons why the Roman Catholic Church grew, the practice of auricular confession would be one of them. The requirement of auricular confession under Innocent III was probably the most important legislative act in the history of the church.

Certain Protestant churches, the Lutheran and those of the Anglican Communion, including the Protestant Episcopal Church in the United States, have kept some form of the confessional. The Lutherans have a sacrament of confession in their Church Creed and the Episcopalians in their Book of Daily Prayer. Martin Luther expressed his emphatic approval of auricular confession: he said "he would rather lose a thousand worlds than suffer it to be thrust out of the Church." Article XI of the Augsburg Confession, under which the Lutheran church functioned, stated that "private absolution ought to be retained in the churches; although an enumeration of all our offenses is not necessary in confession." The formulary of the Church of England contains this: "Almighty God the Father of our Lord Jesus Christ, who desireth not the death of a sinner, but rather that he may turn from his wickedness and live; and hath given power and commandment to his ministers to declare and pronounce to his people, being penitent, the absolution and remission of their sins: He pardoneth and absolveth all of them that truly repent and unfeignedly believe his holy Gospel."

Many of the Protestant clergy will agree that confession, as the Catholic Church practices it, constitutes a powerful attraction to people. Indeed, periodically different Protestant divines, including Dr. Harry Emerson Fosdick, feeling that the Protestant Churches were needlessly depriving themselves of an effective technique, have suggested a return to some form of private, individual confession. In May 1952 the German Lutherans did return to it. The General Synod of the United

Evangelical Lutheran Church restored the kind of private confession which Luther in his day had emphasized as an important means to salvation. This kind still differed from that of the Roman Catholic Church in two respects: it was voluntary; and any Christian, whether ordained or not, could hear another's confession and grant absolution.

Other religious groups, although they may not have the formal institution of confession, have the phenomenon. The Quakers, the Presbyterians, and the Methodists furnish good illustrations—the very word quaker was applied originally in derision of the emotional manifestations of contrition on the part of the confessants. The Methodists were even more intense in their confessions than the Quakers. One of the followers of the Wesleys declared that he was "froward" from his mother's womb, loving cards and "affecting to look rakish"; but then he was suddenly overwhelmed with the inward darkness of terror, the sweat pouring from him in his agony of prayer. Another lamented his sins "howling like a wild beast." The Rev. Henry Alline, a Presbyterian, had a conscience which "would roar night and day." Revival and camp meetings have witnessed distraught and even frenzied confessions.

Most churchgoers engage in some form of confessions of sins. They differ only as to the manner of confessing. Most Protestants and Jews confess their specific sins privately to God and are absolved publicly by means of a liturgical formula. Roman Catholics and some Anglicans confess their sins at regular intervals to a priest. German Lutherans have gone back to this type of confession. Reflecting on all these confessions one may recall some lines from Hervey Allen's "The Priest and the Pirate: A Ballad of Theodosia Burr":

> For I have heard, these fifty years,
> Confessions muttered at my ears,
> Till every mumble of the wind
> Is like tired voices that have sinned.

11 *Alcoholics Anonymous*

PUBLIC CONFESSION OF ERRORS in group meetings of believers has also characterized the procedure of the organization known as Alcoholics Anonymous. This organization, whose aim is the rehabilitation of alcoholics, has a twelve-step program of recovery based on the experiences of cured alcoholics which stresses confession along with a call upon some power greater than one's self:

"Half measures availed us nothing. We stood at the turning point. We asked His protection and care with complete abandon.

"Here are the steps we took, which are suggested as a Program of Recovery: . . .

"5. Admitted to God, to ourselves, and to another human being the exact nature of our ways." The organization emphasizes the importance of this step: "If we skip this vital step, we may not overcome drinking. Time after time newcomers have tried to keep to themselves certain facts about their lives. Trying to avoid this humbling experience, they have turned to easier methods. Almost invariably they got drunk."

Such confessions have furnished the basis for AA meetings. According to one writer: ". . . Seated in the intimate circle of friends who understand and sympathize, it is easier to talk freely than anywhere else or to anyone else. At meetings a member's remarks are only tributaries to the main stream of conversation. He won't say anything the others haven't heard before. Most of his friends can match anything he brings up, and some of them can probably top him.

"There isn't much doubt that the chief value of the regular meetings lies in the opportunity they afford alcoholics to talk.

AA members will give up almost anything for a chance to sit around for two or three hours and talk. . . .

"Swapping stories discussing one another's problems, arguing over the interpretation of one of the Steps in the program, members find a strength that seems to come in no other way. No one feels self-conscious. There's no reason to. Almost from the beginning, a new member finds himself unfolding the details of his life with all the pathos, tragedy, and bitter humor that only alcoholics know. His listeners are sympathetic. Everything that ever happened to him happened to others. Every excuse he ever used has already been worn threadbare. Every lie he ever told has been told many times over. And every hiding place he ever used for his whisky is already known. As he unburdens himself, the alcoholic begins to feel *good!* Confession he discovers, is medicine for the soul."

Yet other of the twelve tested steps involved confessions: "8. Made a list of all persons we had harmed, and became willing to make amends to them all. 9. Made direct amends to such people wherever possible, except when to do so would injure them or others." If an injured person is one whom an alcoholic hates, the organization explains: ". . . It is harder to go to an enemy than to a friend, but we find it much more beneficial to us. We go to him in a helpful and forgiving spirit, confessing our former ill feeling and expressing our regret . . . Simply we tell him that we will never get over our drinking until we have done our utmost to straighten out the past. . . ."

As for an alcoholic's debts: "Most alcoholics owe money. We do not dodge our creditors. Telling them what we are trying to do, we make no bones about our drinking; they usually know it anyway, whether we think so or not. . . ."

If an alcoholic has been unfaithful to his wife he should usually confess this to her, though without details and without naming names. Even when he has committed a penal offense he should confess: ". . . Reminding ourselves that we have decided to go to any lengths to find a spiritual experi-

ence, we ask that we be given strength and direction to do the
right thing, no matter what the personal consequences may be.
We may lose our reputation or face jail, but we are willing.
We have to be. We must not shrink at anything."

Step 12 involves confession along with proselytism. A cured
alcoholic must carry the message to others still afflicted and in
doing so tell of his own experiences: "nothing will so much
insure immunity from drinking" as this.

Two of the best known members of Alcoholics Anonymous
are Lillian Roth, the singer, and Col. Gregory ("Pappy") Boyington, one of the great fighter pilots of World War II. She
has written two books about her life, *I'll Cry Tomorrow* and
Beyond My Worth; and he so far has written one, *Baa Baa
Black Sheep.* In her first book she narrated her marital ven-
tures and described in painful detail what alcohol had done
to her. Boyington, like Miss Roth, detailed the consequences
of his drinking and heaped blame upon himself for the brawling, violent individual he became. Miss Roth near the beginning of her first book related how an old man with a cigar
in his mouth took sexual liberties with her when she was five:

"Now, in preparation for my first job, she (her mother)
undressed me and a fatherly looking old gentleman with a
cigar clenched in his teeth started to paint me with white
body makeup. When lunch time came, Katie (her
mother) left me in his charge while she and Ann (Miss Roth's
sister, who was two and a half years younger than she) went
out to buy sandwiches for all of us, including the old gentleman. Left alone with me, he went to the door, looked outside, and locked it. 'Cold in here,' he said. I had been standing
on a box, 'Better lie down, where it's warm,' he said, taking
me in his arms and carrying me to a couch near the stove.
He painted my thighs, then worked his brush upwards and
began painting me where it made me uneasy.

"He daubed me with the brush, again and again, on the
same part of my anatomy. The cigar moved from one corner

of his mouth to the other, and then back again. 'Only five years old,' he said. 'My, you're a nice little girl.'

"I covered my eyes with my hands. I knew there was something wrong in what he was doing, but I couldn't stop him or cry for help. If Katie found out, something terrible would happen. She would scream, her face would contort, and I could not bear to hear her scream or to see her face like that.

"When he heard footsteps in the hall, he hurriedly unlocked the door and stood me up on the box again; he was just finishing my feet when Katie came in and spread out our lunch.

"An unknown fear held my tongue. I never told her. . . ."

12 *Autobiographical Confessions*

A GREAT VARIETY OF PEOPLE other than ex-communists have given us autobiographical confessions. Indeed such confessions range all the way from royal memoirs to the comics. Two of the best known are those by St. Augustine, the bishop of Hippo (to be distinguished from the St. Augustine who converted the English), and Jean Jacques Rousseau. St. Augustine confessed to stealing, lying to his mother, and various fornications. "I will now call to mind my past foulness, and the carnal corruptions of my soul, not because I love them, but that I may love Thee, O my God . . . boiled over in my fornications . . . Behold with what companions I walked the streets of Babylon, in whose filth I was rolled, as if in cinnamon and precious ointments." He and some of his young companions stole pears. "Yet I had a desire to commit robbery, and did so, compelled neither by hunger, nor poverty, but through a distaste for well-doing, and a lustiness of iniquity . . . It was foul, and I loved it. I loved to perish . . . O rottenness! . . . Could I like that which was unlawful only because it was unlawful?" Concerning his first mistress he wrote: "I befouled, therefore, the spring of friendship with the filth of concupiscence, and I dimmed its lustre with the hell of lustfulness; and yet, foul and dishonorable as I was, I craved, through an excess of vanity, to be thought elegant and urbane. I fell precipitantly, then, into the love into which I longed to be ensnared." His mother caused him to send his first mistress back to Africa, had him engaged to a young girl who lacked two years of being of marriageable age, and while he was waiting for her he took on a second mistress. "Meanwhile my sins were being multiplied . . . a slave to lust . . .

and Thou didst set me face to face with myself, that I might behold how foul I was, and how crooked and sordid, bespotted and ulcerous."

Rousseau in his confessions made himself appear mean, petty, ridiculous, and even depraved. He told how he sent his five illegitimate children to a foundling hospital. His list of offenses included urinating in Madame Clot's saucepan, exhibiting himself as a boy to little girls, lying, stealing, masturbating, and various sexual experiences. "I have taken the first and most difficult step in the dark and dirty labyrinth of my confessions . . . I have never brought myself, even when on most intimate terms, to ask women to grant me the only favor of all which was wanting. This never happened to me but once—in my childhood, with a girl of my own age; even then it was she who first proposed it . . . I learnt to covet in silence, to dissemble, to lie, and, lastly, to steal . . . I descended from the sublimity of heroism to the depths of worthlessness . . ." He stole a ribbon and blamed the theft on an innocent girl. "This burden has remained to this day upon my conscience without alleviation; and I can affirm that the desire of freeing myself from it in some degree, has greatly contributed to the resolution I have taken of writing my Confessions." As for exhibiting himself: "I haunted dark alleys and hidden retreats, where I might be able to expose myself to women in the condition in which I should have liked to have been in their company . . . The foolish pleasure I took in displaying it before their eyes cannot be described . . . I exhibited to the girls who came to the well a sight more laughable than seductive . . ." He related eating a piece of bread that one of his future mistresses had had in her mouth. He admitted abandoning a friend in a fit in the middle of a street. He narrated various proposals to him to engage in homosexual practices. One of these was for mutual though separate masturbation. He fled "trembling as if I had just committed a crime. I was addicted to the same vice . . ." He described his first act of sexual intercourse with a woman. ". . . I felt as if I had been guilty of incest." He and another man shared the same woman. He had intercourse with a prostitute and was afraid for three weeks that he had contracted a venereal disease. He and another man arranged to take a girl between eleven and twelve years in order that both would have her sexually when she got a little older. He and two other men had dinner together and then they all had intercourse with the part time mistress of one of them. "In my singular and unique situation, I owe too much to truth to owe anything further to anyone else. . . . intercourse with women distinctly aggravated my ill-health; the corresponding vice, of which I have never been able to cure myself completely, appeared to me to produce less injurious results."

Catherine II, the Great, in a memoir indicated that her son Paul, who succeeded her, was illegitimate. In a letter to Potemkin she listed her affairs and told him he was only her fifth and not her fifteenth lover: "Now, Sir Hero, can I hope after this confession to receive forgiveness for my sins? You will deign to see that there were not fifteen but only one-third of that. The first, against my will, and the fourth taken out of desperation, can not at all be set down to frivolity. Of the other three only think rightly."

Benjamin Franklin in his autobiography confessed: "The breaking into this money of Vernon's was one of the first great errata of my life . . . that hard-to-be-governed passion of youth hurried me frequently into intrigues with low women that fell in my way, which were attended with some expense and great inconvenience, besides a continual risque to my health by a distemper which of all things I dreaded, though by great good luck I escaped it."

Frank Harris, Isadora Duncan, and Theodore Dreiser related in great detail their sexual experiences. Both Harris and Dreiser confessed to masturbation and all three related their first act of intercourse. Harris told how on one occasion a girl bled after he deflowered her. Duncan gave an account of the birth of her third and last child, illegitimate as were the others, and how she was flowing three ways, tears, milk, and blood. Concerning her first lover she wrote: "Often he cried to me, 'Ah, you are my sister.' And I felt that in our love was some criminal incestuousness."

One can name many other well-known confessants: Madame Du Barry, mistress of Louis XV, Polly (Pearl) Adler, the madam, Alexander Hamilton, Oscar Wilde, André Gide, Jerome Cardan, Samuel Pepys, George Sand, John Bunyan, Maxim Gorki, Ellen Terry, Thomas De Quincey, Leo Tolstoi, Norbert Wiener, Philip O'Connor, Ethel Waters, Ethel Barrymore, her niece Diana Barrymore, Fannie Hurst, Richard Maney, Hjalmar Schacht and Drew Pearson. Schacht called his effort *Confessions of "the Old Wizard"*, and Pearson his piece *Confessions of "an S.O.B."* Some of the other recent titles are equally arresting: Adler, *A House is Not a Home;* Maney, *Fanfare: The Confessions of a Press Agent;* Hurst, *Anatomy of Me;* and O'Connor, *Memoirs of a Public Baby.*

Miss Adler, who has a penchant for the words whore and whorehouse, in addition to describing her business, which involved bribery and perjury as well, also admitted that on one occasion she bought a shoplifted handbag. She further related how before she got into her business she was raped and had an abortion. While she was at work on her story one of her friends told her "that the confessional slant was sure fire."

One of the sadder of the more recent confessionals is Diana Barrymore's *Too Much, Too Soon.* She was the daughter of John Barrymore and Blanche Oelrichs Thomas of Newport society, who was better known under her pen name of Michael Strange. Miss Barrymore related her first sexual experience as well as that of her father. She recounted her many other sexual affairs and how her third husband twice called her a whore. She described her and her father's drinking. She told of her brawling and her attempt at suicide. She referred to some of the sexual affairs of both her parents. She disclosed that she was conceived before her parents were married and while her mother was still married to another. According to a story which she narrated, her father's first sexual experience was with a woman who was in turn his father's mistress. According to the same account her father's father would come "reeling down Broadway, drunk, a chorus girl on either arm." She had this comment about the escorts of her debutante days: "Their sex experience, what they had had of it, was usually limited to a few uncomfortable visits to Polly Adler's establishment in midtown Manhattan."

Tolstoi confessed: ". . . I killed men in war, and challenged men to duels in order to kill them; I lost at cards, consumed the labor of peasants, sentenced them to punishments, lived loosely and deceived people. Lying, robbery, adultery of all kinds, drunkenness, violence, murder—there was no crime I did not commit, and for all that people praised my conduct, and my contemporanies considered and consider me to be a comparatively moral man.

"So I lived for ten years."

One is tempted to add the names of Casanova and Benvenuto Cellini, but they narrated their experiences with such an air of bravado that one hesitates. Cellini confessed, among other things, to three murders, spending the night with a girl of thirteen or fourteen, stealing, getting the "French Disease," and cutting some new beds to shreds in malice.

The compulsion to confess is a subtle force, and has trapped even those who are experts in the field of unconscious motivations. It has deceived such an expert as Dr. Theodor Reik, a student of Freud, and one of the ablest of psychoanalysts. Reik, although he quoted Freud to the effect that there was a discretion one owed one's self which kept one from broadcasting everything, in the course of a book about Goethe's confessions was tempted, in violation of this very dictum, to make unnecessary and indiscreet confessions about himself. For instance, he told about his affairs with two mistresses and of an act of intercourse with a prostitute. He described an act of intercourse with his first mistress, Vilma. She was seated on a table in a dark bathroom and he was standing. Her mother was in the next room. These confessions served no useful purpose in the book. Yet despite the fact that an old friend, to whom he had submitted his manuscript for an appraisal, tried to persuade him not to send the manuscript to the publisher in that form, Reik insisted on going ahead. His friend asked him whether he had thought what his daughter Theodora "would say when she reads this once?" But Reik did not heed his friend's advice. In his book he wrote: "The psychoanalyst who explores his own emotional processes is thus as distant from Goethe's artistic aim as from Rousseau's self-flagellation." But in the table incident he did do what Rousseau did. Again he stated: "The offering need not be self-sacrifice." Yet it was at times.

Autobiographical confessions are so numerous that any large library will have many volumes of them. The card catalogues of two, the New York Public Library and the Library of Congress, will yield, in addition to those we have already considered, the confessions of an engaged couple, the new married couple, a wife, a young wife, an older wife, a rebellious wife, a lawyer's wife, a business man's wife, a useless wife, an author's wife, a husband, a daddy, a young mother, a successful mother, a matchmaking mother, a woman, an elderly lady, an old maid, a pretty woman, a laywoman, a worldly woman, a well-meaning woman, a magdalen, a frivolous girl, a female inebriate, a chorus girl, a prima donna, a princess, the Countess Anne, the Czarina, a club woman, a débutante, a debutant, an immigrant's daughter, that little English girl, a grass widow, of Tibbie Law, *d'une femme, femme du monde, fille, jeune fille, jolie femme, opiomane, abbesse du XVIᵉ siècle, courtisane devenue, des femmes, de la marquise,* a flirt, a male flirt, an inconstant man, a bachelor, a school master, a schoolmaster, an obscure teacher, a layman, an elderly gentleman, an old priest, a French Catholic priest, a clergyman, an agnostic clergyman, a puzzled parson, an actor, a young man, another young man, a sportsman, an agi-

tated sportsman, a policeman, a congressman, a layman, a little
man during great days, a railroad man, a railroad signalman,
a Pullman conductor, a drone, a society man, a seaman, a
working man, a master mason, a quartermaster, two brothers,
a con man, a confidence man, a tolerant man, a tradesman,
a former customers' man, a bond salesman, a trust magnate,
*d'un abbé, Jésuite, curé de village, enfant du siècle, enfant
d'hier, homme d'aujoud'hui, homme de cour, amant, ouvrier,
pecheur, conte,* Bohemian, *ex-libre penseur,* of two, of two
malefactors, a tenderfoot, a Whitefoot, an English hashish-
eater, an American opium-eater, a hyphenated American, an
American citizen, a collector, an incurable collector, an attorney, an uncommon attorney, a minister, a Negro preacher, a
physician, an M.D., a young artist, an old aesthete, a book
agent, a book-lover, a Browning lover, a lover of romance, a
violinist, a clarinet player, a convert, a converted infidel, a reformed cannibal, an apostate, an agnostic, an atheist, a detective, a New York detective, a convict, a criminal, a seafaring
blackmailer, an ancient poacher, a rum-runner, a scoundrel, a
gamester, a rogue, a thug, a nazi spy, a barbarian, a beach-
comber, a China-hand, a twentieth century hobo, a Macedonian
bandit, a planter in Malaya, an imp, a rebel, an individualist,
an inquiring spirit, an economic heretic, an innkeeper, a house-
keeper, a caretaker, an undertaker, a ghost hunter, a ghoul, a
suicide, a drunkard, a reformed inebriate, a parasite, a parlor
socialist, a novice, a player, a journalist, a quill driver, a war
correspondent, a scribbler, a caricaturist, a copy writer, a publisher, a reformed dramatic critic, a poet, a modern poet, an
opera singer, a magnetizer, a modern Midas, a monopolist, a
commercial senator, a capitalist, a speculator, a dealer, a hyp-
notist, a medium, a debunker, a scientist, a unionist, a sometime kindergartner, a European intellectual, an Etonian, an oc-
togenarian, an industrial insurance agent, an afterdinner
speaker, an extension lecturer, a candidate, a Whig, a social
secretary, an aide-de-camp, a jailer, a spotter, a climber, a

drummer, a reformer, a green-tea drinker, a summer colonist, a water patient, a village tyrant, a neurasthenic, a congress delegate, a fool, a child of the century, a patent-medicine man, a phoenix, an old log, of Sir Cupid, St. Valentine, Claude Leigh, Colonel Sylvester, Paul Gosslett, of boyhood, *d'un demi-siècle, poète, voleur, pendant la valse,* a country mouse in the city, *du chat,* of love, in art, in prose, to a heathen idol, of the power trust, of crime, of a keyhole, a pencil-case, the confessions and opinions of Ralph Restless, and the confessions of Mrs. Smith.

In the month that the manuscript of this volume went to the printer the *New York Times Book Review* contained reviews of no less than four or more autobiographical volumes in every issue. October 5: in addition to Hurst, *Anatomy of Me,* there were reviews of Angna Enters, *Artist's Life;* Gladys Brooks (Mrs. Van Wyck Brooks), *Gramercy Park;* and Heather Jiménez, *But I Wouldn't Want to Live There.* Earlier Miss Enters had produced *First Person Plural* and *Silly Girl.*

The following week's issue contained no less than five more reviews of further such volumes: Elinor Goulding Smith (Mrs. Robert Paul Smith), *Confessions of Mrs. Smith;* Agnes de Mille, *And Promenade Home;* Ezio Pinza, with Robert Magidoff, *Ezio Pinza;* Ike Blasingame, *Dakota Cowboy;* and a three-volume work entitled *The Complete Letters of Vincent Van Gogh.* Miss de Mille previously wrote *Dance to the Piper.* In addition, the Best Seller List contained Boyington's *Baa Baa Black Sheep,* and Mrs. Eleanor Roosevelt's *On My Own;* and there were advertisements for Mrs. Roosevelt's book, that of Miss de Mille, as well as Ivy Baker Priest's *Green Grows Ivy.*

October 19: Jane R. Barkley, as told to Frances Spatz Leighton, *I Married the Veep;* James F. Byrnes, *All in One Lifetime;* Leonard Covello and Guido D'Agostino, *The Heart Is the Teacher;* Raymond B. Fosdick, *Chronicle of a Generation;* Dr. Donald T. Atkinson, *Texas Surgeon.* Closely related volumes were Michel del Castillo, *Child of Our Times;* Farley

Mowat, *Coppermine Journey (Selected from the Journals of Samuel Hearne); and Arthur Goodfriend, *Rice Roots.* Previously Byrnes had written *Speaking Frankly.*

October 26: *The Autobiography of Mark Van Doren;* Gloria Vanderbilt and Thelma Lady Furness, *Double Exposure: A Twin Autobiography;* Lady Diana Cooper, *The Rainbow Comes and Goes;* Alice Sligh Turnbull, *Out of My Heart.*

The need to confess is so general that there are periodicals catering to it, such as *True Confessions, True Experience, True Life Stories, True Romance, True Story Magazine,* and *Modern Romances.* There are even books on how to write confessional stories. Indeed, there are even true confessions comics. One of the books on how to write confessional stories has a chapter entitled, "Sin, Suffer and Repent." In it the author explained: "In every confessional we watch the heroine sin, suffer and repent. As a matter of fact those three words cover the very keynote of all exciting and interesting confessional stories! . . . In most confessional stories the word sin has to do with sins of sex." Another such book has ten ingredients for a good confession story which boil down to the same thing. They include: "I Narrator's Character Flaw . . . IX Narrator's Remorse and Her Attempt to Make Restitution . . . X How Narrator's Remorse and Attempt to Make Restitution Unexpectedly Bring Her Happiness After All . . . The narrator on realizing her fault humbles herself."

The editor of one of these confession periodicals recently wrote: "Laugh at the old sin, suffer and repent theory if you like, but laugh softly for it holds good today just as in the past."

Autobiographical confessions have been presented in countless diaries and memoirs: there are almost as many different volumes called diaries as there are those called confessions. They have been recorded in novels. Examples are Stendhal's *The Red and the Black,* Somerset Maugham's *Of Human Bondage* and, more recently Han Suyin's *A Many-Splendored Thing.* One is tempted to add Albert Camus' *The Fall,* and

Yukio Mishima's *Confessions of a Mask*. Indeed, many novels, particularly first ones, are autobiographical.

A request for autobiographical confessions is a standard technique in English classes, and in language classes in other countries from the most elementary to the college level. Sometimes selections from such confessions have been published. A recent example is *The Unsilent Generation,* a symposium of eleven autobiographical essays by Princeton seniors, which Otto Butz compiled and edited.

Autobiographical confessions have become part of the interrogation procedure of the Chinese communists. Chinese communist inquisitors hit upon the technique of requesting those who were in custody or in some way suspect to write their biographies or to keep diaries. They found this device to be surprisingly effective, for the materials which it produced not only contained confessions but also enabled them to extract still more confessions. They therefore stressed its use. When American prisoners of war came into their hands they pressured them to submit autobiographies. Those who complied were on their way to assisting the enemy's propaganda efforts. Of the same order as this device was the requirement of the American communist party that its officials supply it with detailed autobiographical materials.

13 *Confessions in Literature*

LITERATURE, seeking to portray life, has produced its share of confessions, of the innocent and the guilty alike. In Dostoevski's *Crime and Punishment* Nikolay, who is innocent, as well as Raskolnikov, who is guilty, confess to the double murder which Raskolnikov committed. As to confessions of the innocent, Porfiry, the investigator says: "A man confessed to murder and how he kept it up! It was a regular hallucination; he brought forward facts, he imposed upon everyone and why? He had been partly, but only partly, unintentionally the cause of a murder and when he knew he had given the murderers the opportunity . . . he persuaded himself that he was the murderer. . . . It is not a question of suffering for someone's benefit, but simply 'one must suffer.' If they suffer at the hands of the authorities, so much the better . . . So I suspect now that Nikolay wants to take his suffering, or something of the sort." In Dostoevski's *The Brothers Karamazov* both a guilty and an innocent person confess. Smerdyakov, the murderer, confesses, to Ivan, and so, too, does Ivan, at Dmitri's trial.

Hawthorne's works abound with confessions and the idea of secret sins. In *The Minister's Black Veil* Parson Hooper puts on a black veil and wears it the rest of his life to symbolize the fact that people hide rather than confess their secret sins. The villain in *The Scarlet Letter,* Roger Chillingworth, tries to keep the Reverend Arthur Dimmesdale from confessing that he is the father of Hester's child, Pearl. Hester is the one who wears the scarlet letter and Chillingworth is her husband. During the time that his scheme succeeds Arthur is wretched. Hawthorne has him say: "Of penance I have had

enough! Of penitence there has been none . . . Had I one
friend—or were it worst enemy!—to whom, when sickened
with the praises of all other men, I could daily betake myself,
and be known as the vilest of sinners . . . sick, sin-stained
and sorrow-blackened . . . my own heavy sin and miserable
agony . . ." The author says of him: "He was broken down
by long and exquisite suffering . . . the breach which guilt
has once made into the human soul is never in this mortal
state, repaired." At the end, however, Arthur mounts a scaffold
with Hester and Pearl, confesses, and dies. He was, relates
Hawthorne, as one who in the crisis of acutest pain had won
a victory. In his farewell speech Arthur unburdens himself:
". . . The law we broke!—the sin here so awfully revealed
. . . He hath proved his mercy, most of all in my afflictions.
By giving me this burning torture to bear upon my breast!
By sending yonder dark and terrible old man . . . By bringing me hither to die this death of triumphant ignominy before
the people! Praised be his name! His will be done! Farewell!"
With that he dies: "That final word came forth with the minister's expiring breath." In *The Marble Faun,* the relief which
Hilda feels when she makes her confession Hawthorne describes as unspeakable, as the satisfaction of a great need of
the heart, the passing away of a torture. He has Hilda cry
out about her previous state: "I could not bear it. It seemed
as if I made the awful guilt my own by keeping it hidden
in my heart. I grew a fearful thing to myself. I was going mad."

The most famous confession story in this country is that of
Parson Weems about George Washington: every school child
used to read how the boy George admitted to his father that
he had chopped down his father's cherry tree with his little
hatchet. Just as one can suggest that one of the main reasons
the Catholic Church grew was the practice of auricular confession so here one can suggest that the reason Parson Weems's
story became so widely popular was the fact that it involved
a confession.

Tolstoi in *The Power of Darkness* has Nikita confess at the wedding of his stepdaughter that he knew about the planned murder of his wife's first husband, that he himself had had a child by the bride and killed it. The bride was Nikita's wife's first husband's child by a former marriage.

> *Nikita.* Christian Commune! I have sinned, and I wish to confess! . . .
> *Akim (his father).* Here God's work is being done . . . A man is confessing . . .
> *Akim (with rapture).* Speak, my son! Tell everything —you'll feel better! Confess to God . . .
> *Nikita.* Father, dear father, forgive me too . . .
> *Akim (rapturously).* God will forgive you, my own son! *(Embraces him)* You have had no mercy on yourself; he will show mercy on you!

This play was based on an account of a crime Tolstoi had heard several years before: a peasant confessed to the guests assembled at the marriage of his stepdaughter that he had murdered a child he had had by her and afterwards had attempted to kill his own six-year-old daughter.

In one instance a Russian work portended the future: the novel *Chocolate* by Alexander Tarasov-Rodionov, which came out in 1926 in the early years of Stalin's rule, forecast the confession show trials. The author believed that literature should proselytize for communism. His main character Zudin is the chairman of a provincial Cheka. Zudin's wife innocently accepts gifts of chocolate and stockings from one of his questionable employees. The people murmur about this. A committee of Zudin's old comrades condemn him to death on charges of treasonable activities, for chocolate can come only from abroad. At his secret hearing one of the committee members asks him what the people's impression will be of him because of the common gossip that he has taken bribes through his wife. " 'What impression? . . . The very worst,' he whispered, dropping his head. He could not endure his shame."

A committee member who comes to tell him of its sentence explains: " 'The mass will never understand long justifications. The mass understands only the monosyllabic "Yes" or "No." The whole cause—do you understand?—the whole great cause of fighting for the happiness of millions of people, all that has already been gained with so many sacrifices, so much effort, with the suffering and blood of several generations, right here and now all of this will turn to smoke, burst like a soap bubble, because of the childish carelessness of one unfortunate comrade who grew tired, who tore himself away from the masses, and who quite forgot who he was and where he was! Tell me, what shall we do with him, so we may save our great cause?'

" 'Kill him,' Zudin said in a strained, muffled voice.

" 'Yes, kill him,' Tkacheyev confirmed.

" 'And so we are killing you to save our cause, knowing that you understand all this. . . .' "

Dostoevski earlier supplied an even more macabre touch, if that is possible, when he had his character in *A Gentle Spirit* say: ". . . Cheap heroism is always easy, and even to sacrifice life is easy too; because it is only a case of hot blood and and an overflow of energy, and there is such a longing for what is beautiful! No, take the deed of heroism that is laborious, obscure, without noise or flourish, slandered, in which there is a great deal of sacrifice and not one grain of glory—in which you, a splendid man, are made to look like a scoundrel before every one, though you might be the most honest man in the world—you try that sort of heroism and you'll soon give it up!" This and Zudin's fate must have been in the minds of many of the victims of the mass purge in Russia.

Some confessions are in a lighter vein. Illustrations occur in Mikhail Zoshchenko's *The Wonderful Dog,* and Hermann Sudermann's *The New Year's Eve Confession.*

Zoshchenko was at one time one of the most popular writers in the Soviet Union. But in 1946 he became one of Zhdanov's prime targets. *The Wonderful Dog* will indicate why. Even during the thaw after Stalin's death Zoshchenko remained more or less of an outcast. He died in 1958.

In *The Wonderful Dog* Jeremiah Babkin sends for the bloodhound on the complaint that his fur coat has been stolen. She arrives with her keeper. He shows her some footprints and she singles out a woman from the gathering crowd. The woman falls on her knees and confesses that she took five buckets of chicken feed. But she knows nothing about the fur coat. Again the keeper takes the dog to the footprints. This time she singles out the head of the house committee. He falls on his face and confesses that he embezzled the water money. Next the dog takes hold of a young man. He collapses and admits that he is a slacker: he should be in the army but he altered the date in his identity book 'and is living on the people. At this point Babkin hands the dog's keeper money and tells him to take the bitch away. But now the dog goes up to Babkin and smells his galoshes. Babkin in his turn confesses: he is a hooligan; the fur coat is not his but his brother's; he filched it from him. The people start to scatter. Nevertheless the dog grabs two or three more. They all confess. One lost government money at cards. Another threw an iron at his wife. The third made a statement that does not bear repetition. The yard is empty. The dog goes up to her keeper. He pales, falls down before her, and admits that he keeps for himself two-thirds of the money that he gets for her food. The story ends: "What happened after that I don't know. I washed myself of sin as quickly as I could."

In the *New Year's Eve Confession* two old cronies, a widower and his bachelor friend, are sitting alone. On forty-four previous occasions the widower's wife has made the New Year's Eve punch for the three of them. Now she is gone. The bachelor confesses that for over forty years he has been carrying a guilty secret: he has been in love over the whole period with decedent. The widower snorts in reply that he has known this fact for forty years himself, that the decedent herself told him, and what was more she also said that she loved the bachelor. This was the reason, explained the widower, why he had run after women the way he did until he was an old man.

An old, old story tells how the Amalekite confessed to David that he slew Saul. He may even have been innocent: according to another account Saul slew himself by falling on his sword. In any event the Amalekite confessed to murder.

The prodigal son confessed his sins to his father and his father not only forgave but also lovingly rewarded him: "And he arose, and came to his father. But when he was yet a great way off, his father saw him, and had compassion, and ran, and fell on his neck, and kissed him. And the son said unto him, Father, I have sinned against heaven, and in thy sight, and am no more worthy to be called thy son. But the father said to his servants, Bring forth the best robe, and put it on him; and put a ring on his hand, and shoes on his feet: And bring hither the fatted calf, and kill it; and let us eat, and be merry: For this my son was dead and is alive again; he was lost, and is found. And they began to be merry."

In *A Tale of Two Cities* by Charles Dickens, Sidney Carton, who is in no trouble with the authorities, has himself substituted for Charles Darnay, who has been condemned to the guillotine. Dickens has Sidney do this because of his love for Lucy Manette, who in turn loves Charles. The name Charles Darnay is close to that of the author: the given name as well as the initials are the same. Sidney's action may be compared with a former Chinese practice which permitted a condemned person to procure a substitute.

Recent additions to confessional literature include Richard Condon's *The Oldest Confession,* and Myles Connolly's *Three Who Ventured.* The latter volume's third main character is a murderer who, like Dostoevski's Raskolnikov, confesses his sin and embraces his punishment. Condon put on the frontispiece of his volume these lines attributed to *The Keener's Manual:*

> The Oldest Confession
> Is one of Need,
> Half the need love,
> The other half greed.

14 *Miscellaneous Confessions*

Delayed and Deathbed Confessions

MANY PEOPLE HAVE CONFESSED their offenses shortly after they have committed them. Some have waited. From time to time the newspapers have carried accounts of persons who finally confessed to offenses that they had committed anywhere from a few years to as many as or more than twenty-five years previously. One is reminded of Daniel Webster's successful argument for the prosecution in *Commonwealth* v. *Knapp,* a murder case in which one of the participants committed suicide. "Those who shed blood seldom succeed in avoiding discovery. . . . the guilty soul cannot keep its own secret. It is false to itself; or rather it feels an irresistible impulse of conscience to be true to itself. A vulture is devouring it, . . . The deed must be confessed. It will be confessed; there is no refuge from confession but suicide, and suicide is confession." Yet others who have never confessed to anything during the course of their lives finally have done so in their last hour. This practice was an old one. Even such unexpected people as John Selden, an English jurist and writer, and George Monk, Duke of Albemarle, an English general, have made at least deathbed confessions of secret sins.

Various Confessions of Guilt

THERE HAVE BEEN MANY OTHER KINDS of confessions given by a multitude of people under varying circumstances. Well-known individual instances are those of Francis Bacon, Timothy John Evans, George P. Metesky, known as the mad bomber, 8-year-old Melvin A. Nimer, Jr., and Harry Golden.

Bacon was a rival of Edward Coke. In 1621 Parliament charged him with the acceptance of bribes from suitors in chancery. Before he had seen the charges he wrote: "I do ingenuously confess and acknowledge, that having understood the particulars of the charge, not formally from the House, but enough to inform my conscience and memory, I find matter sufficient and full, both to move me to desert the defence, and to move your Lordships to condemn and censure me."

Neither House was satisfied. The Lords sent a message expressing their discontent and enclosing the full bill of charges. On the last day of April they had their reply:

> "To the Right honourable the Lords Spiritual and Temporal, in the High Court of Parliament Assembled: The Confession and humble Submission of me, the Lord Chancellor. Upon advised consideration of the charge, descending into my own conscience and calling my memory to account so far as I am able, I do plainly and ingenuously confess that I am guilty of corruption; and do renounce all defence, and put myself upon the grace and mercy of your Lordships.
> The particulars I confess and declare to be as followeth. . . ."

Twenty-eight charges were appended, each one copied out by the Lord Chancellor and confessed to. A committee of twelve was sent to inquire if the confession was truly his. It was then that Bacon gave his anguished reply: "My Lords, it is my act, my hand, my heart. I beseech your Lordships, be merciful to a broken reed." Their lordships decided that he should, among other things, undergo a fine of 40,000 pounds and be imprisoned in the Tower during the king's pleasure. The fine was in effect remitted by the king, and his imprisonment in the tower lasted only about four days.

Evans gave confessions to the murder of his wife and child. Their dead bodies were found in the house where they lived in London. In 1950 he was tried and hanged.

In 1953 another tenant in the same house found further human remains. A police search revealed the bodies of six more women, all murdered. A man named Christie, who was a witness for the prosecution in the Evans case, confessed to the killing of all of them. He also confessed to the killing of Mrs. Evans.

Evans at his trial repudiated his confessions. In answer to a question from his own counsel he stated: "Well, when I found out about my daughter being dead, I was upset and I did not care what happened to me then."

On cross-examination this occurred:

> *Q.* . . . you pleaded guilty . . . confessed to the murder of your wife and child because you were upset at learning that your daughter was dead?
> *A.* Yes, sir, because I had nothing else to live for.

It is clear that Evans and Christie did not both participate in the murder of Mrs. Evans. The probabilities are that Evans was innocent. Yet he confessed. His case has been the basis for a renewed demand in Great Britain for the abolition of capital punishment.

For sixteen years, from 1941–1957, New York City was plagued by a series of home-made bombs which someone planted in various public places about the city. In January 1957 Metesky, a former employee of the Consolidated Edison Company, confessed that he was the wrongdoer.

The following year produced the confessions of the Nimer boy and Golden. The Nimer boy confessed that he stabbed both of his parents to death in the night at their Staten Island home. Subsequently he alternately recanted and repeated his confession. The story seems incredible, but whether his confession is true or not, two facts remain: in his mind he conceived of himself as guilty of the murder of both his parents; and he confessed.

In the same month Golden confessed. He was then the publisher of a tabloid newspaper, *The Carolina Israelite,* and author of a best-selling book, *Only In America.* He confessed that he was Harry L. Goldhurst, who in 1929 pleaded guilty to fraud charges and went to prison, serving almost all of a five-year sentence. He had been the operator of a bankrupt bucket shop.

There are the confessions which have been made anonymously. Frequently an individual who is in default in some way, or thinks himself so, will send money to governmental authorities. Recently one such individual sent money to President Eisenhower with an anonymous note expressing the hope that the president would "take care of the matter" and see to it that New York City got the money. It did. Controller Lawrence E. Gerosa reported its receipt. He said that the money might have been sent by a merchant who had not paid the full sales tax, or by a city employee who had made use of city materials, or by someone else who had some reason to repent. Various governmental units have funds, usually called conscience funds, which have arisen from such payments. Needless to say, New York City has such a fund.

There have been the confessions to congressional committees and to Dr. Alfred C. Kinsey and his associates. There have been confessions to one's doctor and one's lawyer, to one's barber and one's hairdresser, to one's parents, one's family, one's teachers, and one's friends. These confessions have been both oral and written. They have occurred in letters.

Vincent van Gogh made his confessions in his letters to his brother Theo. He described his liaison with a prostitute, and told of his visits to brothels. In one letter he referred to his "taking a turn at the brothel." He was the one who cut off one of his ears and presented it as a gift to a woman in a brothel. After his convalescence he wrote Theo: "I went to see the girl I had gone to when my wits went astray."

There have been confessions in speeches at various gatherings. They have occurred on radio and television programs. They have occurred in responses to various columns in newspapers and magazines, such as the column entitled "My Most Embarrassing Moment." Very few things have been more prevalent in the lives of human beings than confessions.

Murder Will Out

THE GUILTY HAVE CONFESSED not only in words but also by various forms of self-betrayal. Even when a deviant has tried to be extremely cautious and has paid particular attention to details he has betrayed himself by his very overcautiousness. Self-betrayal by the guilty has been so common a human trait that it has been embodied in such popular sayings as murder will out, and spilled blood cries to heaven. The former of these has been so general that three of the greatest of writers have used it: Chaucer, "Mordre wol out, certain it wol not faille"; Shakespeare, "Murder, though it have no tongue, will speak With most miraculous organ"; and Cervantes simply, "Murder will out." As for spilled blood cries to heaven, God told Cain that the voice of his brother Abel's blood cried to him from the earth.

Self-betraying clues can be discovered in the manner of the crime, the tools, the time, the locality in which the deed was committed, and in all the accompanying circumstances. For instance, Paul Kneisel was no problem for the police. He and two others broke into a men's outfitting shop in Berlin. They dressed in new suits, and took away three more, which they sold. Kneisel not only left his old jacket behind, but he also forgot to take his police registration out of it. George, the incendiary, was likewise no problem. In all his acts of incendiarism he used his father's automobile, which was painted a conspicuous red. George also returned to the scene of the crime and helped the fire chief put out the fire. In the Gutteridge murder case in England in 1927 not only did an innocent person confess, but also the guilty one rendered his apprehension and conviction easy in more than one way: stolen medical instruments, and the use of obsolete cartridges and black powder. In the Knapp case, in which Daniel Webster was the prosecutor, one of the participants in the murder there involved handed to his father, to be passed on to an investigating committee, a letter which helped to solve the crime. Recently in New York two youths dressed exactly alike with pink shirts and thin black ties, committed a robbery and then continued to wear the same garb until they were apprehended. One suspects that Grammer, who murdered his wife and then put her at the wheel of a car which he sent downhill, unconsciously wanted to betray himself when he wedged a pebble under the accelerator to make the car go faster. The pebble helped to convict him.

Other forms of self-betrayal are the return to the scene of the crime and the dwelling on the act itself in conversation. George, the incendiary, returned. So have many other deviants. One of these was Dr. Price Adams Kirkpatrick, a New York City psychiatrist. He stole some antiques, but he left his own valuable camera and tripod on the porch of the house he had robbed. When he returned to retrieve them he was arrested. He readily admitted his crime. His explanation was that he liked antiques and wanted to outfit his office with them before his marriage. In Dostoevski's *Crime and Punishment* not only does an innocent person confess, as well as the guilty one, Raskolnikov, but Raskolnikov, before he confesses, also revisits the scene of the crime. Earlier he wonders why almost all crimes are so badly concealed and so easily detected and why almost all criminals leave such obvious traces. In an abduction case in the Philippines one of the guilty persons who had not been accused came to the courtroom while his associates were on trial and during the testimony of the person whom they had abducted. She identified him from the witness stand. Guilt-ridden human beings leave themselves almost no way out.

The tendency of self-betrayal has also been one of the underlying concepts in various folk tales in which some animal or insect has been responsible for bringing a guilty person to justice. In Schiller's poem "The Cranes of Ibycus," the dying Ibycus charged the passing cranes to avenge him and the murderer betrayed himself when he saw them flying over the theatre. The myth of Ibycus of Rhegium had a German parallel in the tale of St. Meinrad and his ravens. The birds pursued the murderer. Making a terrific noise they clustered about his head, thus solving the crime and bringing him to justice. The Germans have another folk tale in which some flies made a murderer betray himself. In this country an almost comparable case actually occurred. Early one morning Walter Breese poisoned his millionaire uncle by gas. What trapped him was the hour of the murder, and this was determined to be early dawn because dead flies and midges were all found on the window-sill. Had the murder been committed in the dark of the night the flies and midges would have been scattered about the room.

Talking Too Much

IT NOT INFREQUENTLY has happened that when the authorities have questioned an individual about some event, transaction, or charge about which he has known nothing, he has volunteered information, often damaging, about some unrelated matter. For example, when George Popoff was questioned by the communists in Russia about some vague counter-revolutionary charges, he felt impelled to tell them about an illegal diamond transaction in which he brought a seller and buyer together. He almost told them that his brother was a White Guard officer.

Dr. Charles Berg, a medical psychologist, told of the woman who had a mad desire to tell her mother everything that passed through her mind. If she had been out with a young man, she told her mother everything she had done and every word they had said and then she was still uneasy lest she had thought something she had not disclosed. She never seemed to be able to satisfy her need to confess. Dr. Berg entitled his case history of her, *Compulsion to Confess.*

Many members of our armed forces who were taken prisoners by the communists, and we are not referring here to those who confessed to something, but only to those who did not, talked too much, both about themselves and their fellow prisoners. Talking too much is a common human trait and failing. Nearly all of us are guilty of it.

Confessions of Faith

HUMAN BEINGS have used confessions to prove not only matters of fact but also matters of faith. The main confessions of faith in the early period of the Christian religion were the Apostles' Creed, the Nicene Creed and the Quicunque vult or Athanasian Creed. The Apostles' Creed ran:

I believe in God the Father Almighty, Maker of heaven and earth:

And in Jesus Christ his only Son our Lord: Who was conceived by the Holy Ghost, Born of the Virgin Mary: Suffered under Pontius Pilate, Was crucified, dead, and buried: He descended into Hell; the third day he rose from the dead: He ascended into heaven, And sitteth at the right hand of God the Father Almighty: From thence he shall come to judge the quick and the dead.

I believe in the Holy Ghost: The holy Catholic Church; the Communion of Saints: The forgiveness of sins: The Resurrection of the body: And the Life everlasting. Amen.

Other groups of believers have had confessions of faith, Zoroastrians, Buddhists, Mohammedans. The Mohammedan Creed or Kelima consisted of the familiar words: "There is no God but Allah, and Mohammed is his prophet." The communists have a creed too, *The Communist Manifesto*. Marx and Engels drew it up and issued it early in 1848 as the platform of the Communist League, a workingmen's association, first exclusively German, later on international. The League at a congress held in London late the preceding year had commissioned them to do this. The League was dissolved in 1852, but the Manifesto became the credo of the communists.

Western businessmen have been too individualistic to produce a comparable document. However, Louis O. Kelso and Mortimer J. Adler recently produced a volume which they entitled, mirabile dictu, *The Capitalist Manifesto*. A little earlier Clarence B. Randall, the president of Inland Steel Company, wrote a book entitled *A Creed for Free Enterprise*. The jacket described it: "A ringing statement of faith in the American system of free enterprise by the most trenchant spokesman for our heavy industry." Many among us would like such a confession of faith. It would show our belief in capitalism and our opposition to communism and to socialism as well.

Critique

15

A Critique of
Confessions

WITH THE ADMISSION by Khrushchev in his secret speech of February 1956 that during the preceding two years 7,679 persons were rehabilitated in the Soviet Union, many of them posthumously, and the spectacular rehabilitation of Laszlo Rajk in Hungary it is no longer necessary to argue that the confessions to communist inquisitors are not much more reliable than those to clerical inquisitors some centuries earlier. However, the full extent of the fictitious nature of the twentieth-century confessions became apparent only gradually. In the meantime many people were taken in by them. Even so astute an observer as Joseph E. Davies, our ambassador to Russia, was deceived. In his *Mission to Moscow* he wrote concerning the Moscow purge trials: "Notwithstanding a prejudice arising from the confession evidence and a prejudice against a judicial system which affords practically no protection for the accused, after daily observations of the witnesses, their manner of testifying, the unconscious corroborations which developed, and other facts in the course of the trial, together with others of which a judicial notice could be taken, it is my opinion so far as the political defendants are concerned sufficient crimes under Soviet law, among those charged in the indictment, were established by the proof and beyond a reasonable doubt to justify the verdict of guilty of treason and the adjudication of the punishment provided by Soviet criminal statutes." Later Vyshinsky cited Davies' statements to support his assertions about the validity of the Moscow trials.

Nevertheless certain dramatic falsities in the evidence at these trials were established almost immediately. In the 1936 trial one of the defendants, Holtzman, confessed that he had

187

a meeting with Trotsky in Copenhagen in the Hotel Bristol in 1932. But the Hotel Bristol had burned down fifteen years before and was never rebuilt. In the 1937 case the principal defendant, Pyatakov, confessed that in December 1935 he flew from the Tempelhof airport at Berlin to the airfield at Oslo, Norway for a meeting with Trotsky. But no plane landed at the airfield at Oslo between September 1935 and May 1936.

These and other similar falsities were substantiated in 1937 within a few months after the 1937 trial by a commission of inquiry headed by John Dewey, the educator and philosopher. The Dewey commission was constituted by the American committee for the defense of Leon Trotsky. A subcommission, likewise chaired by Dewey, went to Mexico and took Trotsky's testimony. Trotsky was in exile there. Thereafter the commission made its report entitled *Not Guilty*.

Further falsities in connection with subsequent trials, not only in Russia but also in its satellites, came to light from time to time or were pointed out by discerning students. In 1953 Russia, overlooking the fact that in 1949 it had presented a show trial in which it had undertaken to prove that General Yamada and eleven other Japanese acting on the secret instructions of Emperor Hirohito had engaged in germ warfare, made a reply to President Eisenhower's proposal for an atomic energy pool in which it stated that germ warfare had not been used in World War II. Russia in urging the effectiveness of the Geneva Protocol of 1925 said: ". . . the fact that in the Second World War not a single Government decided to use chemical and bacteriological weapons shows that the aforementioned agreement . . . was of positive importance." But in 1949–50 it had vigorously claimed to have proven just the contrary. Both statements could not be true.

Rajk confessed that he met certain Yugoslav communists, Bebler, Mrazovic, Maslaric and Vukmanovic-Tempo, in French concentration camps after the Spanish civil war and plotted counter-revolution with them. But these Yugoslavs were not where Rajk placed them. Bebler and Mrazovic were both wounded in Spain and were taken directly to Paris and from there to Yugoslavia. The defendants in the *Kostov* case, except Kostov himself, pleaded guilty to an indictment which charged that Kostov "with the knowledge and consent of the British Intelligence service, entered into secret criminal relations with the Yugoslav leaders" in order to "deprive Bulgaria of her national sovereignty, her territorial integrity and independence through her annexation to Yugoslavia." But the draft of an agreement looking to a federation of Bulgaria and Yugoslavia was prepared in Moscow and approved by the Soviet Union.

It was Great Britain who objected to the contemplated federation. Great Britain's objection plus her counter-suggestion for a wider federation to include Albania, Greece, and Turkey led the Soviet Union to soft-pedal for a time the idea of a Bulgarian-Yugoslav federation. However, early in 1948 in Moscow Stalin himself, according to Tito, "imperatively demanded the immediate conclusion of an act of federation between Yugoslavia and Bulgaria, while on the other hand the Soviet was against a federation with Albania." But this was 1948, and the Yugoslavs, rather than working with Kostov, were unwilling to go ahead. They were suspicious. As Tito explained: "We came to the conclusion that the demand was put forward in order to facilitate the overthrow and subjugation of Yugoslavia." What was made out in Kostov's trial to have taken place was just the opposite in many material respects of what actually happened.

Besides these specific instances there was one general circumstance which cast doubt on the show trials: the defendants were presented as the blackest kind of traitors who had never been good communists. In the 1938 Moscow trial Krestinsky confessed that Trotsky authorized him in 1921 to enter into an espionage agreement with the Germans and that he completed such an arrangement in 1922. Pursuant to this arrangement he was a spy for the Germans from 1923. Rosengoltz confessed to being a German spy for the same length of time and a British spy since 1926. Sharangovich confessed to being recruited by the Polish intelligence service in 1921. According to Rakovsky, he himself was a spy for the British since 1924 and for the Japanese since 1934. Chernov, according to his own admission, began his espionage work for the Germans in 1928, and Grinko, by his own testimony, became a spy for both the Germans and the Japanese in 1932. Yagoda admitted that he had under his protection spies from various foreign intelligence services, including the German and the Polish. Had these confessions of espionage been true there would have been corroboration in the Nuremberg and Tokyo war crimes trials; but there was not.

Bukharin, although denying espionage, admitted that he belonged to a "block of Rights and Trotskyites," and that the objectives of this group were the overthrow of the communist regime, the restoration of capitalism, and the dismemberment of the Soviet Union in favor of Germany and Japan and to some extent England. Bukharin also confessed that he and others had a plan in 1918 for the arrest of Lenin, Stalin and Jacob Sverdlov (the chairman of the Soviet Executive Committee). Rajk asserted that he was a Hungarian police spy against the communists as far back as 1931, when he was but 22 years old, and that he also became a spy for the French Deuxième Bureau, the German Gestapo, the American OSS, and the Yugoslav intelligence service. Slansky, a staunch Stalinist, called himself a Trotskyite enemy of Stalin since 1927.

If there was this much treason and espionage afoot in the communist part of the world, then, as Deutscher pointed out, the communist regime in Russia would never have survived. Or as Hamilton Fish Armstrong, speaking of the *Rajk* case, commented: "Were the story unfolded by these characters true it should encourage opponents of Communism no end, for if such trusted chiefs of an old and important Communist Party were free to practice every sort of perfidy their responsible colleagues could not be described except as naïve, careless and ignorant. There evidently was in addition a highly satisfactory degree of inefficiency and corruption in the counter-intelligence and among the spies whom Hungarian Communist leaders employed to watch each other."

Yet other incidents made one question the results of the inquisitional technique in the hands of the communists. In an important instance, that of Captain Shiroky and his assistants, communist inquisitors were publicly purged for extracting false confessions. There was also such a case as that of the person who confessed in a show trial at the beginning of the 1930s that he had had too little timber felled, in order to spare the woods for their former owners, the restoration of whose rights was said to be the aim of an alleged Industrial party. He had been sentenced to ten years' forced labor, but had been released after less than a year and appointed to a higher post. Later he confessed that he had had too much timber felled in order to ruin the forests of the Soviet Union and turn them into steppes. Obviously both confessions could not be true.

After Stalin's death came the reversal of the case against the nine Moscow doctors and finally Khrushchev's speech. One can make no stronger indictment of the confessions to communist inquisitors than that of Khrushchev: "A large part of these cases [in 1937–38] are being reviewed now and a great part of them are being voided because they were baseless and falsified. Suffice it to say that from 1954 to the present time the Military Collegium of the Supreme Court has rehabilitated 7,679 persons, many of whom were rehabilitated posthumously."

The list of those in Russia and its satellites who were publicly rehabilitated or released from prison became a long one: it included the jurists Pashukanis and Krylenko, the economist Voznesensky, the nuclear physicist Peter L. Kapitsa, the novelist Boris Pilnyak, the diplomat Ivan M. Maisky, marshals Mikhail N. Tukhachevsky, Aleksander I. Yegorov and Vasily

K. Bluecher, actor and producer Vsevolod E. Meyerhold, Jewish writers, Isaac E. Babel, Itsik Feffer, and Perets D. Markish in Russia; Laszlo Rajk, Cardinal Mindszenty, Archbishop Groesz, Lutheran Bishop Lajos Ordass, social democrats, Arpod Szakasits and Anna Kethly, and revolutionary leader Bela Kun in Hungary; Traicho Kostov in Bulgaria; Wladyslaw Gomulka, Gen. Marian Spychalski, Stefan Cardinal Wyszynski and Bishop Czeslaw Kaczmarok and his codefendants in Poland; and former deputy foreign ministers Arthur London and Vavro Hajdu as well as former deputy trade minister Evzen Loebl in Czechoslovakia. The last three were the only ones in the Slansky trial to escape the gallows. Czechoslovakia has not yet cleared Slansky and the ten others that it hanged in that case but it has repudiated the defendants' confessions of Titoism and condemned the display of anti-Semitism which the trial produced.

In Hungary the bodies of Rajk, Dr. Tibor Szoenyi, and Andras Szalai, two of his co-defendants who were executed with him, and Maj. Gen. Gyeorgy Palffy, who was condemned to death by a military court, were exhumed from unmarked and dishonored graves and given honorary reburial in a cemetery that was slated to become a national pantheon. The coffins were placed on biers at the entrance of the Kossuth mausoleum. Lajos Kossuth was the leader of the ill-fated revolution of 1848–49, which the Russians also helped to crush. Approximately 200,000 people passed before the coffins. All the members of the Hungarian cabinet with the exception of Erno Gero, who was reportedly still in the Crimea with Khrushchev and Tito, were present. So were Rajk's widow and his eight-year-old son. A week later nine military and police officers, including five generals, were similarly rehabilitated. The rehabilitations in Hungary occurred before the uprising there in 1956.

Not only have confessing defendants, both dead and alive, in criminal cases been declared to be innocent, but also confessants who condemned themselves in so-called self-criticism have received apologies. In June 1958 in an unusual action the Russian Communist party's Central Committee decreed that composers Dmitri D. Shostakovich, the late Sergei Prokofieff, Aram Khachaturian and others were unjustly accused of "formalistic perversion" by the party in 1948 and in "one-sided" editorials in the party press in the years before Stalin's death. Stalin's subjective orders in 1948 and thereafter were now said to be examples of his "cult of personality."

How did communist inquisitors manage to obtain such a multitude of false confessions? The first answer that comes to mind is physical compulsion. This was Khrushchev's answer in his secret speech: "And how is it possible that a person confesses to crimes which he has not committed? Only in one way—because of application of physical methods of pressuring him, tortures, bringing him to a state of unconsciousness, deprivation of his judgment, taking away his human dignity. In this manner were 'confessions' acquired."

And this was the way in which clerical inquisitors in the days of the Inquisition and secular inquisitors in prerevolutionary France did obtain many confessions. But this was not the way in which communist inquisitors usually obtained them. Khrushchev's answer is a gross overstatement. The independent evidence indicates that only for a period of a year or so did communist inquisitors regularly use force. This was from August 1937 until the end of the great purge. There were so many arrests then that the method of protracted questioning took too long. In addition, there were sporadic instances of the use of physical torture. The evidence is good that N. N. Krestinsky, formerly assistant commissar of foreign affairs, and one of the defendants in the 1938 Moscow purge trial, was subjected to it. The record shows that on the first day of the trial he pleaded not guilty. The next day he was very anxious, indeed overanxious, to plead guilty. Something happened to him overnight. According to Alexander Weissberg, when someone asked S. A. Bessanov, another defendant in the 1938 case, why he had not taken advantage of the international publicity at his trial to withdraw his confession, he shrugged his shoulders and replied: "Thanks, I didn't want to go through what Krestinsky went through. He withdrew his confession in court, and that night he was fiendishly tortured for three hours. They put out his left shoulder and he suffered terrible agonies, but outwardly there was nothing to be seen. The next day he confessed again." A fellow prisoner told Weissberg: "Take the case of Krestinsky. He withdrew his confession in court at the Bukharin trial. And what happened? A world scandal? Nothing of the sort. Ulbrich, the Presiding Judge, just ignored him for the rest of the day. During the night the GPU dealt with him and the following day he was back in court as meek as a lamb, declaring that his withdrawal had been a counter-revolutionary maneuver intended to discredit the examination methods. What more do you want?"

Force was used shortly before Stalin's death in order to obtain the confessions of the Moscow doctors. According to Khrushchev's secret speech: "Stalin personally called the investigative judge, gave him instructions, advised him on which investigative methods should be used; these methods were simple—beat, beat and, once again, beat." Stalin like the czars before him did not hesitate to use brutal methods whenever he felt that this suited his purposes. It was on his personal order to Yezhov that the NKVD resorted to force from August 1937 on in the great purge. There is likewise evidence that force was employed in Poland from 1949 to 1953, the last years of Stalin's life: in 1957 the Polish government tried and sentenced to long prison term three former ranking security officials for extracting confessions by the use of "impermissible methods" during this period. The chances are that the same condition prevailed in the other Russian satellites. Force was also used in Poland for a time after the Poznan riots in 1956.

There were some other reports of the use of physical torture. Cardinal Mindszenty is reported to have said that he was beaten for days on end with a rubber hose and questioned for 29 days and nights without sleep.

Vogeler stated that he was subjected to a cold water bath. Robert T. Bryan, Jr., said that he got a spinal injection which took away all his volition. Mrs. Erica Glaser Wallach, a prisoner of the East German and Russian communists, testified to beatings in an effort to get her to confess to spying and the Rev. Fulgence Gross, a prisoner of the Chinese communists, to physical torture. Each appeared before the House Committee of Un-American Activities.

But except for the period of a year and some months beginning in August 1937 and except for sporadic instances, the evidence is against the use of physical torture by the communists. According to Herbert S. Dinerstein, who made a study for the Rand Corporation, surviving witnesses of the Moscow trials of 1936–38 are in general agreement that "physical torture was not used in the examination and interrogation of the main figures. . . ." Oatis wrote: "I should hesitate to say that no suspect ever was beaten in Czechoslovakia. But never in my two years in prison was I beaten, and never did I meet another prisoner who would say he had been beaten or who showed any signs of it." Menachem Begin, who experienced the inquisitional technique of the Russian communists and who later became a member of the Israeli parliament, the Knesset, reported similarly: "I can only say that during all the time I was questioned, not a finger was laid on me, even though I was regarded as a serious 'political criminal' and our 'sessions' were sometimes very stormy. Of the hundreds of prisoners I met later, not one complained of any physical maltreatment. A few of them told me they had heard that others had been beaten." Edgar Sanders, one of Vogeler's co-defendants, stated that the communists never used any pressures on him but mental. They questioned him protractedly, once for 34 hours at a time, but they never physically tortured him.

The story out of China was much the same. Among the civilians the Rev. F. O. Stockwell, Father Harold W. Rigney, rector of the Roman Catholic University of Peiping, who was a prisoner of the Chinese communists for four years, two Roman

Catholic priests, the Rev. John Alexander Houle of Glendale, Calif., and Rev. Charles J. McCarthy of San Francisco, who were their prisoners for a like period, the Rev. Levi A. Lovegren, a Baptist missionary who was their prisoner for almost five years, and Lawrence R. Buol, operations manager for the Civil Air Transport Airline, who was their prisoner for over five years, all reported against the use of physical torture. The Rev. F. O. Stockwell wrote: ". . . There was no evidence of drugs, hypnotism or torture. There didn't need to be . . ." Father Rigney told a reporter that the Chinese communists treated him well during his four-year imprisonment: "They didn't torture me or try to force a confession from me." The Revs. Houle and McCarthy both said their prison life had been miserable, but that beatings and other forms of direct physical maltreatment had not been administered. Father McCarthy added: "They didn't have to."

While military prisoners in the early months of the Korean war experienced brutality at the hands of North Korean captors, the Chinese generally did not resort to it. Dr. Segal wrote:

"What about physical mistreatment? Many Americans believe that collaboration followed brutal, physical abuse—that collaborators signed Communist propaganda petitions, or informed on their fellows, only after they were subjected to excruciating tortures.

"This, again, just is not so. On the contrary, the U.S. Army men who collaborated with the enemy and returned from Korea were rarely the victims of actual mistreatment or physical violence. . . ."

Air Force Col. John A. Booth in a speech to a civic club in Charlotte, North Carolina, in which he said that 70 per cent of the American soldiers captured in Korea became traitors to their country, stated that these American prisoners cooperated with the communists, denounced their own country and in many cases informed on each other without having the communists lay a hand on them. He added that most of

the men were not denied food, placed in solitary confinement
or tortured in any way.

Maj. William E. Mayer, an Army psychiatrist, in explaining to American service men the new code of conduct which
had been prepared for them, said that the chances were 100
to 1 that the individual prisoner would never experience mistreatment or torture in an attempt to break him down mentally.
Dr. Albert D. Biderman, a social scientist at Maxwell Air
Force Base, Alabama, in reporting on three years of Air Force
studies, observed that physical torture was "not a necessary
nor particularly effective method" and where used was "particularly likely to fail completely." However, he noted important effects from "the ever-present fear of violence" and requir-
ing prisoners to stand or sit at attention for "excruciating"
periods.

Doctors Hinkle and Wolff in their study based on the work
they did as consultants to the Department of Defense reported:
"Chinese interrogators and prison guards are more likely to
resort to direct physical brutality than their Russian counter-
parts. When asked to explain the difference between Chinese
methods and those of the KGB, one Russian said simply,
'The Chinese use torture.' This is the exception rather than the
rule in their behavior, but nevertheless it occurs. Angry interrogators may slap or beat prisoners and kick them in the shins.
Guards may do likewise. . . ."

These men testified to this effect in the summer of 1956
before the Permanent Subcommittee on Investigations of the
United States Senate. So did yet others who worked with repatriated American prisoners. Capt. Bert Cumby in response
to a question by Chief Counsel Robert F. Kennedy testified:
"No, sir, Mr. Kennedy, I don't think the interrogation, I don't
think the indoctrination was characterized by brutality or by
torture." A little later in answer to a question by Chairman
John L. McClellan of Arkansas, he said: "When brutality and
torture were used in direct connection with an interrogation

or indoctrination it was the exception rather than the rule; yes, sir. I will stand on that."

Senator McCarthy, as would have most of us, found this testimony difficult to believe. At one point the next day he said to Dr. Segal: "I may be in error, but I think not. I have information that a sizeable number died during interrogation, that they were tortured to the point of death." Dr. Segal answered: "Our data, sir, with regard to interrogation are something that I will go into subsequently, but for the moment I might say that we have no evidence of any deaths which occurred among Army POW's [sic] during the interrogation procedures."

Today communist inquisitors probably do not use force much oftener than our police resort to what we call third degree methods. They may use it occasionally, but only occasionally: the use of force has proven unnecessary. As Doctors Hinkle and Wolff said in their study: "The KGB hardly ever uses manacles or chains, and rarely resorts to physical beatings. The actual physical beating is, of course, repugnant to overt Communist principles, and is contrary to KGB regulations also. The ostensible reason for these regulations is that they are contrary to Communist principles. The practical reason for them is the fact that the KGB looks upon direct physical brutality as an ineffective method of obtaining the compliance of the prisoner. Its opinion in this regard is shared by police in other parts of the world. In general, direct physical brutality creates only resentment, hostility, further defiance, and unreliable statements." Neither do the communists use drugs, hypnotism or other fancy methods.

The French legal scholar Esmein gave as the reason for the many confessions in pre-revolutionary France the system of legal proofs, under which the proof had to be as clear as the noonday sun. But this reason does not explain the many confessions in communist countries, for these countries did not have this system of proofs. They could and did take action against people without any judicial trial at all. Besides, they did not need confessions even in their judicial trials in order to make out a case, especially against political deviants. The provisions of their penal laws were so broad and their rules of evidence so discretionary that almost any kind of evidence would have been sufficient to convict. For instance, the well-known, much-used, and comprehensive section 58 of the Soviet Union's Criminal Code of 1926 made any action directed toward the overthrow, undermining, or weakening of the regime a crime of the gravest type. Or again, the law of Czechoslovakia under which Oatis was convicted made nearly any kind of competent news gathering a crime. Moreover, in these countries intent was not an element of the crime of espionage. All that was necessary was that the accused knew or should have known the consequences of his act. Under such a broad and general structure almost any kind of evidence was good enough. Confessions were not necessary. Yet they abounded.

Neither the system of legal proofs nor the use of physical force will explain the many confessions to communist, French and clerical inquisitors. But there was one thing which the different regimes of these inquisitors had in common: the inquisitional system. There were differences in its application, but the results were the same. Pre-revolutionary France and the Inquisition used physical torture; communist countries as a rule did not. On the other hand, in communist countries the isolation of the individual was more complete than it was in pre-revolutionary France or under the Inquisition, and the interrogation was more protracted. Whatever the differences in application, the results in almost every instance were confessions: the inquisitional process bred them. Here is the crux of the difference between the East and the West so far as confessions are concerned: the inquisitional process and all that this implies, the incarceration and isolation of the individual, his interrogation, the absence of counsel, and the lack of such rights as bail and habeas corpus. This is the reason communist countries deal in confessions and England and the United States as a rule do not.

The communists did not invent the inquisitional technique:

Innocent III did, seven centuries before them. They probably did not even devise the particular use they made of it; rather they stumbled upon it and found it to be effective. The inquisitional technique, borrowed from France, was in use under the czars. The communists simply continued with it, adding the power of the totalitarian state, the complete and utter isolation of the individual for indefinite periods of time, and prolonged interrogation, usually without sufficient sleep, and often at night. The method worked, and became a regular procedure with them. The communists themselves do not know why their system works so well, they just know that it does; they know that it is easy to break the will of human beings.

If one had to speculate as to when the communists hit upon their method, one would suggest that it was under Vyshinsky in the period from 1933, the year of the Metropolitan-Vickers case. We know from a study of the trial records that it was in the three-year period between this case and the 1936 Moscow purge trial that the communists greatly intensified their inquisitional technique. It was probably during this period and the following few years that it also dawned on them that prolonged interrogation of individuals held incommunicado would give them, without more devices, any result they wanted in almost every instance. Vyshinsky himself later unwittingly revealed his awareness of the devastating power of this technique in breaking an individual's will to resist. It was at the 1952 session of the General Assembly of the United Nations. He was addressing himself to the problem of the repatriation of communist prisoners in our hands; and charged that such prisoners would appear before a proposed repatriation commission "with their spirits entirely broken . . . they will come quaking with the fear that will have been implanted in them in the course of that procedure, so that they will be utterly incapable either of asking any questions or of awaiting any answers—because all the questions will have been asked and all the answers will have been forthcoming in advance."

Not only is Khrushchev's statement about the use of force an exaggeration, but it also involves a hidden danger, a danger comparable to that which lies in the false assumption on our side that the right of silence arose as a protest to the use of inquisitorial torture. This erroneous identification of the right of silence with the use of torture led many among us, such as Professor Hook and Judge Ploscowe, to the unsound conclusion that this right was of little value to us today. In converse fashion an acceptance of Khrushchev's misstatement about the use of force will tend to make one unduly receptive to the suggestion that post-Stalin confessions in communist countries are valid; Stalin's successors can argue that they have abandoned his methods. And confessions will continue to be forthcoming. They already have been, for the inquisitional system remains. Indeed Stalin's successors announced that Beria and his aides confessed to treason. The charges against them included the usual one of having been for a long time spies for a foreign power. Khrushchev in the very speech in which he denounced Stalin characterized Beria as "the rabid enemy of our party, an agent of a foreign intelligence service . . . who had stolen into Stalin's confidence." *Plus ça change!*

Communist governments were not the only authoritarian regimes which made an intensive use of the inquisitional technique. Fascist regimes did too. This should not come as a surprise, for inquisitional method is basically authoritarian. The ex-minister of justice of fascist Italy, Rocco, in justifying the practical exclusion of counsel for an accused from the Italian preliminary procedure, wrote: "The presence of the lawyer is demanded by those who mistrust the judge. This is the general attitude in a liberal and democratic state where authority always inspires mistrust, but one which cannot be admitted in a Fascist state because it is in contradiction with the fundamental principles of the regime."

Prior to the confessions in the Korean war we usually refused to recognize how easy it was to break the will of individual human beings. In the Oatis case, for instance, we looked for some other explanation than the simple one that the communists by their inquisitional technique succeeded, as is so easily possible, in breaking his will. We made much of the fact that he did not confess to anything more than the free gathering of news as we understand it in the West. The State Department took the position: "The 'confession' of 'espionage' was in truth but the admission of an American reporter that in the high traditions of his profession he was attempting under the most unfavorable conditions to report a true picture of conditions and events in Czechoslovakia as he saw them." The executive editor of the *Syracuse Herald-Journal*, Alexander F. Jones, asserted that Oatis "had confessed to nothing except that he is an American newspaperman attempting to carry on the normal duties of his occupation." One can readily concede that the point is well taken. The provisions under which Oatis was indicted, paragraph 12 of a law of November 6, 1948, incorporated in the new penal code of 1950, rendered it illegal for anyone to make public any "information regarding any enterprise, institution, installation or measure that is important for the defense of the republic or its allies" as well as information on crimes against the defense of the republic if this information had not been officially released. Under these provisions it was impossible for any western newspaperman in Czechoslovakia to file any kind of story for release without violating one or more of them, even if he did nothing else than quote the current price of shoes, if this was classified economic information. The evidence against Oatis included copies of cables requesting information on the reported disappearance of Vladimir Clementis, formerly Czechoslovakia's foreign minister, who was executed in the Slansky case, and on one or another aspect of Czech life. It was therefore quite in order for one to be disturbed that the free gathering of news should be treated as a crime. However, there was more to the Oatis case than this: it was additionally true that the communists broke his will, and under similar circumstances the same thing would have happened to almost any of us.

The confessions in the Korean war finally brought a measure

of realization of the facility with which a totalitarian state by
the use of the inquisitional technique can induce individuals
to do its bidding. Official public recognition of this fact came
in April 1953 when Allen W. Dulles in his speech to a group
of Princeton University alumni warned us that as a result of
the brainwashing tactics of the communists a group of our
men might be so indoctrinated as to renounce, at least temporarily, country and family. The following September the
Vatican newspaper, *L'Osservatore Romano,* condemned the
confession trial in Warsaw, Poland of the most Rev. Czeslaw
Kaczmarek, Bishop of Kielce, and three Catholic priests as "a
shameful episode aimed at bending not only physical persons
but also consciences to the will of atheistic tyranny."

On the weight to be given to confessions offered in evidence
in judicial proceedings, judges, lawyers and writers have been
poles apart. Some have called them the lowest type of evidence
and others the highest. They were questioned even in the days
of the western Roman empire. Calpurnius Flaccus, a rheto-
rician in the reign of Hadrian commented, "Even a voluntary
confession is to be regarded with suspicion"; and Quintilian
a little earlier stated, "A suspicion of insanity is inherent in the
nature of all confessions." They have been challenged even in
the East. Indeed, one of the severest condemnations of confessions came from the exceptional argument of Dimiter Iliev,
one of the lawyers for Petkov:

"The myth that the confession is the queen of proofs has
been exploded long ago, especially in penal processes. Our
law explicitly provides that the confession can be accepted on
basis of a verdict only then when it does not arouse any
doubt whatever. There are many cases when we look for the
motive which has impelled the defendant to make a certain
confession. They are innumerable, Honorable Judges. I will
remind you of the case described by Dostoevski in an inimi-
table and unique manner in his novel *Crime and Punishment.*
For the murder of the woman committed by Raskolnikov
before the investigating coroner Porfirius appear two more

persons confessing that they have committed the crime; one of them is some kind of religious ascetic who wishes to undergo the torments of a murderer, while the confession of the other is based on entirely different motives. A man standing on the defendant's bench and pressed to the wall by the judicial inquiry can make a confession in order to save his head, or to resort to a smaller punishment, if the law provides a heavy one. Another might confess in order to save a dear one from the judicial investigation. Still another might do it in order to divert the investigation from its right path leading toward the really guilty person, so that he can reserve for himself a certain position of which he can make use in the future."

Bukharin in his last speech referred enigmatically to the confession of an accused as a medieval principle of jurisprudence; but one cannot tell whether he meant to condemn the practice or recommend its use if the confession was fulsome enough.

A British authority, Burn, in his *Justice of the Peace* suggested: ". . . magistrates cannot be too cautious in receiving confessions . . ." An editor in a supplement added: "This kind of evidence I have always found, in the words of that truly learned judge, Sir Michael Foster, to be the most suspicious of all testimony." On the other hand, Starkie called them "one of the surest proofs of guilt." Mr. Justice Grose, in delivering the opinion of the judges in *Lambe's* case, described confessions as "the highest and most satisfactory proof of guilt." Another judge, William Scott, in two different cases gave diametrically opposite estimates. In one he commented: "The court must remember that confession is a species of evidence which, though not inadmissible, is regarded with great distrust . . . though it is evidence which is not absolutely excluded, but is received in conjunction with other circumstances yet it is, on all occasions, to be most accurately weighted." In the other he stated: "Now, I need not observe, that confession generally ranks high, or, I should say, highest in the scale of evidence."

But whatever may have been the estimate of confessions, whenever they have been coupled to the inquisitional method British and American courts have usually excluded them. British courts have usually excluded them if there has been any inquisitional period at all unless an accused has first been advised of his right to remain silent. Our Supreme Court has usually excluded them if there has been any unnecessary delay in taking an accused before a committing authority. In *Haley* v. *Ohio,* involving a fifteen-year-old Negro, the Supreme Court excluded a confession even though the inquisitional period was less than five hours.

Occasionally our courts have commented specifically on the element of breaking a human being's will psychologically and without the use of force. In a recent case Mr. Justice Douglas in a concurring opinion in which Justices Black and Frankfurter joined, in commenting on the police practice of arresting a person on one charge and questioning him on another, stated: "But when it is a pretense or used as the device for breaking the will of the prisoner on long, relentless, or repeated questionings, it is abhorrent." In the *Haley* case, Mr. Justice Frankfurter in a concurring opinion reasoned: "But whether a confession of a lad of fifteen is 'voluntary' and as such admissible, or 'coerced' and thus wanting in due process, is not a matter of mathematical determination. Essentially it invites psychological judgment—a psychological judgment that reflects deep, even if inarticulate, feelings of our society. . . .

"It would disregard standards that we cherish as part of our faith in the strength and well-being of a rational, civilized society to hold that a confession is 'voluntary' simply because the confession is the product of sentient choice . . ."

Such comments were not limited to our federal Supreme Court. Judge Frank in an opinion for the Court of Appeals for the Second Circuit pointed out that psychological torture might be far more cruel than physical brutality. A California reviewing court observed: "While no physical force was used and neither threats nor promises made, there can be no doubt at all but that the repeated questioning of the officers, like the constant dripping of water upon a rock, finally wore through his mental resolution to remain silent."

A study of the inquisitional system in the hands of the communists, especially during the Korean war, should indicate the validity of these comments and the worth of our accusatorial method. A consideration of the compulsion to confess will reinforce these conclusions.

The Compulsion to Confess

16 *The Compulsion to Confess*

Primeval Wellsprings

CONFESSIONS ARE AMONG those common occurrences that we usually accept without much thought about their origin. Not only are they as natural to us as living, but the inner force which produces them also causes us generally to feel that they have a great beneficial value. According to Manu one who confessed was freed from guilt as a snake from its slough. James told the early Christians that by mutual confession and prayer they would be healed. John told them that they would be cleansed from all unrighteousness. Publilius Syrus (c. 42 B.C.) wrote: "Confession of our faults is the next thing to innocence." Even Goethe regarded a confession favorably and credited it with absolution: "I went on with the poetical confession I had begun, that, with this self-tormenting penance. I might attain an inner absolution." The most poignant evaluation came from Oscar Wilde in *De Profundis*. "A man's very highest moment is, I have no doubt, when he kneels in the dust and beats his breast, and tells all the sins of his life." Similar evaluations find popular expression in the sayings, an honest confession is good for the soul, and, a fault confessed is half forgiven.

However, until recently we showed little interest in the nature of the force that has engendered an endless flow of confessions from human beings. Dr. Berg in the title to his case history of the girl who felt the need to tell her mother everything furnished us with a descriptive name for it, *Compulsion to Confess;* but this did not explain its basis. We did not have much curiosity about such an explanation until after we became aware of the confessions to communist inquisitors, more specifically after we learned about the collaboration of American military and civilian prisoners in the enemy's propaganda efforts during and after the Korean War. Doctors Hinkle and Wolff began their study with a brief description of the problem: "The Communists are skilled in the extraction of information from prisoners and in making prisoners do their bidding. It has appeared that they can force men to confess to crimes which have not been committed, and, then, apparently to believe in the truth of their confessions and express sympathy and gratitude toward those who have imprisoned them." Such a condition required an explanation.

Feelings of Guilt and Sin

THE PSYCHOLOGISTS, PSYCHIATRISTS and others who sought to account for the actions of American collaborators recurrently referred to guilt feelings. Doctors Hinkle and Wolff used the expressions "strong feelings of guilt" and "heavy load of guilt." Dr. Wolff testified: "For the most part they were guilt-laden and excessively dependent—guilt-laden for personal reasons having to do with their own backgrounds and family experience." The older way of describing the same phenomenon was feelings of sin. Many people still use it.

Concepts of sin have long been with us. They are at least as old as confessions of sins and such confessions go back thirteen centuries and more before Christ. In the long course of time human beings divided sin into various kinds and grades. First of all there was original, inherited or primeval sin—the old Adam. Then there was a sin which was called unpardonable. It was also known as the sin against the Holy Ghost. After that came such sins as: actual or acquired, as opposed to original; mortal or deadly, as opposed to venial; secret; venial; unknown; and probably yet others. Ideas of inherited sin appear to be as old as any. King Mursilis II of the Hittites asked forgiveness for the sin of his father as well as his own. Ideas of the transmission of a father's sin to his son as well as the transfer of a sovereign's sin to his people and country were both usual to the ancient oriental mind. According to Numbers 14:18 and Deuteronomy 5:9 the iniquity of the fathers was visited upon the children unto the third and fourth generation. Psalm 51:5 says: "Behold, I was shapen in iniquity; and in sin did my mother conceive me." Euripides (484–406 B.C.) in a fragment stated: "The gods visit the sins of the fathers upon the children." The early Greeks also phrased the idea of inherited sin in terms of primeval or original sin. A fragment of Anaximander (611?–547? B.C.) related how the unity of the world was broken by "a sort of primeval sin." According to the Orphic mysteries the Titans, who were the ancestors of human beings, treacherously slew the young god Dionysus-Zagreus and tore him to pieces. The burden of this crime weighed upon them. From the mysteries the idea of a primeval sin spread to the schools of philosophy of ancient Greece. In the Christian religion the original sin was against God the Father.

The sin against the Holy Ghost, or the unpardonable sin, presents a more nebulous concept. The Church Fathers were by no means agreed as to the exact constitution of this sin. Thomas Aquinas thought it consisted of a direct insult to the Holy Ghost. According to the Church itself this sin was "to deny from pure malice the Divine character of works manifestly Divine." Henry Maudsley (1835–1918), an English doctor who studied the human mind, gave this description: "The very mystery of that one stupendous sin, its vague and unknown nature, has an awful fascination for the imagination, which is held by it in a sort of cataleptic trance." A number of confessants admitted either that they had a strong desire to commit this sin or that they were afraid they had committed it. John Bunyan wanted to commit this sin. Catherine Phillips, a young Quaker, was so weighed down by a sense of guilt that she concluded she had sinned against the Holy Ghost. So did others.

Whatever differences there were among Christians as to the nature of certain sins, there was agreement on one point: we were all sinful. No one was without sin, not even saints or newborn babes. Paul in his epistle to the Romans wrote, 3:9–10: ". . . for we have before proved both Jews and Gentiles, that they are all under sin; As it is written, There is none righteous, no, not one." And in his epistle to the Galatians, 3:22: "But the scripture hath concluded all under sin . . ." In 1 John 1:8 we read: "If we say we have no sin we deceive ourselves, and the truth is not in us." St. Augustine, the bishop of Hippo, in his *Confessions* wrote: "For before Thee none is free from sin, not even the infant who has lived but a day upon the earth." Or as *The New England Primer* had it:

> In Adam's fall
> We sinned all.

If one had no mortal or venial sins, then according to Roman Catholic doctrine one had to confess one's self in general terms to be a sinner. Some prayers in other churches asked forgiveness for unknown sins. Moreover, one at all times had to be repentant of one's sinful nature. Psalm 51:3 reads: "For I acknowledge my transgressions: and my sin is ever before me."

Individuals in Rebellion

A SECOND FACTOR which those who studied American prisoners of the Chinese communists brought out with reference to the collaborators was that they were often persons in rebellion. Dr. Wolff testified that those who were especially amenable to Chinese communist indoctrination "seemed to have in common, let us say, evidence of rebellion against their family or church or the society in which they originated—not only Americans, but French, Belgian, and other Europeans." He and Dr. Hinkle wrote concerning them: "They were people who, long before their imprisonment, were in rebellion against their parents and the way of life of the segment of society to which their parents belonged, including many of its standards, beliefs, and practices."

Lack of Love

A THIRD FACTOR observable with reference to those on whom the Chinese communists did their most thorough jobs of brainwashing was paucity both in the number of their human relationships and the amount of affection involved in them. Doctors Hinkle and Wolff wrote: "They were people who had few friends within their homeland, and no place, organization, or occupation there with which they were firmly identified. So far as the native country was concerned, they were emotionally rootless." According to Virginia Pasley, who did a book, *21 Stayed,* on the American soldiers who chose to remain in China after the exchange of war prisoners, ". . . 16 had homes broken by death, divorce or separation . . . 19 of the 21 felt unloved or unwanted by fathers or stepfathers . . . 5 of the 21 lost their mothers when they were young . . . 5 others were away from mothers in early childhood . . . 2 of the 21 had mothers who were problem drinkers. 4 of the 21 had mothers who worked away from home. . . ."

Need for Punishment

A FOURTH NOTICEABLE factor, and one not limited to the cases of confessants to communist inquisitors, was a need for punishment. This need is observable in confessants generally. One can see it, for instance, in those who confessed to clerical inquisitors. There is a connection between this need and confessions. Interestingly enough Dr. Reik has a work, in German, with the significant title, *The Compulsion to Confess and the Need for Punishment.*

Indeed this factor is sufficiently general that one may see it even in those who did not confess. An instance was Dr. Edith Bone, an Hungarian communist who spent seven years in solitary confinement in Hungarian prisons. Hungarian rebels liberated her in 1956. Although she apparently never gave a confession, she nevertheless looked upon her imprisonment as something she somehow deserved. When she was interviewed in London she commented: "For 30 years I had been a Communist. Toward the end of that period I began to have severe guilt feelings—I just couldn't stomach some of the filth. My imprisonment was an atonement, a liberation from guilt feelings."

Again, as in the case of guilt feelings, we have a factor which is well-known once it is designated with the earlier terminology, doing penance. This human characteristic is old and has taken a multitude of forms. It has included fasting, almsgiving, pilgrimages, crusades, prayers, wailing and weeping, and flagellation. It has included self-torment in almost endless ways and finally even martyrdom itself. One who was penitent constantly had to mortify the old Adam. He had to soak his bread and his bed with tears. According to St. Ambrose he had to be as one dead, with no care for the things of this life. Coleridge's ancient mariner did penance in the form of eternal confessions—"The man hath penance done, and penance more will do." And even with all their penances, sufferings and misfortunes human beings still expressed the feeling that they were getting better treatment from God than they deserved: Psalm 103:10 tells us: "He hath not dealt with us after our sins; nor rewarded us according to our iniquities."

The early Christians devised a variety of new forms of self-torment. Some of them, such as the pillarists and the anchorites, spent their time making themselves physically miserable. Simeon Stylites bound a rope about him which imbedded itself in his flesh, and it was said that a horrible stench, intolerable to bystanders, exhaled from his body, and worms dropped from him whenever he moved, and they filled his bed. Benedict rolled himself in thorn hedges. Macarius sat naked on an ant hill. Anthony flagellated himself incessantly. Jerome condemned himself to live in the desert without any cooked food, which he deemed a sinful luxury, and with no companionship other than that of scorpions and wild beasts. Yet others lived in empty dens of wild beasts, or in tombs, without clothes, crawling about like animals, covered only with their hair, which was a mass of matted filth.

Voluntary flagellation was one of the oldest and most widespread forms of penance. It increased greatly in prominence in the eleventh century and broke out in epidemic proportions in the thirteenth and fourteenth centuries. Peter Damian, Cardinal of Ostia, urged the substitution of self-flagellation for the reading of penitential psalms, even setting up a scale of values: a thousand strokes of the lash was to equal ten psalms. The first epidemic of penitential scourging began in Perugia, Italy in 1259. It came in the same year as a big epidemic of the plague. This outbreak of scourging spread through northern Italy and to the northeast as far as Bohemia. Flagellants lashed themselves with scourges made of leather thongs until the blood ran down their bodies, and confessed all manner of sins. The second and more famous epidemic occurred in 1349, and led to the formation of the Brotherhood of the Flagellants, often called the Brotherhood of the Cross. This outbreak was at its height in Germany, and just preceded the approach of the Black Death from the East. The bands of flagellants probably helped to spread the very plague which by their self-torments they sought to avert.

Many early Christians sentenced themselves to death. They become marytrs. Those among them whom the Roman tribunals punished but released could not rest until they too had attained martyrdom. The Christians wrote that they not only did not dread but even provoked the enemies of the faith. Many Christian chronicles reported the provocative behavior of the martyrs as proofs of their eagerness. The word martyr literally meant witness, and was applied to those who confessed their faith in Jesus even though this involved death for them.

The Christians have outgrown the early form of martyrdom, but the phenomenon is still with us. Its modern forms include masochism in a myriad of ways and suicide. In Arthur Miller's play *Death of a Salesman* the principal character displays a fear in the first scene that he will have an automobile accident and toward the end of the play commits suicide by deliberately crashing in his car.

The communists and the ex-communists among us have shown a great need for punishment. Ethel and Julius Rosenberg in the atom bomb spy case subjected themselves to the death penalty. A multitude of others have inflicted upon themselves lesser punishments. It was probably not an accident that Chambers called his book *Witness*.

The need for punishment is so pervasive that, just as in the case of the compulsion to confess, it not only expresses itself in conscious forms but also demonstrates its power in unconscious ways. Examples of the latter are the injuries which accident-prone individuals inflict upon themselves. Such persons injure themselves so frequently that we have a basis for inferring that they seek to be hurt. A six-year study in the state of Connecticut showed that less than four per cent of the drivers involved in traffic accidents were concerned in thirty-six per cent of them. The same relation has been shown to exist in industry. One large company which employed a great number of truck drivers transferred those drivers who had the most

accidents to other jobs. By this simple device it succeeded in
reducing the accident rate to one-fifth of its former level.
However, it found out an interesting thing: the drivers who
had a high accident rate retained their accident habit in their
new job. Moreover, we have discovered that those employees
who have the worst accident records in their jobs also have the
most frequent accidents at home or on the way to work. Indeed, Dr. Franz Alexander, an eminent medical psychologist,
has stated that "most accidents are not accidents at all but
are caused largely by the victim's own disposition": in other
words they are "unconsciously intended."

In doing penance human beings have to make themselves
spectacles of abject humility. They have to abase themselves
to the point of prostration. While they beat their breasts, they
must, if they can, grovel in the dust. They must wear sackcloth
and cover themselves with ashes. Nehemiah tells us that "the
children of Israel were assembled with fasting, and with sackclothes, and earth upon them." Daniel made his confession
while fasting and in sackcloth and ashes. Psalm 51:17 reads:
"The sacrifices of God are a broken spirit; a broken and a
contrite heart, O God, thou wilt not despise." The publican,
"standing afar off, would not lift up so much as his eyes unto
heaven, but smote upon his breast, saying, God be merciful
to me a sinner." Oscar Wilde wrote: "There is only one thing
for me, now, absolute humility." Abbas Paulus the Great asserted that he was in dirt up to his neck. The most admired
saints were those who had become a clotted mass of filth.
Athanasius related with enthusiasm that St. Anthony in his
long life had never been guilty of washing his feet. Self-mortifi-
cation, squalor and physical uncleanliness became esteemed
Christian virtues.

Coming before one's god or gods in a state of utter humility
and confessing one's sins and doing penance were general
human characteristics. There were exceptions, but they only
served to sharpen the severe features of the need for punish-

ment. Omar Khayyám, for instance, in one of the quatrains of his *Rubáiyát,* or at least in one ascribed to him, took a rather equalitarian approach to his god:

> O Thou, who man of baser earth didst make,
> And ev'n with Paradise devise the Snake:
> For all the sin wherewith the Face of Man
> Is blackened—Man's forgiveness give—and take!

However, most Christians would hesitate to take this approach.

Because of their need for punishment human beings have found it necessary to supplement their self-inflicted penalties by a deprivation of earthly pleasures as well. They have not been able to permit themselves to enjoy life, to have any fun. St. Augustine, the bishop of Hippo, is a good illustration. He complained even of the fact that he took pleasure in eating. He knew that he had to take food for nourishment but that he should enjoy it while it was on its way to his stomach disturbed him. ". . . against this sweetness do I fight, lest I be enthralled; and I carry on a daily war by fastings . . . This much hast Thou taught me, that I should bring myself to take food as medicine. But during the time that I am passing from the uneasiness of want to the calmness of satiety, even in the very passage doth that snare of concupiscence lie in wait for me." He did not know to what extent food was necessary for his body's nourishment and what amount was due to a sensual snare of desire. He was unable to resolve the matter. But God protect him from the pleasure of eating. He had less trouble with the pleasure of smell, such as perfumes; these he could rather easily put aside. The pleasures of the ear, for instance, music and singing in church, presented somewhat more of a problem. He was inclined, however, to approve of the use of singing in church, "that so by the delights of the ear the weaker minds may be stimulated to a devotional frame. Yet when it happens to me to be more moved by the singing than by what is sung I confess myself to have sinned criminally, and then I would rather not have heard the singing." God also protect

him from enjoying the delights of the eye, including the light
of day. "The eyes delight in fair and varied forms, and
bright and pleasing colors. Suffer not these to take possession
of my soul . . ." In connection with the eyes there was another form of temptation, more complex in its peril: human
curiosity, the desire to experiment. This desire he called "the
lust of the eyes." The satisfaction from receiving praise for a
good life and for good works was another troublesome item.
"Regarding this matter, Thou knowest the groans of my
heart, and the rivers of mine eyes. For I am not able to
ascertain how far I am clean of this plague, and I stand in
great fear of my 'secret faults,' which Thine eyes perceive,
though mine do not." Praise for one's ability was acceptable
only when one was more delighted with the recognition of the
ability which was praised than with one's self. The ability for
which one was praised one had as a gift from God of course
and was not due to one's self.

Alas for St. Augustine, the memories of his past pleasures
returned to him, in dreams as well as when he was awake.
These memories were strengthless when he was awake, but
when he was asleep the story was different. ". . . but in sleep
they do so not only so as to give consent, but even to obtain
consent, and what very nearly resembles reality."

The early Christian ascetics were constantly on guard
against the pleasurable snares of the devil. For instance, the
monk Pachomius once saw a pack of devils dragging along a
bundle of leaves, pretending that this was costing them great
effort, for no other purpose than to tempt him to the sin of
laughter. Then there was the story of the very holy hermit who,
at the devil's urging, acquired a cock to relieve his loneliness.
This was a little thing, but the cock got lonesome, too, and in a
spirit of charity the hermit supplied it with a hen. As one may
suspect, the combination aroused old ardors in the poor hermit. He soon seduced the young and beautiful daughter of a
neighboring nobleman and, in order to escape the vengeance
of her parents, killed her and hid her body underneath his

couch. His crime was of course discovered and he had to suffer death and eternal damnation—all because he listened to the devil in a little thing.

The Puritans carried on in the Augustinian tradition. They occupied themselves with the constant mortification of the old Adam. Unchastity they held to be one of the deadly sins. Hester Prynne in Hawthorne's *The Scarlet Letter* was a woman stained with sin, bowed down with shame, burdened with a lifelong sorrow. But, according to the Puritans, we were all false and sin-stained creatures of the dust, healed only by the miraculous and unmerited intervention of divine grace. They suspected all forms of beauty as snares of the devil, and re-garded all personal decoration as sinful conceit. They distrusted all art and music, all poetry and romance, as artifices of the devil, with certain exceptions which long tradition authorized and in which the mood was consonant with Christ's descent from the cross. They utterly damned the theatre, disapproved of dancing and card playing, did not fully condone humor, and looked askance even upon laughter. Cotton Mather ap-plied himself to fasting, contrition, abasement, and sorrow for sin. He looked anxiously for what he called the mark of an effectually called person of God. Jonathan Edwards, a great Puritan champion, in early life just after graduating from Yale at the age of 17, went into training to perfect himself in godliness. For several years he recorded in a diary the course of training which he followed. The entries went like this: "38. Resolved, Never to utter anything that is sportive, or matter of laughter, on a Lord's day . . ." In England during the Puritan revolution and in New England during the theocracy the Puritans through the civil authorities prohibited various amusements and other pleasures, and gave us what we variously call sumptuary, Sunday, or blue laws. By successive enact-ments between 1644 and 1656 Parliament prohibited every kind of Sunday recreation, even "vainly and profanely" walk-ing for pleasure. These harsh and gloomy aspects of puritan-ism led Macaulay to remark: "The puritan hated bear baiting, not because it gave pain to the bear, but because it gave pleasure to the spectators." H. L. Mencken and George Jean Nathan modernized Macaulay's jibe by defining puritanism as "the haunting fear that someone, somewhere, may be happy."

Substantial remains of early Christian asceticism and of the negative aspects of puritanism are still with us. We still have our blue laws in one form or another. The Lord's Day Act of Canada makes illegal any unnecessary toil and business conducted on Sunday. The Sabbath Law of New York prohibits all labor on Sunday except "works of necessity and charity." Until 1919 New York also prohibited "all shooting, hunting, playing, horse-racing, gaming or other public sports, exercises or shows" on Sunday. In that year there were certain relaxations as to baseball, the movies and legitimate theatre productions, but even so they could be indulged in only after two o'clock in the afternoon. Subsequently other activities were added to the list—basketball, soccer, hockey and football games as late as 1949, and only after two o'clock of course. The purpose of the Sabbath Law, according to the leading case on it, was to declare any act a nuisance which tended "to profane the day by any unnecessary or noisy, conduct."

Thirty-nine states and many municipalities have Sunday blue measures in some form. In recent years various municipalities in Pennsylvania and New Jersey started on a campaign of enforcement. In December 1957 Allentown, Pennsylvania launched a new effort to enforce obedience of a Pennsylvania no-work-on-Sunday law that has been on the statute books since 1794. Pennsylvania has another law which forbids Sunday movies in any area voting against them in local option elections. The constitutionality of this law was challenged in a case which was appealed to the United States Supreme Court. In 1958 New Jersey enacted a new blue law. Various municipalities in that state have sought to compel compliance with Sunday blue ordinances: Ocean Grove, Saddle River, Paramus, South Orange, West Orange, and Woodbridge Township. In Ocean Grove, New Jersey, every business, amusement and recreational facility must be closed on Sunday. On the beach not even wading is permitted. About the only legal Sunday activity is going to church. Many people are still unable to allow themselves to have any great amount of fun. There are still those who regard dancing and card playing as sins. Until recently various denominations made mortification of the flesh one of the central duties of life. C. H. Cramer in his biography of Robert G. Ingersoll quoted the latter as having written: "When I was a boy Sunday was considered altogether too holy to be happy in . . . Nobody said a pleasant word; nobody laughed; nobody smiled; the child that looked the sickest was regarded as the most pious . . . Dyspepsia was in the very air you breathed . . . The minister asked us if we knew that we all deserved to go to hell, and we all answered, 'Yes.' Then we were asked if we should be willing to go to hell if it was God's will, and every little liar shouted 'yes.' " An article in the *Lutheran Quarterly* talked about the "utter ruin and corruption of our race" and the "necessity of daily repentance and the constant mortification of the old Adam with all his lusts and passions."

Catholics, too, must continue to mortify the flesh. In October 1958, a few days before his death, Pope Pius XII told plastic surgeons that it was morally wrong to operate on a person who wanted surgery "only to satisfy vanity or the caprice of fashion." Plastic surgery was morally wrong for the purpose of enhancing a person's "power of seduction, thus leading others more easily into sin."

Omnipotence of Thoughts

TO THESE FACTORS one must add a concept which Freud aptly designated as the omnipotence of thoughts. Freud attributed this phrase to one of his patients, but the expression the patient actually used was the omnipotence of wishes.

The human mind operates on different levels and in different ways. Parts of it, indeed probably the principal parts of it, are still primitive, archaic and irrational. Dr. Berg gave us this general description of the mind: "Medical students find on dissecting the human body that there are innumerable rudimentary, unnecessary and illogical parts. In the same way psychologists find in the human mind deeper levels full of the most primitive obsolescent structures and mechanisms which have nothing of logic or reason or of those principles with which we are consciously familiar and with which we would like to endow them." Moreover, the irrational parts of the mind are largely unknown: the upper rational layer is just thick enough to obscure them from view.

A part of the mind conceives of wishes and thoughts as being omnipotent. Although this part is obscure to us we can recognize some of its modern remains. Modern man, just as his primitive ancestors, still burns his enemies in effigy. After World War I many communities in this country burnt the German Kaiser, William II, in effigy. In 1953 some students at the University of Toronto did the same thing to Senator McCarthy. One can cite other instances. In primitive societies if a man wished to injure an enemy a very common magical procedure was to make an effigy of him from any convenient material. Then whatever was done to the effigy would happen to the original. Whatever part of the effigy was damaged, the same part of the enemy would become diseased.

We still speak of the magic of art. In primitive times it is probable that art literally was magical. It did not begin for art's sake. A primitive artist did not make pictures of animals in caves in order to please his associates but in order to conjure up the animals he pictured and to have power over them. As Salomon Reinach explained, if the primitive artist's purpose was that of pleasing his associates he would not have put his pictures in the darkest and most inaccessible parts of the caves.

Modern man considers the possibility of mental telepathy and some think there is evidence to support the claims for it. Many modern human beings believe that by concentrating on a thought they can in some way, without more, influence or affect other individuals. Such beliefs also rest on the concept that thoughts are omnipotent.

One sometimes hears the expression "if thoughts could kill." To one part of the mind it literally seems that they can. Fears that they have and that the dead will retaliate help to account for our feelings of awe and dread toward the dead. One does have hostile thoughts toward loved ones. They do die, if for no other reason than that they grow old. To one part of one's mind it seems that one's hostile thoughts had a hand in such deaths. The dead must therefore be propitiated. As an old Eskimo explained to the Danish explorer Knud Rasmussen: "We observe our old customs, in order to hold the world up, for the powers must not be offended . . . we are afraid of the great Evil . . . The people here do penance, because the dead are strong in their vital sap, and boundless in their might." We attribute omnipotence to the thoughts of others as well as to our own, and this even though they are dead. Hence we tend to regard the dead as still having strength. In a murder case in New York a suspect was taken to the body of the decedent and made to touch it. When he got back to the police station he confessed. There is an old belief that the corpse of a murdered person will bleed again if the murderer touches it. We have a popular saying that spilled blood cries to heaven. This is what God told Cain his brother Abel's blood did. In the cases of the dying Ibycus and the passing cranes and St. Meinrad and his ravens the dead did avenge themselves. God put a mark on Cain in order to protect him.

Basis for Confession Compulsion

WITH THE FOUR FACTORS of guilt feelings, inner rebellion, lack of love and the need for punishment, and the concept of the omnipotence of thoughts, one is in a position to explore further the nature of guilt feelings and to suggest the basis of

the compulsion to confess. Confessions are based on guilt
feelings and guilt feelings represent a combination of two
things: "the dread of losing love," to use Freud's words; and
the fear of retaliation at the hands of those against whom one's
own hostile and aggressive wishes as well as acts have been
directed. One's first guilt feelings will involve one's parents.
Later they will additionally involve parent-substitutes, "the
larger human community," to use Freud's words again. More
specifically they will involve the state and its police agencies.

The most powerful force in the world as well as the one in
shortest supply is love. It is the chief factor in the motivation
of human beings. One must not only receive love, but also give
it. Loving one's neighbor is one thing from which one will
not have guilt feelings. The power of love is such that modern
psychology and Christianity are in agreement on its importance.
Christ has been called the first therapist because he assured
those who came to him for help that their sins were forgiven
them. He said to a man sick of the palsy, lying on a bed: "Son
be of good cheer; thy sins be forgiven thee." On the centenary
of Freud's birth *The Church of England Newspaper* in an editorial commented: "Freud's rediscovery of love as the basis
of physical as well as spiritual life is something from which
the church might learn much about the full truth of her own
faith."

One of the reasons Christianity spread was its insistence on
love. Another reason was the doctrine that Christ by his suffering and death took on his shoulders the sins of all of us, thus
securing for us the love of God the Father and protecting
us from his retaliation as well. These reasons plus the practice
of auricular confession and a skillfully organized hierarchy
substantially explain why the Catholic Church established
itself. The Church's emphasis on love along with the doctrine
that Christ by being tormented, tortured, and crucified atoned
for the sins of all of us were also the reasons why the drama
in the form of the Passion Plays in the Middle Ages sprang
into fresh life from the ashes of Greek tragedy. The drama

in Greece was based on the tragic inner conflict in human beings plus their proclivities to the primal crimes of incest and murder. The Passion Plays were based on love and atonement.

The power of love is such that one can see the modern stress on it not only in religion and psychology, but also in history and popular literature, both fiction and nonfiction. Examples are Dr. Karl A. Menninger's *Love Against Hate,* Dr. Erich Fromm's *The Art of Loving,* Dr. Smiley Blanton's *Love or Perish,* Arnold Toynbee's *An Historian's Approach to Religion,* and James Gould Cozzens' *By Love Possessed.* Dr. Blanton's book was on the best-seller lists for almost a year.

Cozzens' opening words are: "Love conquers all—*vincit omnia amor,* said the gold scroll in a curve beneath the dial of the old French gilt clock." Fromm maintains: "If it is true, as I have tried to show, that love is the only sane and satisfactory answer to the problem of human existence, then any society which excludes, relatively, the development of love, must in the long run perish of its own contradiction with the basic necessities of human nature."

Toynbee's book, which contains his Gifford lectures at the University of Edinburgh in 1952 and 1953, argues for Christian love as against the history of Christendom and for Mahayanistic Buddhism as against its Hinayanan counterpart. In his concluding chapter he says: ". . . In the judgment of Christianity and the Mahāyāna, even the extremity of Suffering is not too high a price to pay for following Love's lead; for, in their judgement, Selfishness, not Suffering, is the greatest of all evils, and Love, not release from Suffering, is the greatest of all goods."

The power of love is such that human beings in order to obtain or regain it will give even life itself, their own as well as the lives of others. The early Christian martyrs gave their lives to make sure they had the love of Jesus and their fellow Christians. Bukharin, Zinoviev, Kamenev, Slansky, and others

of the communist leaders who were executed after confession
show trials gave their lives to make sure they had as much as
they could get of the love of the state, the party, and their
fellow communists.

Those who confess are trying to obtain or regain love and
ward off feared retaliation. They are in effect saying: forgive
me and love me again; punish me, beat me, but love me
again. When people confess their sins they want God to forgive them and love them again. When the little boy George
Washington confessed to his father in the apocryphal story
about chopping down his father's cherry tree Parson Weems
in effect had him say, "Father, forgive me and love me again."
When Bukharin in the 1938 Moscow purge trial said that he
was kneeling before the country, before the party, before the
whole people he was in effect saying, do with me what you
wish, kill me if you must, but love me again. Sholem Asch in
The Three Cities had one of his characters say that it was a
positive pleasure to a Russian to confess his sins and beg
someone's forgiveness and he would, if necessary, gratify
this desire by inventing a sin for the occasion because he was
afraid of being alone with himself and had a passion for collectivism. What he really wanted to do was to make sure that
somebody loved him. This was the basis for the Russian custom of so-called criticism and self-criticism.

If the innocent will confess in order to gain love, of course
so will the guilty. That is why there are so many kinds of
confessions. Those who are guilty of some criminal offense are
under such anxiety lest they have lost love and lest there will
be retaliation that they usually confess. One deviant who was
in custody sent for two officers separately, one at eight o'clock
in the morning and the other an hour later and confessed to
each. To the one he said: "If your conscience troubled you
as much as mine did all night, you would want to tell your
story to somebody." To the other: "I have put in a terrible
night. I want to tell you all." Yet another said: "I am not
sorry; the anxiety has been too much"; and on a card wrote,

"I cannot stand the horrors I go through every night any longer." Lady Macbeth walked in her sleep, rubbed her hands as if washing them, and cried: "Out, damned spot! out, I say!"

If it is objected that a person would not confess if this meant death, one can point out that the innocent as well as the guilty have confessed to crimes which involved the death penalty and been executed. The early Christians proclaimed their faith in Christ even though this meant that they would be thrown to the lions. Many communist leaders confessed even though this meant that they would be shot or hanged. St. Augustine could find no pleasures free from vexation except in God, "who teachest by sorrow, and woundest us to heal us, and killest us that we may not die from Thee." Hawthorne had the Reverend Arthur Dimmesdale die a death of "triumphant ignominy." The minister asked the members of Robert G. Ingersoll's Sunday school class if they would be willing to go to hell if it was God's will and they all answered affirmatively. No price is too great to pay for love.

Thus it was no accident that the ones with whom the Chinese communists were the most successful in their brainwashing tactics were those whom Doctors Hinkle and Wolff described as emotionally rootless with reference to their homeland. It was no accident that nearly all of those who stayed felt unwanted by one or both parents. In their important early years they lacked love.

The need for punishment is closely tied in with the compulsion to confess, and the objectives sought to be attained by doing penance are the same as those in making a confession, obtaining love and warding off feared retaliation. As one writer put it: "The penitent craves above all else God's pardon." For God's love penitents will put on sackcloth and ashes. They will prostrate themselves and grovel in the dust. Indeed the very word penitentiary means literally a place where penitents do penance. Those who commit offenses and get sent to the penitentiary for them are doing penance. Freud stated: "It

is a fact that large groups of criminals long for punishment."
Moreover, if people are already suffering much, their parents
not only will be sorry for them and love them again, but also
will refrain from inflicting any further punishments on them.
Often the need for punishment is so great that people condemn
themselves to death. They give their lives. This is what the
early Christian martyrs and many communist leaders did by
means of their confessions. According to Freud the "impulses to suicide in a neurotic turn out regularly to be self-
punishments for wishes for someone else's death."

Because of the need for punishment many people refuse
to enjoy life, or to enjoy it fully, to have the fun and laughter
that the world provides. They became ascetic and puritanical.
They subject themselves and the rest of us to various blue laws.

It sometimes happens that an individual has great anxiety
about an act which it is too painful for him to confess. He
may then commit some illegal act, get caught, and confess the
illegal act, and in this way relieve his anxiety. For example,
in large cities there are gangs of boys who engage in mutual
masturbation. This causes them great anxiety, for masturbation was strictly forbidden in their infancy and childhood.
They are thus afraid that they have lost the love of their parents. In order to assuage their guilt feelings, they steal, get
caught, confess, and get punished for stealing. George, the
incendiary, accomplished the same result by setting fires. To
make doubly sure that he regained the love thought to be lost
he returned to the scene of the crime and helped the fire chief
put out the fires.

The woman Dr. Berg described in his case history *Compulsion to Confess* had had sexual imaginings at twelve which
she had concealed from her mother. Later she told her. She
also felt compelled to tell her everything she thought or did.
To a part of her mind this seemed to accomplish two purposes:
she reassured herself that her mother still loved her; and she
warded off the punishment she feared her mother might mete

out to her. The same two purposes, of reassuring one's self about the love of one's parents and of propitiating them are usually thought to be served when human beings indulge in the common human failing of talking too much.

Those with greater rebellion in their hearts than others have greater fears of having lost love and of encountering retaliatory punishments. This includes the communists and the ex-communists among us. They thus have greater feelings of guilt and of a need for punishment. Consequently they also have greater compulsions to confess. In these respects they are like the Russians.

Greater Russian Ambivalences

WITH THE TATAR YOKE, autocracy and serfdom in Russia went to knout. The reaction of the Russian people to this burden was a wide swing from one extreme to the other, from utter rejection to complete acceptance, from fierce rebellion, which expressed itself in the form of nihilism, to abject submission, even a demand for autocracy. For this mingling of opposites medical psychologists have provided us with an apt word: ambivalence. Great ambivalence characterized the response of the Russian people to their lot.

The Tatar yoke, autocracy and serfdom lent themselves to cruelty. The Tatars abused everyone, the rulers abused the nobles, and the nobles abused the peasants. In Dostoevski's novel, *Crime and Punishment,* Raskolnikov dreams that he sees a group of peasants beat a horse to death. There were also tremendous clashes between contending noble cliques and between generations. The history of the Rurik and Romanov lines was a grisly one. In the Rurik dynasty there were murders of kinsmen and princes in nearly every generation. In the Romanov dynasty, Ivan IV struck his son, Ivan, a blow which proved fatal; Peter I subjected his son, Alexis, to such torture that he died; and Peter III, the husband and predecessor of Catherine II, the Great (1762–96), was deposed and probably murdered.

At the one extreme the response of the Russian people to authoritarian oppression and cruelty involved violence and destruction, murder, assassination and nihilism. There were whole series of assassinations and bombings. Alexander I was party to a plot which resulted in the death of his father, Paul I; nihilists bombed Alexander II to death; and when the communists first came to power in Russia they not only executed Nicholas II and his entire family but also sought to destroy all existing legal and political institutions. Indeed, Marxism appealed to the nihilists in Russia and to highly ambivalent rebels in other countries because it included in its basic dogma such doctrines as these: that capitalism would come to an end, and previous forms of society had done so, because of incompatible internal contradictions; that the communists would smash capitalism and other existing forms of society, by violent means in nearly all, if not all, instances; and that thereafter the state and other organs of authority would wither away.

It was no accident that a Russian writer produced a powerful oedipal story just as did an ancient Greek more than twenty-two centuries earlier: Dostoevski's novel, *The Brothers Karamazov,* matched Sophocles' play, *Oedipus Tyrannus.* No English or American author wrote any comparable work. Shakespeare gave us *Hamlet,* but from an oedipal standpoint it was pretty mild and indirect. In Dostoevski's story the father, Feodor, is in competition with his eldest son, Dmitri, for the same woman, Grushenka, and he is murdered by Smerdyakov, who the author suggests is Feodor's illegitimate son. Yet another son, Ivan, has an unspoken compact with Smerdyakov to do the deed. Dmitri is put on trial for the parricide, and Ivan on the stand, after stating that he incited Smerdyakov, asks, "Who doesn't desire his father's death?" A little later he turns to the audience and charges, "They all desire the death of their fathers. One reptile devours another." The prosecutor in his argument in contrasting the Russians and the English comments, "No, gentlemen of the jury, they have their Hamlets, but we still have our Karamazovs."

But extreme rebellion was countered by its opposite, abject submission. Back in the 800's, according to the account in the Russian *Chronicle,* the Slavs, after rebelling and expelling their oppressors, the Varangians, sent a request to them to have someone come and rule over them. In 1564 Ivan IV went through the motions of abdicating, but the people clamored to have him return. They had to have a father, with all the authoritarianism, suffering, pain, persecution and annihilation that this entailed. Two centuries later Leontiev, who did not like socialism but nevertheless preferred it to liberalism, for it at least contained elements of authoritarianism, wrote plaintively: "Sometimes I dream that a Russian czar may put himself at the head of the socialist movement and organize it, as Constantine organized Christianity."

The great ambivalence of the Russians has expressed itself in other related opposites than that of rebellion and submission, and in literature as well as life. Great destruction has been paired off against great self-sacrifice; great hate against great love; the basest sinfulness against the highest atonement. It is a peculiarly Russian idea that only one who has experienced the lowest depths of sinfulness can attain to the highest morality, that only through sinning can one attain genuine salvation. Take Dostoevski's characters. They are the basest of sinners one moment and saints the next. They throw stones at the temple, and then cross themselves at the tavern. They combine atheism with extreme piety, buffoonery with veneration, mockery with reverence, great hate with great love. They hate to the point of murder and love madly. They are cruel one moment, compassionate the next; wild one moment, gentle the next; ferocious one moment, tender the next; weeping without restraint one moment, shouting with joy the next. Pushkin, laughing, said of Gogol's *Dead Souls,* "Oh, God! How sad our Russia is."

No better example of these extreme ambivalences can be taken from Russian life than Ivan IV. He can almost be said to be an embodiment of the Russian proverb, "He who has not sinned does not know repentance and atonement." He was deliberately sacrilegious, yet pious. He was the unbridled criminal that he felt himself to be, yet he wanted to abandon himself to penance. He had many people killed in one cruel way or another, yet he implored mercy for his sins and had masses said for the souls of those whom he had butchered. He insisted on absolutism, yet he called the first Zemsky Sobor and to it made a public confession of the sins of his youth. He had a high regard for Russia, yet put a low value on women and girls, whom he caused to be publicly tortured and executed. He took a sadistic delight in witnessing the horrors of which he was himself the cause, yet at the end of his days he mortified the flesh, prayed, wept, shrieked and consumed his strength in fear of death and of the last judgment. He was at one and the same time Ivan the Terrible and Ivan the God-fearing. At the close of his life he wanted to abdicate and retire to a monastery—his father, Vasily III, shortly before his death had himself tonsured as a monk.

This wide swing between extremes, between nihilism on the one hand for instance and contrite submission on the other was characteristic of the Russians, and of communists in other countries. Communists in other countries had rebellion in their hearts for their own form of government, their own social structure; but they offset this with submissiveness to the party line, and sometimes to a country other than their own, the Soviet Union. The greater their inner rebellion the more dedicated they were as communists, sometimes even unto death.

Freud suggested in *Totem and Taboo* that "the psychical impulses of primitive peoples were characterized by a higher amount of ambivalence than is to be found in modern civilized man." This suggestion accounts for the biggest difference between the Russians and ourselves. They have greater ambivalences. Autocracy and the knout begot them. Greater ambivalences resulted in greater compulsions to confess.

Greater Russian Compulsions

THE RUSSIANS have not only been subjected to the Tatar knout, autocracy and serfdom, have not only been tormented by the cruel contest between absolutism and nihilism, but they have also been scarred by the bloodshed of the October/November 1917 revolution, the liquidation of the kulaks, the deaths from famine, and the mass purges. For centuries they have lived in a sea of hostile thoughts. The result is a heavy load of guilt feelings, a great need for punishment, and strong compulsions to confess.

Chekhov in one of his letters said: ". . . an indefinite feeling of guilt. It is a Russian feeling. Whether there is a death or illness in his family, whether he owes money or lends it, a Russian always feels guilty. Ivanov [in Chekhov's play with the same name] talks all the time about being to blame in some way, and the feeling of guilt increases in him at every juncture."

Pasternak wrote in *Doctor Zhivago:*

"It was the disease, the revolutionary madness of the age, that at heart everyone was different from his outward appearance and his words. No one had a clear conscience. Everyone could justifiably feel that he was guilty, that he was a secret criminal, an undetected impostor. The slightest pretext was enough to launch the imagination on an orgy of self-torture. Carried away by their fantasy, people accused themselves falsely not only out of terror but out of a morbidly destructive impulse, of their own will, in a state of metaphysical trance, in a passion for self-condemnation which cannot be checked once you give it its head."

In Zoshchenko's story, *The Wonderful Dog,* all the characters whom the dog approaches confess to some offense, although not the one for which the dog was summoned.

Those in custody under communist regimes have shown that they were burdened with guilt feelings. Beck and Godin in *Russian Purge and the Extraction of Confession* wrote: "Nevertheless I was prepared for arrest. Why? Because like all other Soviet citizens, I carried about with me a consciousness of guilt, an inexplicable sense of sin, a vague and indefinable feeling of having transgressed, combined with an ineradicable expectation of inevitable punishment. Thus each one of us had been shaped by sifting and checking, criticism and self-criticism. The arrest of acquaintances, colleagues, and friends who felt just as guilty—or guiltless—as ourselves intensified this state of mind."

An unpublished manuscript by a former Soviet historian based on a detailed investigation of attitudes of Soviet people arrested during the purges contains this: "Why was the prophet Jonah thrown into the sea? In order to find expiation and save all the rest. He was no more guilty than the rest, but it fell to his lot. The Soviet system cost the Russian people dear. Who paid for the famine of 1932 and 1933? Who should answer for all the sacrifices aroused by the imperfection of the system, errors in the plan, faults in the apparatus, inability of executives, etc. Those to whose lot it falls . . . [must answer]. In order to save the system as a whole, in order to divert the wrath of the people from its leaders, it is necessary to sacrifice millions of innocent persons. Furthermore they are only relatively innocent for every Soviet person bears greater or lesser accountability for Bolshevism as a whole and in its parts."

Because of their heavy load of guilt feelings and great need for punishment the communists developed a new cult of misanthropy. For them as for the early Puritans life was grim and life was earnest. They could not without misgivings permit themselves to have too much fun out of it. They frowned upon art for art's sake. Later they added humor for humor's sake and play for play's sake. Circus clowns in Russia were not to be amusing in the Western fashion. The Czechoslovak central communist organ *Rude Pravo* warned: "Humor is part and parcel of satire but its unrestrained expression must not mislead the author to indulge in humor for humor's sake, which results in a lack of ideological content." The Chinese communists forbade humor and consigned it to the "decadent and rotten values of the old society." Those who took up athletics were as serious about it as those who engaged in agriculture or industry. An article in Russia urged the people to avoid evil doing, filthy thoughts, and bad, obscene, or cursing language. In a love story the woman married the man, not because they had declared their love for each other, but because he was a stakhanovite worker.

The greater ambivalences and more severe confession compulsions of the Russians are still further illustrations of the repeatedly noted time-lags between Russia and the West. In yet other related respects the Russians are a number of centuries closer to their primal responses than we are. We have outgrown many of the negative aspects of puritanism. They are in the throes of them. They tend to draw less distinction than we do between the thought and the deed, between the desire to commit an offense and the offense itself. With us the act is the important thing. With them the nexus between any given crime and any given person is rather weak. Every crime must have an accused, but it is not as important as it is with us that he be the one who committed the act, since all in their thoughts are guilty of such a crime. In Dostoevski's *The Brothers Karamazov,* Dmitri, who was innocent, was actually convicted and sent to Siberia. The day before his trial began he said to his brother Alyosha: ". . . I go for all because someone must go for all. I didn't kill father, but I've got to go. I accept it. It's all come to me here, here, within these peeling walls. . . ."

This characteristic, too, helped the Russians to confess to crimes which they did not commit, except perhaps in their thoughts.

In addition the Russians have a greater passion for unanimity than we do. They, and the communists generally, have an intense desire that everyone think alike. They want everyone to join their band of brothers in rebellion against authority. This is the basis for their proselytizing zeal. They then match their rebellion by a great submissiveness to the party and the party line. This insistence on conformity is one of the elements involved in their practice of so-called criticism and self-criticism.

To be sure, these ambivalences are not peculiar either to the Russians or to the communists, except in their degree. We have our ambivalences too. We too have our inner rebellions countered by submissiveness to authority. We too long to submit to a leader. Our acclaim of General MacArthur after President Truman's dismissal of him was one proof of this. We too desire unity and unanimity. Christian communion is evidence of this. So are the proselytizing programs of the various religious denominations, with their missions and societies for the propagation of the faith. So are the efforts of the American Legion to have us all think in an approved fashion. The Legion had a poster showing a man behind barbed wire, his mouth stopped by a strip with a hammer and sickle on it. The caption was: "He Can't Speak Up—But You Can." However, the Legion's idea of freedom approaches that of the communists: it is freedom to say what the Legion thinks is correct.

We too have our love countered by hate and our consequent guilt feelings. Hamlet remarked: "Use every man after his desert, and who should 'scape shipping?" We too have our compulsions to confess. Bukharin was thus partly right in his final plea at the 1938 Moscow purge trial when he said that the confessions of the defendants were not due to the Dostoevski mind, to the Slav soul. But he was also partly wrong. It is a fact that the Russians as a rule have heavier loads of guilt feelings and more severe compulsions to confess than we do.

Our Alien Part

A STUDY OF confessants indicates that the mind is divided against itself. Medical psychologists have adumbrated that it consists of at least four parts: id, superego, ego, and ego-ideal. Whether one agrees with this proposition or not, there can be no doubt but that one part of the mind is, as it were, alien to us and alienated from us. This part is in an unceasing conflict with us, often enough a raging and violent one. One's mind furnishes the battleground for a lifelong Armageddon. All will have to admit this, for all experience it, saints as well as sinners, St. Augustine as well as Dostoevski's Feodor Karamazov. Many describe this conflict as the inner struggle between the voices of good and evil. The Christian says that it is the struggle between the spirit and the flesh. Daniel Webster stated: "A sense of duty pursues us ever. It is omnipresent, like the Deity." Emerson wrote:

> So nigh is grandeur to our dust,
> So near is God to man,
> When duty whispers low, Thou must,
> The youth replies, I can.

A person's conscience Thomas Hood described as "that fierce thing." According to Hamlet "conscience does make cowards of us all." A popular saying admonishes us, "Let your conscience be your guide." A Chinese philosophical work issued about the beginning of the 1700s described one's inner conflict in this arresting fashion: "When you have advanced sufficiently in knowledge of yourself, you will find it a grief. There will be, as it were, two men in your bosom. When you desire to do good, evil will come between. Again, when you wish to do wrong, a sense of shame will oppose you. Thus a battle goes on within you." One of the psychological writers who dealt with this problem, Dr. Menninger, entitled his book *Man Against Himself*, and another, Dr. Erich Fromm, called his book *Man For Himself*. Dr. Berg stated: "Conflict is perhaps one of the most important concepts for the explanation of psychological illness." When this inner conflict gets out of hand we speak of dual and split personalities. In literature on this point we have such works as Stevenson's *Dr. Jekyll and Mr. Hyde*, Goethe's *Faust*, and Oscar Wilde's *The Picture of Dorian Gray*.

Our alien part is so constituted that it can indulge in secret joy at the misfortunes of others—*Schadenfreude*, the Germans call this response. It has caused such inner havoc that people have condemned themselves to death, and to many lesser punishments. It has aroused such animosities that we could conceive of the flesh as burning everlastingly in hell. Dante in his *Divine Comedy* elaborated on this concept. A psychoanalyst explained that it was a "mythological projection of a personal region within the individual in which all one's own 'bad,' cruel, torturing and destructive impulses are raging against the 'badness' of others and vice versa; the fires of Hell too symbolize the guilt and shame, not felt by the persecuted as part of them and arising spontaneously but as attacking them aggressively." Dostoevski in *The Brothers Karamazov* suggested that man created the devil as well as God in his own image.

Omar Khayyam, by way of contrast again, was more at peace with himself. A quatrain ascribed to him has a clay shape in a potter's house saying:

"Why," said another, "Some there are who tell of one who threatens he will toss to Hell The luckless Pots he marr'd in making—Pish! He's a Good Fellow, and 'twill all be well." But many Christians still would not agree with this.

Not only is one part of the mind alien to us but also a part of it does not function in any rational way. The result is that we still burden ourselves with superstitions, taboos, and rituals, have our fetishes and sacred cows, and experience such phenomena as nightmares, unconscious errors, slips of the tongue, and a variety of other abberations. Just as primitive man had a host of taboos, so modern man has a multitude of different superstitions. There are numbers, acts, and incidents which people try to avoid as unlucky. The number thirteen is regarded as unlucky by so many people that scores of tall apartment and office buildings in large cities do not have a floor numbered thirteen. Various people will not start a journey on Friday the thirteenth; they avoid lighting three cigarettes on one match, walking under a ladder, opening an umbrella in a house, breaking a mirror, spilling salt, letting a black cat cross their path, and numerous other things. It takes a volume just to catalog American superstitions. The word superstition comes from the Latin. Its Greek equivalent means literally "fear of superhuman powers." The word taboo is of Polynesian origin and means forbidden or severely restricted because of supernatural penalties which would be incurred.

Primitive man had fetishes, but modern man has them, too. The word fetish comes from a Portuguese word meaning a charm. The Portuguese first applied it to relics of saints, rosaries, and images. Then Portuguese voyagers to West Africa in the latter half of the 1400s employed the term for the wooden figures, stones, and charms used in native rituals. In addition to relics of saints, rosaries, and images, modern man has his good luck pieces, lucky coin, rabbit's foot, horseshoe, charms, talismans, idols, icons, and mascots. Sir Walter Scott wrote a novel *The Talisman* about a talismanic stone set in a medieval coin, the Lee penny. The Navy football team has as a mascot a goat and the Army a mule. To avoid bad luck, modern man will often knock on wood. To bring good luck a bride will wear:

> Something old, something new,
> Something borrowed, something blue.

Such acts attribute to inanimate objects certain supernatural powers. Nearly all will admit that these various practices are irrational. Yet many feel bound to follow them.

Modern adults are not only superstitious; they are animistic and animatistic as well, just as were their primitive and even their primordial ancestors. Animism denotes doctrines of souls, spirits and demons; animatism the attribution to inanimate objects of wills like our own. R. R. Marett suggested that animatism preceded animism, and this would seem likely, but it is impossible to say, for no groups have yet been discovered which are without concepts of spirits. That human beings are still animistic needs no elaboration. As Herbert J. Muller pointed out, our everyday language is alive with its animism: skies still threaten, waters are angry, fires rage, and forests murmur. But we are animatistic as well. We, just as our primitive ancestors, vent our anger on occasion on inanimate objects. How many of us have not jerked at a drawer that was stuck, slammed a door that would not go shut, or yanked at a string that would not come untied, thus attributing to an inanimate object a will in opposition to our own? The mind, at least in its present stage of development, is no match for the inquisitional system.

Technique of Communist Inquisitors

THIS WAS THE WAY then that communist inquisitors obtained their volume of confessions: they used the inquisitional technique backed by the power of modern totalitarian states to make the alien part of the minds of their victims their ally. This was ordinarily not difficult, especially with Russian confessants. Arrest itself was a tremendous trauma. If one added to this, solitary confinement, one subjected a human being to the worst disaster that could befall him so far as the primitive parts of his mind were concerned, for to these parts it appeared as if those dear to him had forsaken him and no longer loved him. Balzac in *The Last Incarnation of Vautrin* gave a good description of what happened:

"It is difficult for those at large to imagine what this sudden isolation is to the accused person . . . This absolute separation, so instantaneously and so easily brought about, causes an upset of all his faculties, and a fearful prostration of mind; above all, when the person happens to be one not familiar, through his antecedents, with the ways of the law. The duel between the accused man and the examining judge is, therefore, all the more terrible because the latter has for auxiliary the silence of the walls. . . .

"These points once explained, the least emotional person will tremble at the effect produced by three causes of terror—isolation, silence, and remorse."

Menachem Begin presented the same picture with reference specifically to incarceration under the communists: ". . . we may look into the minds of Bukharin himself and many others who shared his fate. We shall then see a man whose whole world has suddenly tumbled about him and who finds himself in utter isolation—not only physical, but, what is worse, mental and political isolation. This double isolation is absolute. Such was the isolation of smaller fry like us in Lukishki, such the isolation of the big fry in the Lubishki Prison in Moscow. Solitude. Not a word of what you will say will reach a single person in the world outside. Only what those, whose theory permits no doubting, want the outside world to learn, will pierce the prison walls. In certain countries, at certain times, there exist illegal newspapers which publish news and views that never see the light of day in the legitimate press. Here there is no break of the wall of silence. Nobody will hear, or read . . ." One's isolation was complete. One did not even have the comfort of feeling that at least one's own band of brothers still loved one.

If there is superimposed on this desolation from incarceration incommunicado the authority of a powerful totalitarian state and protracted questioning, usually without sufficient sleep and often at night, the primitive parts of one's mind will almost always without more pressure do the rest of the work for the examining authorities: one's guilt feelings, one's fear of the loss of love, the most painful feeling in the world, and of retaliation and punishment will make almost every human being confess to almost anything. Lack of sleep is probably not an essential ingredient, but it is very helpful. Sleep is a great restorative. As Coleridge put it in *The Rime of the Ancient Mariner:*

> O sleep! it is a gentle thing,
> Beloved from pole to pole!
> To Mary Queen the praise be given!
> She sent the gentle sleep from Heaven,
> That slid into my soul.

The prevention of sleep was a method of torture in earlier times. One form of this torture was known as the Spanish vigil. Robert Pitcairn in his *Ancient Criminal Trials in Scotland* commented with reference to the confession of Elizabeth or Bessie Dunlop in 1576 of witchcraft that the prevention of sleep was probably more effective than physical torture in obtaining such confessions: "She was certainly the dupe of her own overheated imagination. One of the most powerful incentives to confession was systematically to deprive the suspected witch of the refreshment of her natural rest and sleep. . . . This engine of human oppression was perhaps more effective in extorting confessions than the actual application of torture." With the rise of gigantic totalitarian states and a concentration of power in the hands of a ruling group that is greater than any concentration the world has ever known, the prevention of sleep, although still useful, is no longer as essential as it once was: the total isolation of the individual plus protracted questioning is enough.

The method of the communists is as simple as this, and as effective. Under this method even the strongest wills will break, and have. Some individuals hold out a little longer than others, but it is usually only a question of time. Among the defendants in the Moscow purge trials of 1937–38, Radek held out for two and a half months, Bukharin for three, Muralov for almost eight, and Bessanov for ten. One of thirteen defendants put on trial in Prague in 1950 as "war conspirators," Kleinerova, held out for four months. In his final plea he revealed:

"I have nothing to say in my defence . . . I would only like to add in the interest of truth that I did not . . . confess immediately after my arrest. I did not confess for a full four months. . . . I would only like to say that I thank the Security officials for their patience in trying for a full four months to show me that, which I finally clearly understood: the basis of my guilt, its being directed against my nation."

Except for the fact that the defendant was under inquisitional pressure for four months, the contents of this plea remind one of the explanation which some of those accused of witchcraft gave for their confessions: ". . . they telling us, that we were witches, and they knew it, and they knew that we knew it, which made us think that it was so. . . ."

We have wondered how the communists have obtained so many confessions. Rather we should wonder that a few held out and that others resisted as long as they did. We wonder that a few of our men should change sides: their familes cannot believe it. Rather we should wonder that only the merest handful did so. On the communist side the defections ran into the thousands, and many of them.

George Orwell in his *Nineteen Eighty-Four* suggests that the reason the Russians used confessions was to prevent their victims from becoming martyrs. O'Brien, the inquisitor, says to his victim, Winston:

"'The first thing for you to understand is that in this place there are no martyrdoms. You have read of the religious persecutions of the past. In the Middle Ages there was the Inquisition. It was a failure. It set out to eradicate heresy, and ended by perpetuating it. For every heretic it burned at the stake, thousands of others rose up. Why was that? Because the Inquisition killed its enemies in the open, and killed them while they were unrepentant. Men were dying because they would not abandon their true beliefs. Naturally all the glory belonged to the victim and all the shame to the Inquisitor who burned him. Later, in the twentieth century, there were the totalitarians, as they were called. There were the German Nazis and the Russian Communists. The Russians persecuted heresy more cruelly than the Inquisition had done. And they imagined that they had learned from the mistakes of the past; they knew, at any rate, that one must not make martyrs. Before they exposed their victims to public trial, they deliberately set themselves to destroy their dignity. They wore them down by torture and solitude until they were despicable, cringing wretches, confessing whatever was put into their mouths, covering themselves with abuse, accusing and sheltering behind one another, whimpering for mercy. And yet after a few years the same thing happened over again. The dead men have become martyrs and their degradation was forgotten. Once again, why was it? In the first place, because the confessions that they had made were obviously extorted and untrue. We do not make mistakes of that kind. All the confessions that are uttered here are true. We make them true. And, above all, we do not allow the dead to rise up against us. You must stop imagining that posterity will vindicate you, Winston. Posterity will never hear of you. You will be lifted clean out from the stream of history. We shall turn you into gas and pour you into the stratosphere. Nothing will remain of you: not a name in a register, not a memory in a living brain. You will be annihilated in the past as well as in the future. You will never have existed.' "

Winston wonders to himself why the regime has then bothered to torture him. O'Brien guesses his thought and answers:

" 'You are a flaw in the pattern, Winston. You are a stain that must be wiped out. Did I not tell you just now that we are different from the persecutors of the past? We are not content

with negative obedience, nor even with the most abject submission. When finally you surrender to us, it must be of your
own free will. We do not destroy the heretic because he resists
us; so long as he resists us we never destroy him. We burn all
evil and all illusion out of him; we bring him over to our side,
not in appearance, but genuinely, heart and soul. We make
him one of ourselves before we kill him. It is intolerable to us
that an erroneous thought should exist anywhere in the world,
however secret and powerless it may be. Even in the instant
of death we cannot permit any deviation. In the old days the
heretic walked to the stake still a heretic, proclaiming his
heresy, exulting in it. Even the victim of the Russian purges
could carry rebellion locked up in his skull as he walked down
the passage waiting for the bullet. But we make the brain
perfect before we blow it out. The command of the old despot-
isms was "Thou shalt not." The command of the totalitarians
was "Thou shalt." Our command is "Thou art." ' "

But martyrdom and confessions are basically the same thing:
they are both efforts to gain love. Martyrdom is a supreme
effort; confessions may be, Bukharin's was. Accordingly confessions will not prevent martyrdom and Orwell says as much
when he predicts, in the words of O'Brien, that the confessants
in Russian show trials will become martyrs after all.

All roads led to the same conclusion: the primitive and
irrational nature of most of the mind together with the power
of modern states, our own included, make it necessary to abandon not only the inquisitional technique but also any of its
challenged fruits. The world should have done with investigative authorities questioning a suspected individual, like a
powerful parent interrogating a helpless child. The inquisitional system stands in the way of the development of equalitarian societies and the growth of human beings into mature
individuals.

Until that better day arrives, however, the best way for an
individual caught in the toils of the inquisitional system to
defend himself is to refuse to engage in a contest of the

wills with the state's inquisitor. Instead he should insist on a right of silence. Those who prepared the new code of conduct for members of our armed forces while prisoners of war thus prove to have been right in recommending adherence to the Geneva Convention. A prisoner of war should give only his name, rank, service number, and date of birth. Thereafter he should adamantly remain silent. He should stoutly refuse any further collaboration, whether in the form of answering questions, or contributing an autobiographical sketch, or keeping a diary. He will fare no worse than those who collaborate, and he may fare even better. The committee that drafted the new code of conduct reported, referring to the enemy in the Korean war:

". . . Sometimes he showed contempt for the man who readily submitted to bullying. The prisoner who stood up to the bluster, threats and blows of an interrogator might be dismissed with a shrug and sent to quarters as mild as any— if any prison barracks in North Korea could be described as mild.

"All in all, the docile prisoner did not gain much by his docility—and sometimes he gained nothing. The prisoner who defied Pak [North Korea's chief interrogator] might take a beating, but again he might not. The ordeal was never easy. But things weren't easy either for the combat troops battling out there in the trenches."

Notes

Chapter 1

P.13, l.23 Gallery, "We Can Baffle the Brainwashers!", *Sat. Eve. Post,* Jan. 22, 1955, pp. 20, 94.

P.14, l.2 The eleven in the order of their return were Corporals Edward S. Dickenson and Claude J. Batchelor, next Otho G. Bell, William Cowart and Lewis W. Griggs, then Richard R. Tennyson, followed by Arley Pate and Aaron Wilson, and thereafter separately by Samuel David Hawkins, Andrew Fortuna and Sgt. LaRance Sullivan. One of the twenty-three, Rufus E. Douglas, died in China. When Bell, Cowart and Griggs returned they said that the seventeen who then remained likewise wanted to come back.

P.14, l.6 *N.Y. Times,* Dec. 14, 1955, p. 24, col. 3. Another, Hawkins, after crossing the border, said about his prior decision to go to China: "I half-way believed what I was told—we were brainwashed and I was afraid." He gave as the main reason for his decision to return home his abhorrence of "wanton killing by Soviet troops in Hungary," *N.Y. Times,* Feb. 28, 1957, p. 10, cols. 3–4. The last of the eleven, Sullivan, said that he had gone to communist China "in the skin and heart of a Negro," and had been "very happy among soul-stirring and peace-loving people." *N.Y. Times,* March 31, 1958, p. 6, cols. 2–8.

P.14, l.27 *N.Y. Times,* Feb. 28, 1955, p. 1, cols. 6–7, p. 7, cols. 1–5, March 1, 1955, p. 8, cols. 3–5.

P.15, l.6 See *N.Y. Times,* Sept. 16, 1955, p. 1, col. 8, p. 3, cols. 3–4, Sept. 17, 1955, p. 1, col. 5, p. 6, cols. 3–6.

P.15, l.21 See also GENERAL DEAN'S STORY, p. 107–154 (as told to William L. Worden 1954).

P.15, l.25 For the prison diary of one of them, Lieut. Roland W. Parks, see *U.S. News & World Report,* June 24, 1955, pp. 30–33, 36, 38, 40, 130–147.

P.16, l.18 *N.Y. Times,* April 28, 1954, p. 16.

P.16, l.30 *N.Y. Times,* Oct. 27, 1953, p. 1, col. 8, p. 4, col. 5, p. 4, cols. 3–4.

P.17, l.11 Lieut. Col. Paul V. S. Liles, Majors Harry Fleming and Ronald E. Alley, M/Sgt. William H. Olson, Sgts. William E. Banghart and James C. Gallagher, Corporals Edward S. Dickenson, Claude J. Batchelor and Harold M. Dunn, Pvt. Rothwell B. Floyd and Thomas Bayes, Jr.

Corporals Dickenson and Batchelor were the first to come back of the twenty-three who changed sides. Ironically enough, their early return drew for them sentences of ten years and life, respectively. Batchelor's life sentence was later reduced to twenty years. To the remaining twenty-one the Army gave dishonorable discharges. This precluded the Army under a subsequent Supreme Court decision from ever bringing them before courts-martial. Toth v. Quarles, 350 U.S. 11 (1955). When Bell, Cowart and Griggs, more of those who changed sides, returned, the Army at first took them into custody but then released them. *N.Y. Times,* Nov. 9, 1955, p. 14, cols. 1–2, Nov. 17, 1955, p. 2, cols. 3–4. Civilian courts here cannot try them either, for they committed their alleged offenses abroad.

Most of those convicted appealed, but so far without relief. All but one of the appellants, Gallagher, had their convictions sustained. United States v. Alley, 8 U.S.C.M.A. 559, 25 C.M.R. 63 (1958); United States v. Bayes, 7 U.S.C.M.A. 798 (1957) (petition for review denied); United States v. Fleming, 7 U.S.C.M.A. 543, 23 C.M.R. 7 (1957); United States v. Olson, 7 U.S.C.M.A. 460, 22 C.M.R. 250 (1957); United States v. Batchelor, 7 U.S.C.M.A. 354, 22 C.M.R. 144 (1956); United States v. Floyd, 6 U.S.C.M.A. 817 (1955) (petition for review denied); United States v. Dickenson, 6 U.S.C.M.A. 438, 20 C.M.R. 154 (1955). Dickenson also applied for habeas corpus but it was denied him. Dickenson v. Davis, 245 F.2d 317 (10th Cir. 1957), *affirming* 143 F.Supp. 421 (D. Kan. 1956), *cert. denied,* 355 U.S. 918 (1958). In Gallagher's case an Army Board of Review decided that the court-martial which tried him had no jurisdiction, but the Court of Military Appeals reversed and held that the court-martial did have jurisdiction. United States v. Gallagher, 7 U.S.C.M.A. 506, 22 C.M.R. 296 (1957).

The three acquitted were Major Ambrose H. Nugent, Lieut. Jefferson D. Erwin and Sgt. John L. Tyler.

P.17, l.12   Sgt. Frank J. Paige.

P.17, l.15   See, *e.g.,* the cases of Sgt. Douglas .E. Stephens and Corp. Spencer W. Welsh. *N.Y. Times,* Feb. 8, 1956, p. 20, col. 3; *N.Y. Post,* March 30, 1956, pp. 3, 47, April 6, 1956, pp. 4, 22. In the case of Stephens the Army later reversed itself and gave him an honorable discharge. *N.Y. Times,* June 30, 1956, p. 37, col. 2.

P.18, l.6   *N.Y. Times,* Aug. 18, 1955, p. 1, col. 8, p. 8, col. 3, pp. 10–11.

P.19, l.2   *N.Y. Times,* Aug. 21, 1955, p. 30, cols. 3–4.

P.19, l.12   *N.Y. Times,* Sept. 27, 1955, p. 31, cols. 1–7.

P.19, l.22   *N.Y. Times,* Aug. 21, 1955, p. 30, col. 4.

P.19, l.32   *N.Y. Times,* Sept. 4, 1956, p. 27, col. 5.

P.21, 1.25   REPORT OF COURT PROCEEDINGS IN THE CASE
OF THE ANTI-SOVIET "BLOC OF RIGHTS AND TROTSKY-
ITES," 777–779 (Moscow, 1938).

P.22, 1.31   VERBATIM RECORD OF THE TRIAL 1, 96–97 (U.S.
State Dept.).

P.23, 1.5   *N.Y. Times,* May 17, 1953, p. 1, col. 8.

P.23, 1.17   *N.Y. Times,* May 18, 1953, p. 1.

P.23, 1.21   *N.Y. Times,* May 19, 1953, p. 1.

P.24, 1.9   Edward Hunter, a newsman and writer, takes credit for
giving currency to the word. He testified before the Senate Permanent Subcommittee on Investigations of the Committee on Government Operations: "I am happy to say I brought the word into use.
I was the first man to put the word into writing in any language.
I was the first person to use the spoken word in any language—
except in Chinese. The word came out of the sufferings of the
Chinese people. * * * A young man came out of Red China
whose family I had known before as an editor in China, and
who let slip the Chinese for brainwashing—Hsi Nao. I immediately pinned him down to find out what that meant and that
gave me the clue that linked together a number of what seemed
almost wholly irrelevant events and developments." *Hearings,*
84th Cong., 2d Sess. 56 (1956). He has also written two books
on the subject: BRAINWASHING (1956); BRAIN-WASHING
IN RED CHINA (new and enlarged ed. 1953).

P.24, 1.25   Dennis v. United States, 341 U.S. 494, *affirming* 183
F.2d 201. In addition to Dennis those convicted were John B.
Williamson, national labor secretary; John Gates, editor of the
Daily Worker; Irving Potash, fur union official; Carl Winter,
Michigan chairman; Jack Stachel, director of agitation, propa-
ganda and education; Benjamin J. Davis, Jr., former New York
City Councilman; Gus Hall, former Ohio chairman and acting
national chairman; Henry Winston, national organization sec-
retary; Robert Thompson, New York State chairman; and Gilbert
Green, Illinois chairman. A pretrial motion to quash the indictment
on the ground, among others, that the Smith act was unconstitu-
tional, was denied. United States v. Foster, 80 F.Supp. 470
(D.S.D.N.Y. 1949).

The government repeatedly tried to bring Foster to trial, but
was never successful in doing so. Six times court-appointed physi-
cians examined him to this end. In each instance the physician
reported that Foster suffered from arteriosclerosis affecting his
heart and cerebral circulation. See *N.Y. Times,* April 26, 1956,
p. 12, cols. 3–4.

P.25, 1.9   United States v. Flynn, 216 F.2d 354, *cert. denied,* 348
U.S. 909. After the Supreme Court's decision in the Dennis case

four from that case, Hall, Thompson, Winston and Green, and four from the Flynn case, Sidney Stein, James E. Jackson, Jr., William Norman and Fred M. Fine, staged a mass flight. Hall, Thompson and Stein were apprehended. The rest voluntarily surrendered at various times thereafter. The four fugitives in the Dennis case, who had already been convicted and sentenced on their indictment, also drew sentences for criminal contempt. Green, Winston and Hall each drew three years, and Thompson four. Green and Winston v. United States, 356 U.S. 165 (1958), *affirming* 241 F.2d 631 (2d Cir. 1957), *affirming* 140 F.Supp. 117 (D.S.D.N.Y. 1956); United States v. Thompson, 214 F.2d 545 (2d Cir. 1954), *affirming* 117 F.Supp. 685 (D.S.D.N.Y. 1953), *cert. denied,* 348 U.S. 841 (1954); United States v. Hall, 198 F.2d 726 (2d Cir. 1952), *affirming in part* 101 F.Supp. 666 (D.S.D.N.Y. 1951), *cert. denied,* 345 U.S. 905 (1953).

P.25, l.11   When these cases reached reviewing courts they fared indifferently. The first three judgments of conviction were sustained. In addition to the Dennis and Flynn cases, arising out of the first two Foley Square prosecutions, the Baltimore Smith Act conspiracy conviction was sustained. Frankfeld v. United States, 198 F.2d 679 (4th Cir. 1952), *affirming* 101 F.Supp. 449 C.D. Md. 1951), *cert. denied,* 344 U.S. 922 (1953). The six defendants included Philip Frankfeld, Maryland chairman, Mrs. Regina Frankfeld and Maurice L. Braverman.

But the rest so far have been reversed:

Cleveland: Brandt v. United States, 265 F.2d 79 (6th Cir. 1958), *reversing* 139 F.Supp. 367 (D.N.D. Ohio 1955), and sending the case back for a new trial.

Denver: Bary v. United States, 248 F.2d 201 (10th Cir. 1957), *reversing* and sending the case back for a new trial. One of the defendants in this case was Patricia Blau. Prior to the Denver Smith Act conspiracy prosecution she and her husband successfully insisted on their right of silence or, as it is usually called, privilege against self-incrimination, in cases which went all the way to the federal Supreme Court. Patricia Blau v. United States, 340 U.S. 159 (1950); Irving Blau v. United States, 340 U.S. 332 (1951).

Detroit: Wellman v. United States, 354 U.S. 931 (1957), *vacating judgment* in 227 F.2d 757 (6th Cir. 1955). Thereafter the Court of Appeals for the Sixth Circuit reversed and remanded the case for a new trial. Wellman v. United States, 253 F.2d 601 (1958).

In another case which involved Wellman the court held that communist party membership, even though active and meaningful, did not work a forfeiture of a veteran's service-connected disability benefits. Wellman v. Whittier, 259 F.2d 163 (D.C. Cir. 1958).

Honolulu: Fujimoto v. United States, 251 F.2d 342 (9th Cir. 1958), reversing with instructions to enter judgment in favor of all defendants. In this case Circuit Judge Chambers commented:

"One may as well recognize that the Yates decision leaves the Smith Act, as to any further prosecution under it, a virtual shambles—unless the American Communist Party should witlessly set out to reconstitute itself again with a new 'organization'." At 342. But Circuit Judges Hastie and Hamley said:

"We concur in Judge Chambers' opinion, except in so far as it refers to the effect of the Yates decision upon future prosecutions under the Smith Act. In our view, this statement is unnecessary to the decision." *Ibid.* Before the trial the Supreme Court denied a motion for leave to file a petition for a writ of prohibition or mandamus. Fujimoto v. Wiig, 344 U.S. 852 (1952).

Los Angeles: Yates v. United States, Schneiderman v. United States, Richmond v. United States, 354 U.S. 298 (1957), *reversing* 225 F.2d 146 (9th Cir. 1955). The fifteen defendants included William Schneiderman, Loretta Starvus Stack, Oleta O'Connor Yates and Al Richmond. All but one, who was severed because of ill-health, were convicted. The Supreme Court ordered an acquittal as to five of the defendants and a new trial as to the remaining nine. Subsequently the government procured the dismissal of the indictment on the ground that the prosecution "cannot satisfy the evidentiary requirements laid down by the Supreme Court in its opinion reversing the convictions." See United States v. Yates, 1958 F.Supp. 480, 481 (D.S.D. Cal. 1958).

On a previous petition the Supreme Court gave relief as to bail requirements. Stack v. Boyle, 342 U.S. 1 (1951), *reversing* 192 F.2d 56 (9th Cir.).

On previous denials of motions for a new trial and in arrest of judgment see United States v. Schneiderman, 106 F.Supp. 906 (D.S.D. Cal. 1952). Schneiderman was involved in another famous case, in which the Supreme Court refused to invalidate his naturalization certificate. Schneiderman v. United States, 320 U.S. 118 (1943), *reversing* 119 F.2d 500 (8th Cir. 1941). The court divided five to three (Mr. Justice Jackson did not participate) with Mr. Justice Murphy writing the majority opinion and Mr. Chief Justice Stone the dissenting one. Wendell L. Willkie, Republican candidate for president in 1940, argued the case for Schneiderman. In the Dennis case the defendants relied on the majority opinion and the government on the dissenting one.

Yates further received various contempt sentences, some of which were reversed and some affirmed on appeal. One of those which was affirmed went to the Supreme Court, and the Court, although sustaining the conviction on one specification, vacated the sentence and remanded the case to the district court for resentencing. Yates v. United States, 355 U.S. 66 (1957), *vacating judgment in* 227 F.2d 851 (9th Cir. 1955). See also Yates v. United States, 227 F.2d 848 (9th Cir. 1955); Yates v. United States, 227 F.2d 844 (9th Cir. 1955). Subsequently the district court, after reconsidering the matter in the light of the Supreme Court's opinion again imposed a sentence of one year on the defendant. United States v. Yates, 158 F.Supp. 480 (D.S.D. Cal. 1958). The Court of Appeals for the Ninth Circuit again affirmed. Yates v. United States, 252 F.2d 568 (1958). But the Supreme Court again vacated the judgment. Yates v. United States, 356 U.S. 363 (1958). This time the Court remanded the case to the district court with directions to reduce the sentence on the petitioner to the time already served.

New Haven: United States v. Silverman, 248 F.2d 671 (2d Cir. 1957), *cert. denied,* 355 U.S. 942 (1958), *reversing* with directions to dismiss the indictment.

New York: There was a third Foley Square Smith Act conspiracy trial. It involved seven of the defendants in the second conspiracy indictment there. They were Stein, Jackson, Norman and Fine, who decamped with four of the defendants in the Dennis case, Alexander Trachtenberg and George Blake Charney, who obtained a new trial because of Harvey Matusow's recantations, and Mrs. Marion Bachrach, who won a severance because she suffered from cancer. They went to trial in 1956. This time the trial took three months. The judge directed an acquittal as to Mrs. Bachrach. The remaining six were convicted. However, on appeal the Court of Appeals for the Second Circuit reversed. The court was unanimous in reversing, and by a two to one vote directed the dismissal of the indictment. United States v. Jackson, 257 F.2d 830 (2d Cir. 1958).

Stein was at one time held in bail of $125,000. This was for two prosecutions, one of them this one. In one his bail was $75,000 and in the other, $50,000. The Court of Appeals for the Second Circuit reduced the $50,000 bail to $30,000. United States v. Stein, 231 F.2d 109 (1956), *modifying* 18 F.R.D. 248 (D.S.D.N.Y. 1955), *cert. denied,* 351 U.S. 943 (1956). Mr. Justice Douglas reduced the $75,000 amount first to $45,000, with the consent of the government, and then to $10,000. Stein v. United States, 76 S.Ct. 822 (1956). But Stein's total bail was still $40,000.

Philadelphia: United States v. Kuzma, 249 F.2d 619 (3d Cir. 1957), *reversing* with directions to enter a judgment of acquittal as to four of the defendants and leave to take further proceedings as to the remaining five. Thereafter District Judge J. Cullen Ganey dismissed the indictment. *N.Y. Times,* May 17, 1958, p. 8, col. 5.

Pittsburgh: Stephen Mesarosh, also known as Steve Nelson v. United States, 352 U.S. 1 (1956), *reversing* 223 F.2d 449 (3d Cir. 1955), *affirming* 116 F.Supp 345 (D.W.D.Pa. 1953). Nelson was also involved in a state prosecution in which the Supreme Court invalidated a Pennsylvania sedition law, and cast doubt on such laws of other states, on the ground that the federal Smith Act preempted the field. Pennsylvania v. Nelson, 350 U.S. 497 (1956), *affirming* 377 Pa. 58, 104 A.2d 133 (1954), *reversing* 172 Pa. Super. 125, 92 A.2d 431 (1952).

St. Louis: Sentner v. United States, Forest v. United States, 253 F.2d 310 (8th Cir. 1958), *reversing* with directions to grant a new trial. Subsequently the government dropped the case on the ground that the Yates decision left it with no other alternative. *N.Y. Times,* Oct. 11, 1958, p. 11, col. 6.

Seattle: Huff v. United States 251 F.2d 342 (9th Cir. 1958), *reversing* with an instruction to enter judgment in favor of all the appellants. It was in this case that one of the defendants, Mrs. Barbara Hartle, abandoned her appeal, and served twenty and a half months of a five-year sentence. She was formerly a leading communist party organizer in the Pacific northwest.

In addition, there are separate indictments under the membership clause of the Smith Act against the defendants in the Dennis case and eight more individuals singly. The cases of two of the eight have been before the Supreme Court. Claude Mack Lightfoot v. United States, 355 U.S. 2 (1957), *reversing* 228 F.2d 861 (7th Cir. 1956); Junius Irving Scales v. United States, 355 U.S. 1 (1957), *reversing* 227 F.2d 581 (4th Cir. 1955). Lightfoot was a party functionary in Chicago, and Scales was North Carolina chairman. In each case the Court in a per curiam opinion ruled: "Upon consideration of the entire record and the confession of error by the Solicitor General, the judgment . . . is reversed. *Jencks* v. *United States,* 353 U.S. 657." Scales has again been tried and convicted, his conviction has again been affirmed by the Court of Appeals for the Fourth Circuit, and the Supreme Court has again granted certiorari. Scales v. United States,. 260 F.2d 21, *cert. granted,* 27 U.S.L. WEEK 3186 (Dec. 15, 1958). One of the witnesses against him was Mrs. Hartle.

The remaining six are United States v. Blum (D.S.D. Ind.); United States v. Dr. Albert Emanuel Blumberg (D.E.D. Pa.); United States v. Hellman (D. Mont.); United States v. John Francis Noto (D.W.D. N.Y.); United States v. Russo (D. Mass.); United States v. Max Morris Weiss (D.N.D. Ill.). Blumberg, Noto and Hellman have been tried and convicted and their cases are pending on appeal.

In Noto v. United States, 76 S.Ct. 255 (1955), Mr. Justice Harlan fixed bail at $10,000 after the district court had fixed it at $30,000 and the Court of Appeals for the Second Circuit had refused to change it. The Supreme Court confirmed his ruling. Noto v. United States, 351 U.S. 902 (1956), *reversing* 226 F.2d 953 (2d Cir. 1955) (opinion by Judge Medina). In United States v. Blumberg, 136 F.Supp. 269 (D.E.D. Pa. 1955), the court overruled a motion to dismiss the indictment.

P.25, l.15   Even Mrs. Hartle did not plead guilty. Rather she stood by her associates during the trial but then contacted the FBI and withdrew her appeal. See Scales v. United States, 260 F.2d 21, 31 (4th Cir. 1958).

P.25, l.18   Huff v. United States, 251 F.2d 342 (9th Cir. 1958). There were seven defendants in this case. Another renounced communism and was acquitted by the jury. See *N.Y. Times,* Feb. 11, 1956, p. 3, col. 4. A third committed suicide during the trial. See *N.Y. Times,* Jan 21, 1958, p. 13, col. 1. The remaining four were convicted, appealed, and went free.

P.25, l.25   *N.Y. Times,* Feb. 2, 1956, p. 26, cols. 6–7. In June 1954 she was the star witness before the House Committee on Un-American Activities and identified more than 400 persons she had known as party members.

P.25, l.33   United States v. Flynn, 130 F.Supp. 412 (D.S.D.N.Y. 1955). In United States v. Flynn, 131 F.Supp. 742 (D.S.D.N.Y. 1955), the court denied a motion of the remaining eleven for reargument of their motion for a new trial.

Of all the more than a hundred American communist party leaders convicted in Smith Act prosecutions, only 29 served their sentences; eleven from each of the first two Foley Square prosecutions, six from the Baltimore case, and Mrs. Hartle.

P.26, l.9   Harris v. South Carolina, 338 U.S. 68; Turner v. Pennsylvania, 338 U.S. 62; Watts v. Indiana, 338 U.S. 49.

P.26, l.10   338 U.S. at 54.

Chapter 2

P.33, l.9   1 LEA, A HISTORY OF THE INQUISITION OF THE MIDDLE AGES, 328 (1888); TURBERVILLE, THE SPANISH INQUISITION, 7–8 (1949).

P.33, l.10   1 LEA, *op. cit. supra* at 345; 1 LEA, A HISTORY OF THE INQUISITION OF SPAIN 158 (1906); MAYCOCK, THE INQUISITION FROM ITS ESTABLISHMENT TO THE GREAT SCHISM, 219 (1927).

P.33, l.15   1 LEA, A HISTORY OF THE INQUISITION OF SPAIN, 157–160 (1906).

P.35, l.22   See 1 LEA, A HISTORY OF THE INQUISITION OF THE MIDDLE AGES, 387–394; 2 *id.* at 104; MAYCOCK, *op. cit. supra* at 166–172.

P.35, 1.25   See 4 LEA, A HISTORY OF THE INQUISITION OF SPAIN, 517–518; SABATINI, TORQUEMADA AND THE SPANISH INQUISITION, 439 n.1 (rev. ed. 1924).

P.35, 1.27   See 4 LEA, *op. cit. supra* at 518–519.

P.37, 1.12   CONWAY, THE CONDEMNATION OF GALILEO, 12, 16, 17 (1913).

P.37, 1.18   GEBLER, GALILEO GALILEI AND THE ROMAN CURIA 78 (Sturge transl. 1879).

P.37, 1.23   MACDONELL, HISTORICAL TRIALS 120 (1927).

P.38, 1.3   *Id.* at 122–123.

P.38, 1.12   GEBLER, *op. cit. supra* at 183.

P.38, 1.19   BERTI, IL PROCESSO ORIGINALE DI GALILEO GALILEI 16 (1876).

P.38, 1.23   GEBLER, *op. cit. supra* at 203–205.

P.38, 1.29   *Id.* at 215.

P.39, 1.5   *Id.* at 227.

P.39, 1.16   *Id.* at 243.

P.39, 1.23   MACDONELL *op. cit. supra* at 111.

P.39, 1.28   For a brief but moving account of her life see 1 CHURCHILL, A HISTORY OF THE ENGLISH-SPEAKING PEOPLES, THE BIRTH OF BRITAIN, 413–423 (1956). For accounts of her interrogation and trial see 3 LEA, A HISTORY OF THE INQUISITION OF THE MIDDLE AGES, 359–378; COULTON, INQUISITION AND LIBERTY, 249–260 (1938).

P.42, 1.4   MACDONELL, *op. cit. supra* at 24.

P.42, 1.13   MARTIN, THE TRIAL OF THE TEMPLARS, 30–33 (1928).

P.42, 1.29   3 LEA, *op cit. supra* at 262.

P.43, 1.3   *Id.* at 281; 2 FINKE, PAPSTTUM UND UNTERGANG DES TEMPLERORDENS, 152–153 (1907).

P.43, 1.15   1 MICHELET, PROCÉS DES TEMPLIERS, 90 (1841).

P.43, 1.21   MARTIN, *op. cit. supra* at 51.

P.43, 1.30   *Id.* at 53.

P.44, 1.3   *Id.* at 55–56.

P.44, 1.9   3 LEA, *op. cit. supra* at 321–322.

P.44, 1.17   *Id.* at 262, 300; see MARTIN, *op. cit. supra* at 58–61.

P.44, 1.21   MARTIN, *op. cit. supra* at 58.

P.45, 1.5   3 LEA, *op. cit. supra* at 480–481.

P.45, 1.23   *Id.* at 223.

P.45, 1.36   *Id.* at 231.

P.46, 1.13   *Id.* at 234.

P.46, 1.21   MACDONELL, *op. cit. supra* at 68.

P.46, 1.25   *Id.* at 72.

P.46, 1.29   BERTI, VITA DI GIORDANO DA NOLA 349 (1868).

P.46, 1.34   *Id.* at 357.
P.47, 1.3   *Id.* at 373.
P.47, 1.7   *Id.* at 384–385.
P.47, 1.29   As quoted in MACDONELL, *op. cit. supra* at 82–83.

Chapter 3

P.49, 1.6   26 Hen. 8, c. 13, §2.
P.49, 1.24   As quoted in Smith, *English Treason Trials and Confessions in the Sixteenth Century,* 15 *Jour. Hist. Ideas,* 471, 477 (1954).
P.50, 1.10   *Ibid.*
P.50, 1.18   *Id.* at 478.
P.50, 1.24   *Id.* at 474.
P.50, 1.29   1 HALL, HENRY VIII, 226 (Whibley ed. 1904).
P.51, 1.4   5 FOXE, THE ACTS AND MONUMENTS, 402 (Cattley ed. 1838).
P.51, 1.21   2 BREWER, THE REIGN OF HENRY VIII, 379 (Gairdner ed. 1884). It was Wolsey who said immediately before he died: ". . . But if I had served God as diligently as I have done the King, He would not have given me over in my grey hairs." FERGUSON, NAKED TO MINE ENEMIES, 498 (1958).
Shakespeare transmuted this into:
> "Had I but serv'd my God with half the zeal
> I serv'd my king, He would not in mine age
> Have left me naked to mine enemies."

KING HENRY VIII, Act 3, sc. 2, 1.456.
P.52, 1.4   2 HALL, *op. cit. supra* at 259.
P.52, 1.13   5 FROUDE, HISTORY OF ENGLAND, 360 (1873).
P.52, 1.29   2 TYTLER, ENGLAND UNDER THE REIGNS OF EDWARD VI AND MARY, 230–231 (1839).
P.52, 1.34   2 BAYLEY, THE HISTORY AND ANTIQUITIES OF THE TOWER OF LONDON, xlix (1825).
P.53, 1.6   THE CHRONICLE OF QUEEN JANE 73 (Nichols ed., 48 Camden Soc. Pub. 1850).
P.53, 1.10   6 FOXE, *op. cit. supra* at 545.
P.53, 1.14   See Rowse, *Robert Devereux, Earl of Essex* in THE GREAT TUDORS 553, 562–564 (Garvin ed. 1935).
P.54, 1.15   See BOWEN, THE LION AND THE THRONE 160–162 (1956); 1 JARDINE, CRIMINAL TRIALS, 377–379 (1832); 2 SPEDDING, LETTERS AND LIFE OF FRANCIS BACON, 233–237 (1862).
P.54, 1.36   1 HOW. ST. TR., 1409, 1416 (1601).

Chapter 4

P.55, l.6   3 INST. *44.

P.55, l.12   3 LEA, A HISTORY OF THE INQUISITION OF THE MIDDLE AGES, 549 (1888).

P.55, l.27   2 EVIDENCE §572 (1st Am. ed. from the 6th London ed., Morgan 1876).

P.56, l.1   3 PITCAIRN, ANCIENT CRIMINAL TRIALS IN SCOTLAND, 602–16 (1833); PAGET, JUDICIAL PUZZLES, 53–57 (1876).

P.56, l.11   3 PITCAIRN, *op. cit. supra* at 616–618.

P.58, l.7   1 *id.* at 209–223, 230–241.

P.58, l.20   1 *id.* at 217. In his three-volume work Pitcairn has numerous witchcraft cases with confessions: 1 *id.* pt. 2, at 49–58 (Elizabeth or Bessie Dunlop, confession, burned, 1576); 1 *id.* at 76 (Violet Mar, confession 1577); 1 *id.* at 161 (Alesoun Peirsoun, confession, burned, 1588); 2 *id.* at 25–29, 52–53 (Jonet Stewart, Christian Lewingstoun, Bessie Aiken, Christian Saidler, confessions, all strangled and burned except Bessie; in 1598 Bessie was banished from the realm, 1597); 2 *id.* at 477–479 (Patrik Lowrie, produced a witness who testified that he got his father's curse, but that he was ordained to make his repentance and that he had done so; strangled and burned, 1605); 2 *id.* at 535–536 (Bartie Patersoun, confession, strangled and burned, 1607); 2 *id.* at 537–538 (Issobell Haldane, confession, 1623); 3 *id.* at 267 (Robert Erskine and his three sisters, Helene, Issobell and Anna, witchcraft and murder, Robert confessed, all beheaded except Helene, who was banished, 1614); 3 *id.* at 508–536 (Margaret Wallace, partial confession and repudiation; strangled and burned, 1622); 3 *id.* at 599 (Manie Haliburton, confession; she had carnal copulation with the devil, his nature being cold; he desired her to renounce Christ and become his servant, which she did, 1649); 3 *id.* at 601 (Jonet Watsone, confession; her devil was in the shape of a pretty boy in green clothes; another time he was in the shape of a black dog; and yet another time he wore green clothes and a black hat, 1661).

For a novel about the investigation of witches in Scotland in 1590 see WILLIAMS, THE WITCHES (1957). His book is based on the thesis that the witch cult, with its covens and sabbaths or assemblies, was the old religion which Christianity displaced. For a fuller treatment of this thesis see MARGARET MURRAY, THE GOD OF THE WITCHES (1933); and THE WITCH-CULT IN WESTERN EUROPE (1921). The word coven is a derivative of convene. A coven usually consisted of thirteen: twelve members and a chief or "devil." "The God of the old religion becomes the Devil of the new."

P.59, l.3   ARNOT, CELEBRATED CRIMINAL TRIALS IN SCOT-LAND, 401–403 (1812).

P.59, l.6   *Id.* at 404–405.

P.59, l.8   *Id.* at 403–404. According to another account it would appear that Weir's difficulty was incest with his sister. Both confessed to witchcraft as well, and both were executed. SINCLAIR GEORGE, SATAN'S INVISIBLE WORLD DISCOVERED, postscript (1685).

P.59, l.11   ARNOT, *op. cit. supra* at 405–411. At 390–391 Arnot reports the case of "Alison Pearson." Pitcairn, under the spelling "Alesoun Peirsoun," reports the same case. According to Arnot she confessed that she had associated with the Queen of Elfland for many years. She was present at a meeting of witches which took place just before sunrise. The witches prepared their charms in pans over a fire. She was strangled and burned.

P.60, l.18   4 How. St. Tr., 856.

P.61, l.18   4 *id.* at 839–840.

P.61, l.21   4 *id.* at 836.

P.61, l.27   *The several Informations, Examinations, and Confessions of Witches in the County of Essex,* 4 *id.* 817–858 (1645).

P.61, l.34   4 *id.* at 837–838.

P.61, l.35   4 *id.* at 839.

P.62, l.4   4 *id.* at 854–855.

P.62, l.8   4 *id.* at 853.

P.62, l.11   4 *id.* at 852–853.

P.62, l.15   4 *id.* at 853–854.

P.62, l.30   4 *id.* at 855–856.

P.63, l.6   2 *id.* 1049, 1059–60 (1616).

P.63, l.25   8 *id.* 1017, 1038.

P.64, l.15   PITT, CONFESSIONS OF WITCHES UNDER TORTURE (1886).

P.66, l.3   1 LEA, MATERIALS TOWARD A HISTORY OF WITCHCRAFT 232–256 (Howland ed. 1939); 2 *id.* at 848–850; BURR, RELIGIOUS CONFESSIONS AND CONFESSANTS, 217–218 (1914). See HUXLEY, THE DEVILS OF LOUDON (1952).

P.66, l.13   BURR, *op. cit. supra,* at 218–21.

P.66, l.20   *A note to A Trial of Witches, at the Assizes held at Bury St. Edmond's for the County of Suffolk,* before Sir Matthew Hale, Lord Chief Baron of the Court of Exchequer, 6 HOW. ST. TR. 647–702 (1665). See STARKEY, THE DEVIL IN MASSACHUSETTS (1949).

Chapter 5

P.67, l.10   Abramson, *Why Innocent People Confess to Crimes,* 1 *Why,* Jan. 6, 1952, pp. 110, 114.

P.67, l.13   Abramson put the number at sixteen. *Op. cit. supra* at 112. Subsequent news accounts added still one more.

P.67, l.16   69 U.S.L. REV., 625 (1935).

P.67, l.17   *Ibid.*

P.67, l.24   SMITH, MAN AND HIS GODS, 211 (1952).

P.68, l.1   2 BEST EVIDENCE §559 (1st Am. ed. from the 6th London ed., Morgan 1876); WHARTON, A TREATISE ON THE CRIMINAL LAW OF THE UNITED STATES §683 (6th ed. 1868). See PAGET, JUDICIAL PUZZLES 52 (1876). This portion of Paget's book is a reprint of an article from 88 BLACKWOOD'S MAG. 54 (1860).

P.68, l.8   14 HOW. ST. TR. 1312–24; PAGET, *op. cit. supra* at 37–52.

P.68, l.11   6 HOW. ST. TR., 807 (1666); 4 THE LIFE OF LORD CLARENDON, by himself, 160–163 (1798).

P.68, l.31   2 BUNYAN'S WORKS 737 (1692); 1 WHARTON, *op. cit. supra,* §683.

P.69, l.20   PAGET, *op. cit. supra* at 65.

P.69, l.28   2 LIFE OF SIR SAMUEL ROMILLY, by himself, 42–43 (3d ed. 1842).

P.69, l.35   WHARTON, INVOLUNTARY CONFESSIONS 22 (1860).

P.70, l.3   COCKBURN, MEMORIALS OF HIS TIME, 216–217 (1856).

P.70, l.5   6 Am. St. Tr., 73; BORCHARD, CONVICTING THE INNOCENT, 15–22 (1932); PEARSON, STUDIES IN MURDER, 265–85 (1926), 275–94 (Modern Library 1938); WHARTON, INVOLUNTARY CONFESSIONS, 16–7 (1860); Robach, "The Psychology of Confessions," 16 *Univ. Mag.,* 265 (1917); Hudson, "Problems Relating to Criminal Confessions of Innocent Persons," 18 *Medico-Legal Jour.* 84 (1900); "Confession of Crime—Its Value," 5 *Overland Monthly,* 251 (1870).

P.70, l.30   2 BEST, *op. cit. supra,* §569.

P.71, l.8   Shellenberger v. State, 97 Nebr. 498, 506, 510, 150 N.W. 643, 647, 648 (1915).

P.71, l.16   At 54 (1931).

P.71, l.18   At 263.

P.71, l.27   "The State v. Harold Israel," 15 *Am. Inst. of Crim. Law and Criminology Jour.,* 406 (1924).

P.72, l.2   App. 1 at 299 (1929).

P.72, l.6   Monck, "The Confessions of the Innocent," 18 *Medico-Legal Jour.*, 536 (1901).

P.72, l.11   WHARTON, INVOLUNTARY CONFESSIONS, 23.

P.72, l.18   Abramson, *op. cit. supra* at 113.

P.72, l.28   Bratuscha confessed that he stifled his 12-year-old.daughter, and part by part consumed her. He said his wife was his accomplice. She denied it at first, but after going to confession told the same story as her husband: the priest had denied her absolution until she confessed the truth. But both confessed falsely. The child was alive. Robach, *op. cit. supra* at 273; GROSS, CRIMINAL PSYCHOLOGY, 32 (Kallen transl. 1911).

The trial in Scotland in 1705 of Captain Thomas Green and members of his crew for piracy, robbery and murder produced three innocent confessants. Green was the master of an English vessel, the *Worcester,* and was forced by stress of weather into a Scottish port. This proved unfortunate for him: there were extreme rivalries at the time between Scottish and English commercial companies; also, Scotland was severely divided over the pending treaty of union with England. The report spread that Captain Green and his crew were pirates, and that they had murdered a Captain Drummond and seized his vessel. Fifteen went on trial, of whom fourteen were convicted. Three of the crew gave confessions: Thomas Linsteed, assistant to the supercargo; George Haines, steward; and John Bruckly, seaman. Two of these confessions were fairly detailed, and included a supplemental statement with still further details. Captain Green and two of his crew were executed. Several months later letters arrived from Captain Drummond and from the very ship for whose alleged seizure Captain Green was executed. 14 HOW. ST. TR., 1199; 5 HARGRAVE ST. TR., 571–610; 10 COBBETT, PARLIAMENTARY HISTORY OF ENGLAND, 284–285 (1812).

At Nuremberg in 1787 two women, Maria Schoning and Anna Harlin, falsely charged themselves with a capital crime. They were convicted and executed but, according to the account, one died on the scaffold through excitement and grief at witnessing the death of her friend. 2 BEST, *op. cit. supra,* §570; CAUSES CÉLÈBRES ÉTRANGÈRES, 200 (Paris 1827).

In May 1833 Miss Catherine Elmes was murdered in Chelsea, England. James Sharpe, who was innocent of it, confessed his complicity. Later he retracted his confession, explaining that he had given it because of jealousy of his wife, whom he had seen standing with another man. He added: "Some time ago three of my children died, and it preyed on my mind; and one night I gave myself up for murdering them, when it was all false; and, on another occasion, I gave myself up for a robbery." ANNUAL REGISTER, CHRONICLE 74 (1833).

In December 1837 a flotilla of five British boats on the Niagara River captured *The Caroline*, a little steamboat owned by an American, killed one person, removed the crew, set the boat on fire and sent her burning over the falls. In 1841 Alexander McLeod, a Canadian, claimed in Buffalo that he was a member of the raiding party and the one who was the killer. He was indicted and tried, but then was able to prove a clear alibi. 7 AM. ST. TR., 61, 86–90.

In Springfield, Illinois, in 1846 Henry Trailor confessed that his brothers William and Archibald killed one Fisher. He gave a detailed account how he helped them dispose of the body in a pond outside of the city. The authorities searched the pond but could find no body. Word came that Fisher was still alive. Henry persisted in his confession. Fisher himself had to be produced before the case was finally disposed of. 4 *Western L. Jour.* 25; *Chicago Daily Law Bull.*, Dec. 14, 1904.

In 1856 a clergyman in England gave himself up to justice, declaring that he had been guilty of forging certain bills of exchange, that they were about to come due, that he was unable to pay, that detection was inevitable, and that he wished to anticipate the blow and make such reparation as was in his power by a full acknowledgment of his guilt. There was not the slightest truth in the story. There was no forgery, and no such bills of exchange as the clergyman described were ever in existence. PAGET, *op. cit. supra* at 63–64.

One afternoon in July 1874 a woman of 22 was brought to the Boston City Hospital with fearful and bloody injuries about her head. She finally recovered. In May 1876 a condemned murderer, a few days before his execution, made a confession of many of his misdeeds, and claimed this assault as one of the number. But the facts showed that he could not possibly have done it. Cotting, *A Murderer's Dying Confession Disproved*, 121 *Boston Medical and Surgical Jour.* 3 (1889).

During the winter in 1908 the Rev. James Larry Smith of Nanseland County, Virginia disappeared. The Rev. Ernest Lyons confessed to his murder. After Lyons had been in prison about two years, Smith was found alive. He had disappeared across the state line into North Carolina with about $45 of church money which had been collected to be sent to a conference in Suffolk. McLemore, "The Strange Case of Reverend Ernest Lyons Who Falsely Confessed Murder and Suffered Accordingly," 17 *Va. L. Rev.*, 369 (1931).

One Fanning confessed repeatedly in Topeka, Kansas, in 1909 that he had poisoned a Mrs. Short with arsenic. Medical and chemical testimony showed this to be impossible and indicated heart trouble as the cause of death. *Topeka Capital*, Nov. 16, 1909. John A. Johnson in Madison, Wisconsin confessed that in September 1911 he murdered Annie Lemberger, aged seven, and threw her body into Lake Manona. He was later proven to be innocent and after ten years in prison, pardoned. BORCHARD, *op. cit. supra* at 112–122.

In Louisiana Leland Walker confessed that he murdered Nelson McManus by hitting him on the head with an ax. McManus had disappeared from his home in Jena. Three and a half months later McManus returned. In Indiana, Seth Nichols gave an account of the way in which he slaughtered Dr. Knabs, an Indianapolis woman physician. Investigation showed that he could not have done this murder. "Untrue Confessions," 19 CASE & COM. 841 (1913). Mrs. Jean E. McCleary, a pretty blonde from Ferndale, Michigan repeatedly confessed to murders. Once she went to Chicago to confess to a killing in which the murder weapon was a pair of scissors. Abramson, *op. cit. supra* at 114–115.

Selma Graaf, aged 15, was clubbed to death with an iron pipe by an intruder in the bedroom of her Brooklyn home. Newspapers carried the story of the murder. In a few days the police had a call from a pay station in a Brooklyn cafeteria. "I want to surrender," the caller said nervously. "I killed that little girl Selma Graaf. I'll wait here till you pick me up." The police raced to the spot and took into custody James Goarke, a 31-year-old auto thief on probation, who was involved in house-breaking as well. Yet he was innocent. *Id.* at 116. A New York servant girl, Elizabeth Baksa, confessed to the murder of her employer, Mrs. Helen Hamel. But she was innocent. The real murderer turned out to be a convict at Sing Sing. *Id.* at 116, 118.

In 1951 a deputy sheriff in Indianola, Mississippi and his new assistant obtained detailed confessions from three Negroes to the murder of a person whose mother had reported him as missing. They confessed that they murdered the missing person with a brick and threw his body into the Sunflower River. The officers started dragging the river, without success. The next morning the mother of the alleged victim got a letter from him from East St. Louis. The press located him there. His comment was that he certainly was not dead.

A patient at the Worcester Hospital in Massachusetts begged Dr. H. R. Storer to have him hanged for an alleged murder which had never occurred. 18 *Medico-Legal Jour.*, 84, 132 (1900). An inmate of an asylum in England told a magistrate that he was committed for the murder of his wife, and that it was necessary for him to be under restraint or his impulse would return. But his wife was alive. PAGET, *op. cit. supra* at 66.

An East Bronx factory fire that killed six firemen and injured fourteen more, immediately brought forth a confessant. He was a seven-year-old tenement boy. He not only gave an account of his "crime" but also buttressed it with a spurious re-enactment near the rubble-strewn scene of the disaster. Yet he was innocent. *N.Y. Times*, April 6, 1956, p. 1, col. 1, p. 22, col. 8.

In China there existed the practice, and that in cases involving capital punishment, of permitting the condemned person to procure a

substitute. MEADOWS, DESULTORY NOTES ON THE GOVERN-
MENT AND PEOPLE OF CHINA, Note XIII, "On Personating
Criminals," 172–174 (1847); 2 BERNCASTLE, A VOYAGE TO
CHINA, 167 (1851). Sometimes he did this by the payment of a sum
of money. At other times juniors in families impersonated their deviant
seniors, and domestic serfs their guilty masters. This custom supplied
the plot for James Payn's novel, BY PROXY (1878).
P.73, l.6   As quoted in PAGET, *op. cit. supra* at 66–67.
P.73, l.20   INVOLUNTARY CONFESSIONS 16, 21.
P.73, l.23   §683.

Chapter 6

P.74, l.23   1 GSOVSKI, SOVIET CIVIL LAW 156 (1948); BER-
MAN, JUSTICE IN RUSSIA 23 (1950). On this decree Kucherov
commented: "Decree No. 1. on Courts of the Council of People's
Commissars, dated November 24, 1917, abrogated all the existing
judicial institutions and the guild of lawyers. It is one of the
supreme ironies of history that the free Russian lawyer and the
democratic administration of justice were born by the will of an
autocratic Tsar and destroyed by a decree of a revolutionary government, as the life of Alexander II himself, who was the creator
of the greatest democratic reforms in Russian history, was destroyed by revolutionaries.

"The abrogation of the institution of lawyers and of the bar had its
precedent in history: the French Constituante declared in its Decrees of
August 16 and September 2, 1790, that those who 'call themselves
avocats may no longer form a class, or association, or wear special
clothes during the performance of their duties.' " COURTS, LAWYERS
AND TRIALS UNDER THE LAST THREE TSARS, 314 (1953).
P.75, l.2   Quoted in ZELITCH, SOVIET ADMINISTRATION OF
CRIMINAL LAW, 116 (1931).
P.75, l.4   1 GSOVSKI, SOVIET CIVIL LAW, 852 (1948); BER-
MAN, JUSTICE IN RUSSIA, 23 (1950).
P.75, l.26   1 GSOVSKI, SOVIET CIVIL LAW, 235 (1948);
SCHLESINGER, SOVIET LEGAL THEORY, 77 (1945).
P.75, l.33   See 1 GSOVSKI, SOVIET CIVIL LAW, 157 (1948).
P.76, l.4   *Ibid;* SCHLESINGER, SOVIET LEGAL THEORY, 68
(1945).
P.76, l.9   See BERMAN, JUSTICE IN RUSSIA, 24 (1950); 1
GSOVSKI, SOVIET CIVIL LAW, 170 (1948); HAZARD and
WEISSBERG, CASES AND READINGS ON SOVIET LAW 2
(Columbia Univ. mimeograph 1950).
P.76, l.18   As quoted in 1 GSOVSKI, SOVIET CIVIL LAW, 170
(1948); and BERMAN, JUSTICE IN RUSSIA, 21 (1950).

P.76, l.22   SCHLESINGER, SOVIET LEGAL THEORY, 202 (1945). See also BERMAN, JUSTICE IN RUSSIA, 37 (1950).

P.76, l.31   As quoted in SCHLESINGER, SOVIET LEGAL THEORY, 156 (1945). See also BERMAN, JUSTICE IN RUSSIA, 21 (1950).

P.76, l.34   "The General Theory of Law and Marxism" (3d ed. 1927), in SOVIET LEGAL PHILOSOPHY, 201 (Babb transl., 5 The 20th Century Legal Philosophy Series 1951).

P.77   BAUER, THE NEW MAN IN SOVIET PSYCHOLOGY, 35–37 (1952); BERMAN, JUSTICE IN RUSSIA, 24–29 (1950); 1 GSOVSKI, SOVIET LEGAL THEORY, 160, 172–175, 247 (1948); HARPER and THOMPSON, THE GOVERNMENT OF THE SOVIET UNION 30–33, 237 (2d ed. 1949); SKELSEN, THE COMMUNIST THEORY OF LAW (1955); SCHLESINGER, SOVIET LEGAL THEORY, 105–121 (1945); Fuller, "Pashukanis and Vyshinsky: A Study in the Development of Marxian Legal Theory," 47 *Mich. L. Rev.*, 1157 (1949).

P.77, l.17   As quoted in 1 GSOVSKI, SOVIET CIVIL LAW, 853 (1948).

P.77, l.25   As quoted in 1 *id.* at 280.

P.78, l.14   For a description of the procuracy see BERMAN, JUSTICE IN RUSSIA, 168–173 (1950); 1 GSOVSKI, SOVIET CIVIL LAW, 846–851 (1948).

P.78, l.27   AGABEKOV, OGPU ix (1931).

P.78, l.32   See SCHLESINGER, SOVIET LEGAL THEORY, 106 (1945); 1 GSOVSKI, SOVIET CIVIL LAW, 236 (1948).

P.79, l.3   As quoted in 1 GSOVSKI, SOVIET CIVIL LAW, 172 (1948).

P.83, l.14   SOVIET LEGAL PHILOSOPHY 235 (Babb transl., 5 The 20th Century Legal Philosophy Series 1951). See also, 1 GSOVSKI, SOVIET CIVIL LAW, 173 (1948); BERMAN, JUSTICE IN RUSSIA, 34–35 (1950).

P.83, l.18   SCHLESINGER, SOVIET LEGAL THEORY, 147–148 (1945).

P.84, l.4   See WRECKERS ON TRIAL, A RECORD OF THE TRIAL OF THE INDUSTRIAL PARTY (Workers' Library Publishers 1931).

P.84, l.6   See THE MENSHEVIK TRIAL (Workers' Library Publishers 1931).

P.84, l.23   SUKHANOV, THE RUSSIAN REVOLUTION 1917, xi-xii (Carmichael ed. and transl. 1955).

P.84, l.32   The four other English defendants were Allan Monkhouse, John Cushny, Charles Nordwall and A. W. Gregory. See MONKHOUSE, MOSCOW 1911–1933, chs. 21–22 (1934); WRECKING ACTIVITIES AT POWER STATIONS IN THE SOVIET

UNION, 85, 169, 258, 259, 427, 502, 515, 676, 677, 776 (Moscow, State Law Publishing House 1933).

P.85, l.22 MONKHOUSE, MOSCOW 1911–1933, 269–270 (1934).

P.87, l.16 MEISEL and KOZERA, MATERIALS FOR THE STUDY OF THE SOVIET SYSTEM, 205–206 (1950). Nikita S. Khrushchev, the Russian communist party boss, in his speech in February 1956 at a secret session of the party's twentieth congress accused Stalin of acting without consultation in getting out a directive on this decree: "On the evening of Dec. 1, 1934, on Stalin's initiative (without the approval of the Political Bureau, which was passed two days later, casually) the secretary of the Presidium of the Central Executive Committee, Abel S. Yenukidze, signed the following directive: '. . . 2. Judicial organs are directed not to hold up the execution of death sentences pertaining to crimes of this category in order to consider the possibility of pardon, because the Presidium of the Central Executive Committee of the U.S.S.R. does not consider as possible the receiving of petitions of this sort. 3. The organs of the Commissariat of Internal Affairs are directed to execute the death sentences against criminals of the above-mentioned category immediately after the passage of sentences.' " *N.Y. Times,* June 5, 1956, p. 14, col. 3.

P.88, l.11 DEUTSCHER, STALIN, A POLITICAL BIOGRAPHY, 357 (1941).

P.88, l.21 STALIN, PROBLEMS OF LENINISM, 522 (authorized English transl. from 11th Russian ed. 1947).

P.89, l.1 *The Current Digest of the Soviet Press,* Aug. 22, 1956, p. 15.

P.89, l.26 See THE CASE OF THE TROTSKYITE-ZINOVIEVITE CENTRE, 164 (Moscow, 1936).

P.90, l.1 See BECK and GODIN, RUSSIAN PURGE AND THE EXTRACTION OF CONFESSION, 169 (pseudonyms, Mosbacher and Porter transl. 1951); WEISSBERG, THE ACCUSED, 12, 421 (Fitzgerald transl. 1951).

P.90, l.8 See DELBARS, THE REAL STALIN, 188 (Miall transl. 1953).

P.90, l.13 STALIN, PROBLEMS OF LENINISM, 625 (authorized English transl. from 11th Russian ed. 1947).

P.90, l.20 *N.Y. Times,* June 5, 1956, p. 15, col. 8, p. 16, col. 7.

P.91, l.12 MEISEL and KOZERA, MATERIALS FOR THE STUDY OF THE SOVIET SYSTEM, 261 (1950).

P.91, l.16 *Ibia.*

P.91, l.19 Art. 114.

P.91, l.20 Art. 115.

P.91, l.35 As quoted in 1 GSOVSKI, SOVIET CIVIL LAW, 173–174 (1948). Earlier in the form of self-criticism he confessed a series of errors, but tried to hang onto his idea about the withering away of the state and law. See his *The Soviet State and the Revolution of Law* (1930), in SOVIET LEGAL PHILOSOPHY, 243–273 (Babb transl. 5 The 20th Century Legal Philosophy Series 1951).

P.92, l.1   MEISEL and KOZERA, MATERIALS FOR THE STUDY OF THE SOVIET SYSTEM, 240 (1950).

P.92, l.14   As quoted in 1 GSOVSKI, SOVIET CIVIL LAW 174 (1948).

P.92, l.20   *N.Y. Times*, Sept. 7, 1956, p. 4, col. 5.

P.92, l.25   At 53, 54 (Babb transl. 1948).

P.92, l.26   "The Fundamental Task of the Science of Soviet Socialist Law" (1938), in *Soviet Legal Philosophy* 304 (Babb transl. 5 The 20th Century Legal Philosophy Series 1951). In the same piece he referred to the "provocateur theory of Pashukanis" at 307, and again condemned a nihilistic attitude to Soviet law: "One of the objectives of the people's foes who busied themselves in the theoretical arena in the domain of law and state was to disarm the proletariat . . . through cultivating a nihilistic attitude toward soviet law, the soviet state, and the soviet statute." At 314.

P.92, l.29   BERMAN, JUSTICE IN RUSSIA, 199 (1950)

P.93, l.15   WRECKING ACTIVITIES AT POWER STATIONS IN THE SOVIET UNION, 751, 762–764 (Moscow, 1933).

P.93, l.33   MOSCOW 1911–1933, 313–314 (1933).

P.94, l.4   WRECKING ACTIVITIES AT POWER STATIONS IN THE SOVIET UNION, 716 (Moscow, 1933).

P.94, l.9   *Id.* at 502.

P.94, l.22   *Id.* at 674, 676–677.

P.95, l.2   *Id.* at 690.

P.95, l.8   *Id.* at 682.

P.95, l.26   REPORT OF COURT PROCEEDINGS IN THE CASE OF THE ANTI-SOVIET TROTSKYITE CENTRE 517 (Moscow 1937).

96, l.1   *Id.* at 523.

P.96, l.10   *Id.* at 533.

P.96, l.15   REPORT OF THE COURT PROCEEDINGS IN THE CASE OF THE ANTI-SOVIET "BLOC OF RIGHTS AND TROTSKYITES," 705–706 (Moscow 1938).

P.96, l.22   At 329 (1951). He quoted Braude in the same language as that set forth in what purported to be a verbatim report of the case. TRIAL OF THE ORGANIZERS, LEADERS AND MEMBERS OF THE POLISH DIVERSIONIST ORGANIZATIONS, ETC., 211 (1945).

P.97, l.9   At 330.

P.97, l.23 THE TRIAL OF TRAICHO KOSTOV AND HIS GROUP, 561 (Sofia 1949).

P.97, l.30 *Id.* at 564.

P.98, l.4 *Id.* at 572.

P.98, l.9 ARMSTRONG, TITO AND GOLIATH, 210 (1951).

P.98, l.15 *N.Y. Times,* Sept. 17, 1953, p. 11, col. 8.

P.98, l.34 "Prison Diary of Lt. Parks," *U.S. News & World Report,* June 24, 1955, p. 146.

Chapter 7

P.99, l.7 THE CASE OF THE TROTSKYITE-ZINOVIEVITE CENTRE, 68–69 (Moscow 1936).

P.100, l.28 *Id.* at 44, 171.

P.102, l.14 *Id.* at 166–168, 170–172.

P.105, l.16 REPORT OF COURT PROCEEDINGS IN THE CASE OF THE ANTI-SOVIET TROTSKYITE CENTRE, 233, 539, 541–543, 549–551, 557, 559, 561–563, 567, 568 (Moscow 1937).

P.110, l.16 REPORT OF COURT PROCEEDINGS IN THE CASE OF THE ANTI-SOVIET "BLOC OF RIGHTS AND TROTSKY-ITES," 716, 718–722, 724, 729, 730, 736, 737, 740, 741, 743, 750, 751, 757, 758, 760, 766, 777–779, 785, 787, 791 (Moscow 1938).

In addition to ARTHUR KOESTLER, DARKNESS AT NOON (Hardy transl. 1940), and VICTOR SERGE, THE CASE OF COMRADE TULAYEV (Trask transl. 1950), see a recent novel on the confessions during the mass purge, N. NAROKOV, THE CHAINS OF FEAR (1958).

P.110, l.31 See LAUTERBACK, THESE ARE THE RUSSIANS, 298–304 (1944). For this and most of the subsequent cases the author has also relied on news accounts in the *New York Times.*

P.111, l.18 Chaps. 11–17 (1951). See also TRIAL OF THE OR-GANIZERS, LEADERS AND MEMBERS OF THE POLISH DIVERSIONIST ORGANIZATIONS, ETC. (1945); MOSCOW TRIAL OF 16 POLISH DIVERSIONISTS (Soviet News 1945).

P.112, l.9 See THE TRIAL OF NIKOLA D. PETKOV, RECORD OF THE JUDICIAL PROCEEDINGS (Sofia 1947).

P.112, l.20 See LASZLO RAJK AND HIS ACCOMPLICES BE-FORE THE PEOPLE'S COURT (Budapest 1949).

P.112, l.22 See THE TRIAL OF TRAICHO KOSTOV AND HIS GROUP (Sofia 1949).

P.113, l.13 EVANS, THE TRIAL OF CARDINAL MINDSZENTY (Birmingham, England).

P.113, l.15 THE TRIAL OF THE FIFTEEN PROTESTANT PASTOR-SPIES (Sofia 1949).

P.114, l.7 *Hungarian Bulletin,* no. 97, pp. 358, 363, 364.

P.114, l.31 MATERIALS ON THE TRIAL OF FORMER SERV- ICEMEN OF THE JAPANESE ARMY CHARGED WITH MANUFACTURING AND EMPLOYING BACTERIOLOGI- CAL WEAPONS, 5–37, 284, 516, 517, 518, 521 (Moscow 1950).

P.116, l.21 R. VOGELER, E. SANDERS AND THEIR ACCOM- PLICES BEFORE THE CRIMINAL COURT 279 (Budapest 1950).

P.116, l.30 VOGELER, with LEIGH WHITE, I WAS STALIN'S PRISONER, 158 (1952).

P.116, l.32 DOSTOEVSKI, THE BROTHERS KARAMAZOV, 305 (Constance Garnett transl. Modern Library 1943).

P.117, l.13 "A Ransomed U.S. Airman Tells Story of His Ordeal," *Life,* Jan. 14, 1952, p. 104.

P.117, l.18 WHITE, THE CAPTIVES OF KOREA, 148–149, 167– 171 (1957).

P.117, l.26 *N.Y. Herald Tribune,* June 12, 1952, p. 9, col. 8.

P.117, l.35 *N.Y. Times,* Nov. 25, 1952, p. 9, col. 2.

P.118, l.21 See her 7 YEARS' SOLITARY, 34 (1957).

P.120, l.30 *Commentary,* Jan. 1953, pp. 1–18.

P.122, l.6 As quoted by Arthur Krock, "Allen W. Dulles Describes 'Warfare for the Brain'," *N.Y. Times,* April 16, 1953, p. 28, col. 5.

P.122, l.15 See *Communist Interrogation, Indoctrination and Exploi- tation of American Military and Civilian Prisoners, Hearings be- fore the Permanent Subcommittee on Investigations of the Com- mittee on Government Operations,* 84th Cong., 2d Sess. 148–150 (1956); Hinkle and Wolff, "Communist Interrogation and In- doctrination of 'Enemies of the State'," 76 *Archives of Neurology and Psychiatry,* 115, 168 (1956).

P.122, l.19 *Hearings, op. cit. supra* at 89. See also S. REP. No. 2832, 84th Cong., 2d Sess. (1956).

P.122, l.26 *Id.* at 88, 89.

P.122, l.34 *Id.* at 90, 92, 95. See also Segal, "Were They Really 'Brainwashed'?" *Look,* June 26, 1956, p. 101.

P.123, l.6 *Treatment of British Prisoners of War in Korea* iv, 34, 35 (London 1955).

P.123, l.15 *N.Y. Times,* Sept. 15, 1953, p. 9, col. 1.

P.123, l.23 *N.Y. Times,* May 30, 1956, p. 1, col. 8, p. 4, cols. 4–5.

P.123, l.26 *N.Y. Times,* June 22, 1956, p. 1, col. 8, July 21, 1956, p. 4, cols. 6–7, Sept. 15, 1956, p. 3, col. 4.

P.123, l.30 *N.Y. Times,* Oct. 13, 1956, p. 2, col. 3.

P.124, l.6 *N.Y. Times,* July 4, 1956, p. 3, col. 8.

P.124, l.8 *N.Y. Times,* June 18, 1956, p. 2, col. 3.

P.124, l.17 Hinkle and Wolff, *op. cit. supra* at 174; *Hearings op. cit. supra* at 34.

P.124, l.21 *N.Y. Times,* July 11, 1955, p. 1, cols. 2–4.

P.125, l.15 *N.Y. Post,* Jan. 16, 1957, p. 3.

P.125, l.17 *N.Y. Times,* March 8, 1957, p. 5, cols. 5–6.

P.125, l.28 *N.Y. Times,* June 23, 1957, p. 2, cols. 3–5.

P.126, l.2 *N.Y. Times,* Feb. 19, 1957, p. 12, col. 3.

P.126, l.11 *N.Y. Times,* June 22, 1957, p. 17, cols. 1–5.

P.127, l.7 THE COUNTER-REVOLUTIONARY CONSPIRACY OF IMRE NAGY AND HIS ACCOMPLICES 11, 19–20, 96 (Budapest 1958).

P.127, l.16 *N.Y. Times,* Aug. 2, 1957, p. 1, col. 2.

P.127, l.18 *N.Y. Times,* April 13, 1958, p. 3, cols. 2–4.

P.127, l.21 *N.Y. Times,* April 25, 1958, p. 3, cols. 2–4.

Chapter 8

P.128, l.16 Kozlov, "Criticism and Self-Criticism Is a Law of Development of Soviet Society," *USSR Information Bull.,* May 18, 1951. See GORDAY, VISA TO MOSCOW, 214 (Woods transl. 1952).

P.128, l.18 Kozlov, *op. cit. supra.*

P.128, l.21 Corbett, "Postwar Soviet Ideology," 263 *Annals of the Am. Acad. of Pol. and Soc. Sci.* 45, 48 (1949).

P.128, l.24 Kozlov, *op. cit. supra.*

P.129, l.7 "The Soviet State and the Revolution of Law" (1930), in SOVIET LEGAL PHILOSOPHY 250–265 (Babb transl., 5 The 20th Century Legal Philosophy Series 1951).

P.129, l.22 Feuer, "Dialectical Materialism and Soviet Science," 16 PHIL. OF SCIENCE 105, 121 (1949).

P.130, l.36 "Thought Control in the Soviet Union," 25 *Dept. of State Bull.* 895, 901 (1951).

P.131, l.6 *N.Y. Times,* February 16, 1948, p. 7, col. 2; December 31, 1948, p. 10, col. 7.

P.131, l.13 "Thought Control in the Soviet Union," 25 *Dept. of State Bull.* 895, 901 (1951).

P.131, l.23 *N.Y. Herald Tribune,* February 19, 1948.

P.132, l.1 Feuer, *op. cit. supra* at 122.

P.132, l.9 Cook, "Walpurgis Week in the Soviet Union," 68 *Science Monthly,* 367, 369 (1949).

P.132, l.15 Wolfe, "Science Joins the Party," 10 *Antioch Rev.* 47, 58 (1950).

P.132, l.28 Yakobson, "Postwar Historical Research in the Soviet Union," 263 *Annals of the Am. Acad. of Pol. and Soc. Sci.* 123, 129–30 (1949).

P.133, l.29 *N.Y. Times,* March 23, 1949, p. 20, col. 3.

P.133, l.36 *N.Y. Herald Tribune,* March 23, 1949; *N.Y. Times,* May 7, 1949.

P.134, l.13 *N.Y. Times,* Oct. 31, 1949, p. 6, col. 6.

P.134, l.21 "Thought Control in the Soviet Union," 25 *Dept. of State Bull.* 895, 897 (1951).

P.134, l.29 Schwartz, "Statistics Barred in Soviet Science," *N.Y. Times,* March 9, 1952.

P.134, l.32 *N.Y. Times,* July 31, 1951, p. 3, col. 3.

P.135, l.10 *N.Y. Times,* Oct. 16, 1951, p. 15, col. 3.

P.136, l.20 *N.Y. Times,* Dec. 25, 1952, Jan. 2, 9 and 17, 1953.

P.136, l.32 *N.Y. Times,* Oct. 9, 1955, p. 1, cols. 6–7, p. 31, cols. 1–3, p. 32, cols. 1–2.

P.136, l.36 GORDAY, VISA TO MOSCOW, 152–5 (Woods transl. 1952).

P.137, l.6 *Id.* at 155–9.

P.137, l.7 *Id.* at 142–6.

P.137, l.15 As quoted in MEAD, SOVIET ATTITUDES TOWARD AUTHORITY, 76 (1951).

P.137, l.29 *N.Y. Times,* Aug. 18, 1954, p. 6, col. 3.

P.137, l.34 *N.Y. Times,* March 14, 1954, p. 85, cols. 4–5.

P.138, l.6 See *N.Y. Times,* Jan. 3, 1955, p. 7, col. 1.

P.138, l.26 *N.Y. Times,* Oct. 15, 1957, p. 8, cols. 3–4.

P.138, l.28 *N.Y. Times,* Dec. 30, 1957, p. 2, col. 3.

P.139, l.1 *N.Y. Times,* Nov. 3, 1957, p. 1, col. 5.

P.139, l.12 COOKE, A GENERATION ON TRIAL, 38 (1950).

P.139, l.21 *N.Y. Times,* Nov. 6, 1958, p. 4, cols. 3–6. In the closing days of 1958, ex-Premier Nikolai Bulganin, one-time traveling companion of party boss Khrushchev, came to a meeting of the Communist Party Central Committee in Moscow and confessed: "Everything Comrade Khrushchev said in his report on the anti-party group about Malenkov, Molotov, Kaganovich and about me and Shepilov was true." *Wall Street Jour.,* Dec. 19, 1958, p. 1, col. 3.

P.140, l.31 *N.Y. Times,* June 9, 1958, p. 1, col. 5. For further material on Russian confessions of errors, see BAUER, THE NEW MAN IN SOVIET PSYCHOLOGY, 36–37, 154 (1952); Corbett, "Postwar Soviet Ideology," 263 *Annals of the Am. Acad. of Pol. and Soc. Sci.,* 45 (1949); CRANKSHAW, CRACKS IN THE KREMLIN WALL, 137, 226–7 (1951); EISENSTEIN, FILM FORM, 147, 245 (Jay Leyda transl. 1949); EISENSTEIN, THE FILM SENSE (1948); EPSTEIN, "Soviet Philosophy and Modern Science," 151 THE 20th CENTURY, 333 (1952); Moseley, "Soviet Research in the Social Field," 94 *Am. Phil. Soc. Proc.* no. 2, 105 (1950); SETON, SERGEI M. EISENSTEIN (1952);

"Thought Control in the Soviet Union," 25 *Dept. of State Bull.* 719, 844 (1951).

P.141,l.15   *N.Y. Times,* Sept. 24, 1956, p. 7, col. 6; Sept. 30, 1956, §E, p. 7, cols. 3–6.

P.142,l.4   *N.Y. Times,* July 16, 1957, p. 12, cols. 3–5.

P.142,l.7   *N.Y. Times,* Jan. 20, 1958, p. 3, col. 8.

Chapter 9

P.143,l.12   Washington v. McGrath, 341 U.S. 923 (1951), *affirming* 182 F.2d 375 (D.C. Cir. 1950) (loyalty investigation); Bailey v. Richardson, 341 U.S. 918 (1951), *affirming* 182 F.2d 46 (D.C. Cir. 1950) (*ibid.*); Joint Anti-Fascist Refugee Committee v. McGrath 341 U.S. 123 (1951) (attorney general's blacklist of organizations, compiled without any hearings); Adler v. Board of Education, 342 U.S. 485 (1952) (Feinberg Law of New York, relating to the public school system, which provided that the board of regents was to establish its own blacklist of organizations and in so doing to make use of any similar authorized blacklist of any federal agency or authority); Shaughnessy v. United States *ex rel.* Mezei, 345 U.S. 206 (1953) (alien resident of this country seeking to return after a trip abroad held entitled to no hearing at all); United States *ex rel.* Knauff v. Shaughnessy, 338 U.S. 537 (1950) (alien war bride held entitled to no hearing); Ludecke v. Watkins, 335 U.S. 160 (1948) (alien ordered banished without a hearing); Carlson v. Landon, 342 U.S. 524 (1952) (alien denied bail without a hearing); United States v. Nugent, 346 U.S. 1 (1953) (draft status of conscientious objector); Jay v. Boyd, 351 U.S. 345 (1956) (exercise of attorney general's discretionary power of suspension of deportation of an alien).

P.144,l.18   United States v. Hiss, 185 F.2d 822 (2d Cir. 1950.), *cert. denied,* 340 U.S. 948 (1951); United States v. Hiss, 201 F.2d 372 (2d Cir. 1953), *affirming* 107 F.Supp. 128 (D.S.D.N.Y. 1952), *cert. denied,* 345 U.S. 942 (1953). See also COOKE, A GENERATION ON TRIAL (1950).

P.144,l.26   At 3–5.

P.144,l.36   At 13, 17.

P.145,l.7   At 21–22.

P.145,l.16   At 455–456.

P.145,l.18   At 462. Silone wrote that he made the statement jokingly. THE GOD THAT FAILED, 113 (Crossman ed. 1949).

P.145,l.28   At 714–715.

P.145,l.32   At 762.

P.146,l.22   At 222. A recent autobiography by an ex-communist is

The Story of an American Communist (1958) by John Gates, former editor of *The Daily Worker*. Although substantially, as Earl Browder stated in a foreword, "Gates gives us nothing of the breast-beating confessions of sin that have made most of the writings of ex-communists so stale and boring to the point of nausea," he did admit thefts, a passport violation, and going AWOL, and described how the American communist party submissively followed the line of the Russian one. Concerning his childhood he wrote: "I was a stubborn and opinionated child, it seems. * * * I would drink only from my own cup—and the contents had to be stirred clockwise. When my grandmother once stirred my milk counter-clockwise, I became furious and called upon God to punish her." He related how he fell "deeply in love" with the woman he married while she was in the process of separating from her then husband. At viii-ix, 8, 43, 54–55, 73–75, 88–89, 99, 112–113, 166–169.

P.146, l.30 Christoffel's first conviction was reversed by the United States Supreme Court in the last opinion which Justice Murphy wrote. Christoffel v. United States, 338 U.S. 84 (1949), *reversing* 171 F.2d 1004 (D.C. Cir. 1948). The Supreme Court divided five to four. On a retrial Christoffel was convicted again. He again appealed and the Supreme Court again sent the case back to the trial court, but this time for resentencing rather than another trial. Christoffel v. United States, 345 U.S. 947 (1953), *vacating judgment in* 200 F.2d 734 (D.C. Cir. 1952). For a discussion of the first Christoffel trial see ROGGE, OUR VANISHING CIVIL LIBERTIES, c. 15 (1949).

P.147, l.1 See p. 366.

P.147, l.11 Natvig v. United States, 236 F.2d 694 (D.C. Cir. 1956) *cert. denied,* 352 U.S. 1014 (1957); United States v. Matusow, 244 F.2d 532 (2d Cir. 1957), *cert. denied,* 354 U.S. 942 (1957). Matusow was also held in contempt of court in Texas for recanting testimony which he had previously given there, but this judgment was reversed on appeal. Matusow v. United States, 229 F.2d 335 (5th Cir. 1956). He gave his former testimony in a criminal case accusing Clinton E. Jencks, an officer of one of the branches of the International Union of Mine, Mill and Smelter Workers, of filing a false noncommunist affidavit with the National Labor Relations Board. Jencks was convicted but the Supreme Court reversed his conviction and sent the case back for a new trial. Jencks v. United States, 353 U.S. 657 (1957), *reversing* 226 F.2d 540 and 226 F.2d 553 (5th Cir. 1955). Thereafter the government dropped its case against Jencks with the statement: "On the available evidence the Government cannot successfully retry this defendant." *N.Y. Times,* Jan. 2, 1958, p. 15, cols. 1–4.

A little over two months after the Supreme Court refused to review Mrs. Natvig's judgment of conviction, the district court suspended her prison sentence and placed her on probation for two years. *N.Y. Times,* April 30, 1957, p. 16, col. 6.

Chapter 10

P.148, 1.16   These figures came from information supplied me by the Administrative Office of the United States Courts in communications of June 5, 1953, and December 16, 1954.

P.149, 1.9   An estimate based on information supplied me by the Administrative Office of the Courts in communications of June 11, 1953, and December 10, 1954. The New Jersey statistics are compiled in the form of "cases." A case is a separate charge against an individual defendant. Thus 10 charges against one defendant equal 10 cases, and one charge against 10 defendants equals 10 cases. For the two-year period ending August 31, 1954 the number of cases in which there were pleas either of guilty or non vult amounted to 7209, whereas the number of cases that went to trial amounted to but 2725.

P.149, 1.14   BURR, RELIGIOUS CONFESSIONS AND CONFESSANTS, 216–219 (1914); Cameron, "Inscriptions Relating to Sacral Manumission and Confession," 32 *Harv. Theol. Rev.,* 143 (1939); CERAM (MAREK), THE SECRET OF THE HITTITES, 163–164 (Richard and Clara Winston transl. 1956); Cutter, "Shall Protestants Adopt the Confessional?" 229 *North Am. Rev.* 200 (1930); Kline, "Confession," 54 *Luth. Quar.* 1 (1924); 1 LEA, A HISTORY OF AURICULAR CONFESSION AND INDULGENCES (1896); Pettazzoni, "Confession of Sins and the Classics," 30 *Harv. Theol. Rev.* 1 (1937); PETTAZZONI, "Confessions of Sins in Hittite Religion," in *Occident and Orient* (1936); Shore, "Auricular Confession and the English Church," 37 *The Nineteenth Century,* 71 (1895); Wilson, "Habitual Confession for the Young," 83 *Contemporary Rev.* 834 (1903).

P.149, 1.32   SACRED BOOKS OF THE EAST, "Laws of Manu," c. 11, par. 229 at 477 (Buehler's transl. 1886).

P.149, 1.35   MENZIES, HISTORY OF RELIGION, 376 (1895).

P.151, 1.31   Richard, "Private Confession and Private Absolution in the Lutheran Church," 26 *Luth. Quar.* 336 (1896).

P.152, 1.16   1 LEA, *op. cit. supra* at 515; Cowell, "Confession: Its

Scientific and Medical Aspects," 34 *Contemporary Rev.* 717, 740 (1879).
P.152, l.20   Singmaster, *Confession*, 28 *Luth. Quar.* 334 (1898).
P.152, l.28   Springer, *Confession*, 7 *Luth. Quar.* 81, 82–3 (1877).
P. 153, l.20   BURR, *op. cit. supra* at 154, 199, 206.

Chapter 11

P.154, l.14   ALCOHOLICS ANONYMOUS, 59 (new and rev. ed. 1955).
P.154, l.19   *Id.* at 72–73.
P.155, l.15   TAYLOR, A SOBER FAITH: RELIGION AND ALCOHOLICS ANONYMOUS, 81–82 (1953).
P.155, l.27   ALCOHOLICS ANONYMOUS, 77.
P.155, l.31   *Id.* at 78.
P.155, l.34   *Id.* at 81.
P.156, l.4   *Id.* at 78–79.
P.156, l.8   *Id.* at 89–94.
P.157, l.11   At 17–18 (1954).

Chapter 12

P.158, l.8   THE CONFESSIONS OF ST. AUGUSTINE, bk. 2, chs. 1–4, 6, bk. 3, c. 1, bk. 4, c. 2, bk. 5, c. 8, bk. 6, chs. 13, 15, bk. 8, c. 7 (Pilkington transl. 1927).
P.159, l.9   THE CONFESSIONS OF JEAN-JACQUES ROSSEAU, 16–7, 31, 38, 67–8, 86–7, 90–1, 111, 119, 128–33, 171–2, 203, 212, 251–2, 261, 273, 278, 326, 331–2, 340, 354, 364, 367–8, 412, 456, 518, 543, 561–2, 617 (Modern Library 1945).
P.160, l.15   MEMOIRS OF CATHERINE THE GREAT, 247–250 (Katharine Anthony transl. 1927).
P.160, l.22   *Id.* at 324.
P.160, l.30   At 37, 74 (Modern Library).
P.160, l.34   HARRIS, MY LIFE (Frank Harris Publishing Co.); DUNCAN, MY LIFE, 182–183 (1933); DREISER, DAWN, 246–249, 268 (1931).
P.161, l.4   *Id.* at 307.
P.161, l.14   *Sat. Eve. Post*, Nov. 3, 1956, p. 23, Nov. 10, 1956, p. 38, Nov. 17, 1956, p. 44, Nov. 24, 1956, p. 36.
P.161, l.25   At 25–26, 121, 144–145, 169, 179–197, 369 (1953).
P.162, l.9   FRANK and BARRYMORE, TOO MUCH, TOO SOON, 11–13, 15, 18, 105, 109–110, 269–270, 315 (1957).

P.162, l.18   TOLSTOY, A CONFESSION AND WHAT I BELIEVE, 9 (Aylmer Maude transl. 1921).

P.162, l.24   THE LIFE OF BENVENUTO CELLINI bk. 1, chs. 29, 30, 32, 33, 43, 51, 59, 73, 79, 115, bk. 2, chs. 4, 29, 30, 33–5.

P.162, l.33   FRAGMENT OF A GREAT CONFESSION, 295, 386, 422, 493 (1949).

P.166, l.19   SCHWARTZ, HOW TO WRITE CONFESSIONAL STORIES, 36–41 (1937).

P.166, l.25   COLLETT, WRITING THE CONFESSION STORY (1951).

P.166, l.29   Glay, "True Life Stories," *The Writer*, June 1956, pp. 164, 165.

P.167, l.23   See BUDENZ, THIS IS MY STORY 235 (1947); "The Communist Party of the United States of America," S. DOC. No. 117, 84th Cong., 2d Sess. 25–29 (1956); Richard and Gladys Harkness, "How About Those Security Cases," *Reader's Digest*, Sept. 1955, pp. 202, 213–214.

Chapter 13

P.168, l.16   At 314, 410 (Constance Garnett transl. 1928).

P.168, l.19   Bk. 11, c. 8, bk. 12, c. 5, pp. 834–835 (Constance Garnett transl. Illustrated Modern Library).

P.170, l.20   SIMMONS, LEO TOLSTOY, 417 (1946).

P.170, l.35   At 182 (Malamuth transl. 1933). It was also translated by William Henry and Sonya Chamberlain. 26 ASIA 768–775, 818–822, 890–898, 912–915, 988–994, 1002–1008 (1926).

P.171, l.17   *Id.* at 254–255.

P.171, l.29   At 30 (Constance Garnett transl. Harrison 1931).

P.172, l.28   This story exists in two translations: ZOSHCHENKO, THE WONDERFUL DOG, 1–4 (Fen transl. 2d ed. 1942); RUSSIA LAUGHS, 72–75 (Helena Clayton transl. 1935) (*Dog Scent*).

P.173, l.7   2 Samuel 1.

P.173, l.9   1 Samuel 31.

P.173, l.21   Luke 15:20–24.

Chapter 14

P.175, l.7   7 AM. ST. TR., 395 (1830).

P.175, l.20   "Confession and Absolution," 93 *Sat. Rev.* 421, 422 (1902).

P.176, l.32   7 SPEDDING, THE LETTERS AND THE LIFE OF FRANCIS BACON, 243, 252, 262 (1874).

P.177, l.14 EDDOWES, THE MAN ON YOUR CONSCIENCE 203 (1955); SARGANT, BATTLE FOR THE MIND, 200–208 (1957); Gilmour, "Evans or Christie?" 195 *Spectator* 270 (Aug. 26, 1955).

P.177, l.30 *N.Y. Times*, Jan. 22, 1957, p. 1, col. 1, Jan. 23, 1957, p. 1, cols. 5–8.

P.177, l.34 *N.Y. Times*, Sept. 11, 1958, p. 1, cols. 2–3.

P.178, l.9 *N.Y. Times*, Sept. 19, 1958, p. 54, cols. 5–6.

P.178, l.20 *N.Y. Times*, Sept. 25, 1958, p. 11, col. 2.

P.178, l.25 See their SEXUAL BEHAVIOR IN THE HUMAN FEMALE (1953); SEXUAL BEHAVIOR IN THE HUMAN MALE (1948).

P.178, l.36 DEAR THEO 122–130, 230–233, 238–239, 273–279, 489, 496 (Stone ed. 1937).

P.179, l.19 THE CANTERBURY TALES, "The Prioress' Tale," line 1766.

P.179, l.21 HAMLET, Act 2, sc. 2, 1.630.

P.179, l.22 DON QUIXOTE, pt. 1, bk. 3, c. 8.

P.179, l.32 REIK, THE UNKNOWN MURDERER 22, 62–63 (Dr. Katherine Jones transl. 1945).

P.179, l.36 Simmel, "Incendiarism" in SEARCHLIGHTS ON DELINQUENCY 95–96 (dedicated to Professor August Aichhorn 1949).

P.180, l.5 MOYLAN, SCOTLAND YARD, app. 1, pp. 295–313 (1929).

P.180, l.29 At 157 (Constance Garnett transl. 1928).

P.180, l.31 *Id.* at 66.

P.181, l.21 REIK, *op. cit. supra* at 117–121.

P.181, l.35 POPOFF, THE TCHEKA 70, 91–92 (1925). This book contains a highly sensationalized account of the author's experiences, and the statements in it must be viewed with caution. However, those cited in the text have the ring of truth.

P.182, l.8 In THE CASE BOOK OF A MEDICAL PSYCHOLOGIST, 84–92 (1948).

P.182, l.17 CURTIS, A HISTORY OF CREEDS AND CONFESSIONS OF FAITH (1911); GIBSON, THE THREE CREEDS (1908); A HANDBOOK OF MARXISM, 21–59 (Burns ed. 1935); Muller, "The History of the Apostles' and Nicene Creeds," in CREEDS AND LOYALTIES, 3–22 (1924).

Chapter 15

P.187, l.4 *N.Y. Times*, June 5, 1956, p. 14, col. 8.

P.187, l.5 *N.Y. Times*, Oct. 7, 1956, p. 1, cols. 7–8.

P.187, l.24   At 271–272 (1941).

P.187, l.26   See, *e.g.*, U.N. General Assembly, Off. Rec., Sess. 4, Sept. 20–Dec. 10, 1949, Committee Meetings, Political Resolutions 67, 272 (Oct. 12, 1949).

P.188, l.2   REPORT OF COURT PROCEEDINGS—THE CASE OF THE TROTSKYITE-ZINOVIEVITE TERRORIST CENTRE 98–100 (Moscow 1936).

P.188, l.3   See THE CASE OF LEON TROTSKY 167–173 (1937).

P.188, l.6   REPORT OF COURT PROCEEDINGS IN THE CASE OF THE ANTI-SOVIET TROTSKYITE CENTRE, 56–60 (Moscow 1937).

P.188, l.8   See THE CASE OF LEON TROTSKY, 212–214.

P.189, l.9   THE TRIAL OF TRAICHO KOSTOV AND HIS GROUP, 14 (Sofia 1949).

P.189, l.21   Speech at the opening of the Yugoslav National Assembly, April 26, 1950, *Yugoslav Fortnightly,* Belgrade, May 5, 1950.

P.189, l.35   REPORT OF THE COURT PROCEEDINGS IN THE CASE OF THE ANTI-SOVIET "BLOC OF RIGHTS AND TROTSKYITES," 260–261, 285–286, 630 (Moscow 1938). Krestinsky at first resisted Vyshinsky in the matter of the initial date of his alleged espionage connections with the Reichswehr. Vyshinsky charged that it was in 1920–21. In his speech for the prosecution he stated that Krestinsky admitted that he conducted negotiations with the Reichswehr as far back as 1920–21. At 659. Krestinsky in his final plea did not object.

In these three trials the alleged beginnings of criminal courses of conduct became increasingly earlier in the charges and confessions. In the first trial, Vyshinsky still spoke about the defendants as "these people who were once in our ranks, although they were never distinguished for either staunchness or loyalty to the cause of socialism." At 163. In the third trial he alleged that some of the defendants had betrayed their associates as far back as the early years of the regime and even czarist times. At 7–8.

P.190, l.2   At 259, 630.

P.190, l.3   At 200.

P.190, l.5   At 288–289, 299–308, 630.

P.190, l.7   At 90–100.

P.190, l.8   At 630.

P.190, l.11   At 571, 576–577, 630.

P.190, l.19   At 371, 377–378.

P.190, l.26   LASZLO RAJK AND HIS ACCOMPLICES BEFORE THE PEOPLE'S COURT, 8, 31, 33–81, 257 (Budapest 1949).

P.190, l.31   DEUTSCHER, STALIN: A POLITICAL BIOGRAPHY, 372 (1949).

P.191, l.5   ARMSTRONG, TITO AND GOLIATH, 246 (1951).

P.191, l.19   BECK and GODIN, RUSSIAN PURGE AND THE EX-
TRACTION OF CONFESSION, 113 (1951).

P. 191, l.30   *N.Y. Times,* June 5, 1956, p. 14, col. 8.

P.192, l.31   See *N.Y. Times,* March 30, 1956, p. 1, col. 8, Oct. 7,
1956, p. 1, cols. 7–8, Oct. 14, 1956, p. 1, col. 5.

P.193, l.8   *N.Y. Times,* June 9, 1958, p. 1, col. 5.

P.193, l.17   *N.Y. Times,* June 5, 1956, p. 14, col. 8.

P.193, l.25   See WEISSBERG, THE ACCUSED 408–435 (Edward
Fitzgerald transl. 1951); BECK and GODIN, RUSSIAN PURGE
AND THE EXTRACTION OF CONFESSION, 40, 52, 54
(1951). WEISSBERG'S book was published in Great Britain
under the title CONSPIRACY OF SILENCE (1952).

P.193, l.32   At 36.

P.193, l.33   At 155–158.

P.194, l.7   *Op. cit. supra* at 432.

P.194, l.15   *Ibid.* See also ORLOFF, THE SECRET HISTORY OF
STALIN'S CRIMES (1953). Orloff was a former member of the
NKVD.

P.194, l.21   *N.Y. Times,* June 5, 1956, p. 15, col. 8.

P.194, l.25   See WEISSBERG, THE ACCUSED 408–411 (1951);
N.Y. Times, June 5, 1956, p. 14, col. 8, p. 15, col. 1. According
to Khrushchev, Stalin later attributed this order to the Central
Committee:

"When the wave of mass arrests began to recede in 1939, and the
leaders of territorial party organizations began to accuse the N. K.
V. D. workers of using methods of physical pressure on the arrested,
Stalin dispatched a coded telegram Jan. 20, 1939, to the committee
secretaries of oblasts and krais, to the Central Committees of republic
Communist parties, to the Peoples Commissars of Internal Affairs
and to the heads of N. K. V. D. organizations. This telegram stated:

'The Central Committee of the All-Union Communist party (Bolsheviks) explains that the application of methods of physical pressure
in N. K. V. D. practice is permissible from 1937 on in accordance
with permission of the Central Committee of the All-Union Communist
party (Bolsheviks). It is known that all bourgeois intelligence services
use methods of physical influence against the representatives of the
Socialist proletariat and that they use them in their most scandalous
forms.

'The question arises as to why the Socialist intelligence service should
be more humanitarian against the mad agents of the bourgeoisie,
against the deadly enemies of the working class and of the collective
farm workers. The Central Committee of the All-Union Communist
party (Bolsheviks) consider that physical pressure should still be used
obligatorily, as an exception applicable to known and obstinate enemies
of the people, as a method both justifiable and appropriate.

"Thus, Stalin had sanctioned in the name of the Central Committee of the All-Union Communist party (Bolsheviks) the most brutal violation of Socialist legality, torture and oppression, which led as we have seen to the slandering and self-accusation of innocent people."

P.194, l.30   *N.Y. Times,* July 2; 1957, p. 3, col. 1, Sept. 17, 1957, p. 17, col. 4, Nov. 12, 1957, p. 1, col. 7.

P.194, l.36   Bain, "Cardinal Mindszenty Tells How He Was Tortured," *Look,* Dec. 25, 1956, pp. 21, 24.

P.195, l.1   *Evening Star,* Wash., D.C., Nov. 14, 1951, p. A–24.

P.195, l.3   *N.Y. Herald Tribune,* June 12, 1952, p. 9, col. 8..

P.195, l.7   *N.Y. Times,* March 23, 1958, p. 20, cols. 4–5, June 23, 1957, p. 2, cols. 3–5.

P.195, l.16   Dinerstein, "Purges in the Soviet Union and the Satellites," 5 (The Rand Corporation, p. 421, Aug. 3, 1953).

P.195, l.20   *N.Y. Times,* Sept. 13, 1953, p. 46, col. 6.

P.195, l.29   THE REVOLT 8 (1951).

P.195, l.32   *N.Y. Times,* Aug. 19, 1953, p. 14, cols. 3–5.

P.196, l.9   "What Is Brain-Washing?" 70 *Christian Century,* 104, 105 (1953).

P.196, l.16   *N.Y. Times,* June 23, 1957, p. 2, cols. 3–5.

P.196, l.28   "Were They Really 'Brainwashed'?" *Look,* June 26, 1956, pp. 101, 102.

P.197, l.2   *N.Y. Times,* Nov. 19, 1957, p. 11, cols. 1–2.

P.197, l.7   *N.Y. Times,* Aug. 12, 1956, p. 19, col. 1.

P.197, l.15   *N.Y. Times,* Nov. 14, 1956, p. 18, cols. 4–5.

P.197, l.25   "Communist Interrogation and Indoctrination of 'Enemies of the State'," 76 *Archives of Neurology and Psychiatry,* 115, 155 (1956).

P.197, l.33   "Communist Interrogation, Indoctrination and Exploitation of American Military and Civilian Prisoners, Hearings Before the Permanent Subcommittee on Investigations," 84th Cong., 2d Sess. 56 (1956).

P.198, l.2   *Id.* at 58.

P.198, l.11   *Id.* at 81. See also pp. 99, 101, 119, 120, 146, 207.

P.198, l.27   *Op. cit. supra* at 135.

P.198, l.32   ESMEIN, HISTOIRE DE LA PROCÉDURE CRIMINELLE EN FRANCE, translated in 5 CONTINENTAL LEGAL HISTORY SERIES, ch. 5 (1913).

P.199, l.13   See BERMAN, JUSTICE IN RUSSIA, 82 (1950).

P.200, l.35   *N.Y. Times,* Dec. 10, 1952, p. 34, cols. 2–3.

P.201, l.20   *N.Y. Times,* June 5, 1956, p. 15, col. 8.

P.201, l.32   As quoted in Ploscowe, "The Investigating Magistrate" (Juge D'Instruction) in "European Criminal Procedure," 33 *Mich. L. Rev.* 1010, 1016 (1935).

P.202, l.9   A release of July 4, 1951, *N.Y. Times,* July 5, 1951, p. 16, col. 3.

P.202, l.13   As quoted in *N.Y. Times,* July 4, 1951, p. 8, col. 6. See also the statement of the Associated Press of July 4, 1951, as quoted in *N.Y. Times,* July 5, 1951, p. 16, col. 4: "Even with the callous disregard of fundàmental honesty and equity which marked the procedure, the Czech Government produced evidence which showed only that Oatis was engaged in the legitimate pursuit of news gathering as free people understand it."

P.202, l.21   See *N.Y. Times,* July 2, 1951, p. 7, col. 3.

P.202, l.30   *N.Y. Times,* July 3, 1951, p. 6, col. 2.

P.202, l.35   Of course a number of exceptional individuals held out, or if they did finally yield and give confessions, retracted them. Stypulkowski was one of those who held out. So was Elizabeth Lermolo. See her FACE OF A VICTIM (Talmadge transl. 1955). Stypulkowski was subjected to 141 protracted interrogations, and dragged out of bed for them on 70 nights out of 71. See his INVITATION TO MOSCOW, 268–306 (1951). Yet he did not give in. Petkov held out, and before him, for a long time, one of his chief lieutenants, Peter Koev. Koev finally confessed, but before he did so he prepared a statement that any confession he gave would not be his or the result of his free will. Petkov read this statement in parliament. W. H. Lawrence, "Why Do They Confess?—A Russian Enigma," *N.Y. Times,* May 8, 1949, §6, p. 7. Monkhouse also held out, but he was subjected only to a single interrogation. However, it continued uninterruptedly from breakfasttime until two o'clock the following morning. See his MOSCOW 1911–1933 at 295–296 (1933). The communists had not yet intensified their inquisitional technique to the point that it reached in later years. Kostov, although he gave a confession, at his trial repudiated it.

Likewise, not all communists submitted to the practice of so-called self-criticism. American communist Earl Browder and French communists André Marty and Charles Tillon were examples. One of Browder's comrades, Gilbert Green, communist party chairman for Illinois and later one of those convicted in the first Foley Square Smith Act case, in an attempt to persuade him to "confess whatever sins" had been imputed to him suggested that he read CHOCOLATE. According to an account which Browder later wrote: "Away back in the days of June, 1945 . . . it was none other than Gilbert Green himself, who, having taken the road of confession, gently advised me to read the novel *Chocolate* as the best guide for one in my situation. I had read that book long before, and had decided that it was one of the most poisonous pieces of literature ever written. . . ." MODERN RESURRECTIONS & MIRACLES, 44–45 (1950).

In witchcraft days Urbain Grandier of Loudon refused to confess and Giles Corey of Salem refused to plead.

P.203, l.13   *N.Y. Times*, Sept. 23, 1953, p. 17, col. 1.

P.204, l.12   THE TRIAL OF NIKOLA D. PETKOV, RECORD OF JUDICIAL PROCEEDINGS, 461–462 (Ministry of Information and Arts, Sofia, 1947).

P.204, l.20   Vol. 1 at 566 (Chetwynd's ed.).

P.240, l.24   1 EVIDENCE, *73 (10th Am. ed. 1876).

P.204, l.25   2 LEACH, 629 (3d. ed.).

P.204, l.34   Williams v. Williams, 1 Hagg. Cons. 299, 304 (1798).

P.204, l.36   Mortimer v. Mortimer, 2 Hagg. Cons. 310, 315 (1820).

P.205, l.9   332 U.S. 596 (1948).

P.205, l.20   United States v. Carignan, 342 U.S. 36, 46 (1951).

P.205, l.30   332 U.S. at 603, 606. In a yet more recent case, Fikes v. Alabama, 352 U.S. 191 (1957), Mr. Justice Frankfurter, in a concurring opinion in which Mr. Justice Brennan joined, reasoned:"* * * It is, I assume, common ground that if this record had disclosed an admission by the police of one truncheon blow on the head of petitioner a confession following such a blow would be inadmissible because of the Due Process Clause. For myself, I cannot see the difference, with respect to the 'voluntariness' of a confession, between the subversion of freedom of the will through physical punishment and the sapping of the will appropriately to be inferred from the circumstances of this case— detention of the accused virtually incommunicado for a long period; failure to arraign in that period; horse-shedding of the accused at the intermittent pleasure of the police until confession was forthcoming. * * *" At 198–199.

P.205, l.34   United States ex rel. *Caminito v. Murphy*, 222 F.2d 698, 701 (2d. Cir.), *cert. denied*, 350 U.S. 896 (1955). *Cf.* Brock v. United States, 223 F.2d 681, 685 (5th Cir. 1955).

P.206, l.3   People v. Quan Gim Gow, 23 Cal. App. 507, 511, 138 Pac. 918, 919 (1913).

Chapter 16

P.209, l.11   Maxim 1060 (Darius Lyman transl. 1856).

P.209, l.14   As quoted in REIK, FRAGMENT OF A GREAT CONFESSION, 45 (1949).

P.209, l.17   At 131–132 (1949).

P.210, l.12   "Communist Interrogation and Indoctrination of 'Enemies of the State'," 76 *Archives of Neurology and Psychiatry*, 115, 116 (1956).

P.210, l.21   *Id.* at 141, 162.

P.210, l.24 Communist Interrogation, Indoctrination and Exploitation of American Military and Civilian Prisoners, Hearings Before the Permanent Subcommittee on Investigations, 84th Cong., 2d Sess. 30 (1956).

P.210, l.26 See BURR, RELIGIOUS CONFESSIONS AND CONFESSANTS, 254–267 (1914); 1 LEA, A HISTORY OF AURICULAR CONFESSIONS AND INDULGENCES, 238 (1896); PETTAZZONI, "Confession of Sins in Hittite Religion," in OCCIDENT AND ORIENT (Gaster Anniversary Volume 1936); 2 REINACH, CULTES, MYTHES ET RELIGIONS 75–84 (1905–12); REINACH, "L'Idée de Péché Original," in ANNALES DU MUSEE GUIMET, tome 29, pp. 245–278 (1908); REINACH, ORPHEUS, A HISTORY OF RELIGION, 82 (Florence Simmonds transl. 1930); SMITH, MAN AND HIS GODS, 234–235 (1952).

P.211, l.11 PHRIXUS, fragment 970 (Morris Hicky Morgan transl.).

P.211, l.14 2 REINACH, CULTES, MYTHES ET RELIGION, 76 (1905–12).

P.211, l.21 FREUD in TOTEM AND TABOO, 132–161 (James Strachey transl. 1952), propounded the theory that the original sin was patricide. His theory was an elaboration of the findings and ideas of Charles R. Darwin, J. J. Atkinson, William Robertson Smith and J. G. Frazer.

P.211, l.32 NATURAL CAUSES AND SUPERNATURAL SEEMINGS, 234 (1887).

P.211, l.35 GRACE ABOUNDING TO THE CHIEF OF SINNERS, para. 104.

P.212, l.16 Bk. 1, c. 7 (Pilkington transl. 1927).

P.213, l.3 *Op. cit. supra* at 29.

P.213, l.8 *Op. cit. supra* at 163.

P.213, l.21 *Op. cit. supra* at 163.

P.213, l.29 At 245–248 (1955).

P.214, l.5 GESTÄNDNISZWANG UND STRAFBEDÜRFNIS (1925).

P.214, l.17 *Newsweek,* Dec. 10, 1956, pp. 116, 117. She later wrote a book about her experiences. 7 YEARS' SOLITARY (1957). Her introduction she entitled "I Was Born a Rebel."

P.215, l.2 See SMITH, MAN AND HIS GODS, 210–211, 263–264, 382 (1952); REIK, MASOCHISM IN MODERN MAN, 78, 353–357, 414–415 (1941).

P.216, l.13 In March 1823 Margaret Peter of Wildisbuch, Switzerland, in a religious frenzy helped beat her sister Elizabeth to death, and then had herself physically crucified. Schroeder, *The Wildisbuch Crucified Saint,* 1 PSYCHOANALYTIC REV. 129 (1914). Dr. Reik in his MASOCHISM IN MODERN MAN (1941) pointed

out that masochism and the wearing of sackcloth and ashes involve
the further idea of one's own ultimate victory and exaltation. Out of
one's own self-defeat will come one's own ultimate victory. The greater
one's self-defeat and self-humiliation the greater one's victory and
triumph. The Via Dolorosa becomes a triumphal road. One takes one's
place at the right hand of Jesus. Indeed Jesus himself took God, the
Father's place. The idea that one's self-abasement will lead to one's
exaltation occurs repeatedly in the New Testament: Luke 14:11:
"For whosoever exalteth himself shall be abased; and he that humbleth
himself shall be exalted"; Matthew 19:30: "But many that are first
shall be last; and the last shall be first." The publican who stood afar
off and said, God be merciful to me a sinner, without as much as lift-
ing up his eyes, would be exalted for he humbled himself. The early
Christians took the hint. St. Patrick declared: "I, Patrick, a sinner,
the rudest and least of all the faithful, and most contemptible to very
many." BURR, RELIGIOUS CONFESSIONS AND CONFESSANTS
60 (1914). The habitual pronouncement of the pious is that we are all
miserable sinners. But one can be sure that they all secretly expect
to sit beside Jesus.

P.216, l.34 "The Accident-Prone Individual," 39 *Amer. Jour. of
Public Health,* 1036 (1949).

P.217, l.5 Alexander, "The Accident-Prone Individual," 64 U.S.
PUBLIC HEALTH REP. 357 (1949).

P.217, l.11 *Id.* at 358.

P.217, l.18 Ch. 9:1.

P.217, l.19 Daniel 9:3–4.

P.217, l.24 Luke 18:13.

P.217, l.25 DE PROFUNDIS, 78 (1949).

P.219, l.23 CONFESSIONS, bk. 10, ch. 30–37.

P.220, l.3 SMITH, MAN AND HIS GODS, 261–262.

P.220, l.4 See PERRY, PURITANISM AND DEMOCRACY, 190–
256 (1944); SMITH, MAN AND HIS GODS, 377–380.

P.220, l.28 PERRY, *op. cit. supra* at 256.

P.221, l.2 1 HISTORY OF ENGLAND FROM THE ACCESSION
OF JAMES II, 129 (Everyman's Library).

P.221, l.4 "Clinical Notes," *American Mercury,* Jan. 1925, p. 59.

P.221, l.18 N.Y. PENAL LAW, §§2145–52, as amended, and
§2154.

P.221, l.21 People v. Dunford, 207 N.Y. 17, 21, 100 N.E. 433,
434 (1912).

P.221, l.28 18 PA. STAT. ANN. §4699.4 (Purdon's 1945) ("Who-
ever does or performs any worldly employment or business whatsoever on the Lord's day, commonly called Sunday (works of
necessity and charity only excepted) . . . shall, upon conviction
thereof . . . be sentenced to pay a fine of four dollars . . . or in

default of the payment thereof, shall suffer six (6) days' imprisonment.").

P.221, l.30   4 PA. STAT. ANN. §60 (Purdon's) (1957 Supp.).

P.221, l.32   Commonwealth v. Grochowiak, 184 Pa. Super. 522, 136 A.2d 145, *appeal dismissed*, 27 U.S. *Law Week* 3110 (Oct. 13, 1958). Yet another case involving the constitutionality of a Sunday blue law, this time of Ohio, was appealed to the federal Supreme Court in 1958. State v. Kidd, 167 Ohio St. 521, 150 N.E. 2d 413, *appeal dismissed*, 27 U.S.L. WEEK 3175 (Dec. 8, 1958).

P.22.1, l.32   N.J. Laws 1958, c. 138. The act may well be invalid because it excludes from its operation Atlantic, Cape May and Ocean Counties. Governor Meyner signed the measure but indicated that he questioned this exclusion as well as several other provisions. He signed it because he said he believed it to be in the best interests of the state to do so. However, he called upon the legislature to act promptly to correct the defects contained in the law.

The previous statute contained no penalty. See Auto-Rite Supply Co. v. Woodbridge Twp., 25 N.J. 188, 195, 135 A.2d 515, 518 (1957).

P.221, l.36   The New Jersey Supreme Court voided the ordinances of Woodbridge Township and South Orange because they permitted the sale of certain items which the statute forbade. Auto-Rite Supply Co. v. Woodbridge Twp., 25 N.J. 188, 135 A.2d 515 (1957), *affirming* 41 N.J. Super. 303, 124 A.2d 612 (1956). The New Jersey statute there considered forbade all "worldly employment or business, except works of necessity and charity." N.J. STAT. ANN. 2A:171-1.

P.222, l.17   ROYAL BOB: THE LIFE OF ROBERT G. INGERSOLL, 22–23 (1952).

P.222, l.20   Jacobs, *The Confessional Principle and the Confessions*, 11 *Lutheran Quar.*, 14, 19–20 (1881).

P.222, l.27   *N.Y. Times*, Oct. 7, 1958, p. 6, col. 4.

P.222, l.33   TOTEM AND TABOO, 85–90 (James Strachey transl. 1952).

P.222, l.35   2 JONES, THE LIFE AND WORK OF SIGMUND FREUD, 266 (1955).

P.223, l.10   THE CASE BOOK OF A MEDICAL PSYCHOLOGIST, 247–248 (1948).

P.223, l.12   A human being from the standpoint of the operations of his mind has been called an idiot genius. Sillman, "The Genesis of Man," 34 International Jour. of Psycho-Analysis, 146 (1953). He is a genius in his perception of the external world of things. He is a near idiot in his perception of his own motivations and those of others. As James H. Breasted succinctly put it ". . . man is morally still a mere child playing in a nursery full of the most dangerous toys. . . ." THE DAWN OF CONSCIENCE, 406 (1933).

P.223, l.33   See his 1 CULTES, MYTHES ET RELIGIONS, 125–136; FREUD, TOTEM AND TABOO 90–91.

P.224, l.17   THE PEOPLE OF THE POLAR NORTH, 124 (1908).

P.224, l.22   People v. Johnson, 2 Wheeler's Cr. C. 361, 378 (N.Y. 1824).

P.225, l.3   CIVILIZATION AND ITS DISCONTENTS 107 (Riviere transl. 1930). Dr. Ernest Jones, Freud's biographer, in discussing the latter's CIVILIZATION AND ITS DISCONTENTS, thus summarized Freud's views:

"The most characteristic way of dealing with this matter of aggression is to internalize it into a part of the self called the super-ego or conscience. This then exercises the same propensity to harsh aggressiveness against the ego that the ego would have liked to exercise against others. The tension between the two constitutes what is called the sense of guilt. A sense of guilt begins, not from an inborn sense of sin, but from the fear of losing love. In adult life this may be called 'social anxiety,' fear of public opinion. Many people are prepared to do 'wicked' things so long as they are sure they will not be found out, but when the super-ego is firmly established, then fear of its disapproval becomes stronger than fear of other people's disapproval. Mere renunciation of a forbidden act no longer absolves the conscience, as saints well know, because the wish still persists. On the contrary, privation, and, even more, misfortune intensifies the sense of guilt because it is felt to be a deserved punishment ('sackcloth and ashes' was the ancient answer to misfortune). At this point Freud put forward the novel idea that the sense of guilt is *specifically* the response to repressed aggressiveness. Since it is to a large extent unconscious its manifest expression is a feeling of uneasiness, of general discontent or unhappiness." 3 THE LIFE AND WORK OF SIGMUND FREUD, 341–342 (1957).

P.225, l.8   *Op. cit. supra* at 107.

P.225, l.19   Matthew 9:2.

P.225, l.24   *N.Y. Times,* May 27, 1956, p. 27, col. 1.

P.225, l.26   Curiously enough, the ones who seemed to end up with the most love were the ones who were the biggest sinners. The best example of this was the story of the prodigal son.

P.226, l.21   At 133 (1956).

P.226, l.31   At 293 (1956).

P.227, l.35   WIGMORE, THE SCIENCE OF JUDICIAL PROOF, 629–630 (3d ed. 1937).

P.228, l.13   CONFESSIONS, bk. 2, ch. 2.

P.228, l.30   O'Brien, "Psychiatry and the Confessional," 98 *Ecclesiastical Rev.* 223, 231. (1938).

P.229, l.1   *Op. cit. supra* at 233.

P.229, l.10   TOTEM AND TABOO, 154 n. 1.

P.230, l.29   At 50–55 (Constance Garnett transl. 1928).

P.231, l.36   At 834–835 (Constance Garnett transl., The Illustrated Modern Library 1943).

P.232, l.3   At 870.

P.232, l.17   As quoted in CRANKSHAW, RUSSIA AND THE RUSSIANS 50 (1948).

P.233, l.17   See, *e.g.*, ECKHARDT, IVAN THE TERRIBLE (Catherine Alison Phillips transl. 1949).

P.233, l.35   At 66 (James Strachey transl. 1952).

P.234, l.22   LETTERS OF ANTON CHEKHOV TO HIS FAMILY AND FRIENDS, 113 (Garnett transl. 1920).

P.234, l.34   At 457 (Max Hayward and Manya Harari transl. 1958).

P.235, l.14   At 181.

P.235, l.30   Quoted in MEAD, SOVIET ATTITUDES TOWARD AUTHORITY, 93 (1951).

P.236, l.19   WALKER, CHINA UNDER COMMUNISM, 58 (1955).

P.236, l.35   At 720.

P.237, l.8   Dr. Reik wrote: "The proselytizers have both homosexual and rebellious instincts. They strive to unite all the brothers. But it cannot be completely concealed that even this all-embracing love for God is essentially nothing but a reaction to extreme rebellious impulses. The eagerness to convert derives from these repressed aggressive impulses." FROM THIRTY YEARS WITH FREUD, 151–152 (Winston transl. 1940).

P.237, l.32   Act 2, sc. 2.

P.238, l.1   For a psychoanalytic interpretation see Bonnard, "The Metapsychology of the Russian Trials Confessions," 35 *International Jour. of Psycho-Analysis,* 208 (1954).

P.238, l.22   6 WORKS 105 (20th ed. 1890).

P.238, l.29   LAMIA, sc. 7.

P.238, l.30   Act 3, sc. 1.

P.239, l.2   29 THE CHINESE RECORDER, 240 (1898).

P.239, l.7   *Op. cit. supra* at 55. Because the mind is a divided substance human beings can change from antagonist to protagonist. They can turn from one position to its opposite. Saul of Tarsus, who became St. Paul, turned from persecutor of the Christians to a proselytizer for them. St. Augustine, the bishop of Hippo, gave up the satisfaction of earthly pleasures and became an ascetic. Gautama, known after his conversion as the Buddha (=the enlightened), put behind him a life of luxury and became a wandering monk. Budenz went from Catholicism to Communism and back again. Benito Mussolini changed from socialism to fascism, and Pierre Laval from socialism to collaboration with the Nazis.

P.239,1.25   Riviere, "The Unconscious Phantasy of an Inner World Reflected in Examples from English Literature," 33 *International Jour. of Psycho-Analysis* 160, 170 (1952).

P.239,1.27   At 283.

P.239,1.33   No. 88 (Fitzgerald transl. 5th ed.).

P.240,1.15   LYS, A TREASURY OF AMERICAN SUPERSTITIONS (1948).

P.241,1.9   "Pre-Animistic Religion," 11 Folk-Lore 162 (1900). See also FREUD, TOTEM AND TABOO 91.

P.241,1.15   THE USES OF THE PAST, 45 (1952).

P.241,1.22   For further material on the mind and its ways see AICHHORN, WAYWARD YOUTH (1935); BARUCH, ONE LITTLE BOY (1952); BERG, PSYCHOTHERAPY (1948); Bergler, "Is Psychic Masochism an Oversimplification?" 9 *American Imago,* 79 (1952); Desmond, "Psycho-Analysis and Legal Origins," 34 *International Jour. of Psycho-Analysis,* 52 (1953); Eliasberg, "He Murdered to Get Hanged," 39 *Psychoanalytic Rev.* 164 (1952); Evans, "Early Anxiety Situations in the Analysis of a Boy in the Latency Period," 33 *International Jour. of Psycho-Analysis* 93 (1952); Freud, "The Economic Problem in Masochism," in 2 COLLECTED PAPERS, 255 (1950); Hart, "Displacement Guilt and Pain," 34 *Psychoanalytic Rev.* 259 (1947); Hart, "Masochism, Passivity and Radicalism," 39 *Psychoanalytic Rev.* 309 (1952); Johnson, "Some Etiological Aspects of Repression, Guilt and Hostility," 20 *Psychoanalytic Quar.* 511 (1951); Jones, "Fear, Guilt and Hate," 10 *International Jour. of Psycho-Analysis,* 383 (1929); Keiser, "The Fear of Sexual Passivity in the Masochist," 30 *International Jour. of Psycho-Analysis* 162 (1949); Moloney, "Mother, God, and Superego," 2 *Jour. of the Amer. Psychoanalytic Ass'n.,* 120 (1954).

P.242,1.31   THE REVOLT 8 (1951).

P.243,1.18   Augustin Nicholas, president of the Parlement of Dijon, wrote in 1682, as quoted in ESMEIN, *op. cit. supra:* "The Spanish vigil, which compels a man to keep himself suspended in the air for a space of seven hours, so that he may not lean upon a sharpened iron which would puncture him in the rear . . ." At 356.

P.243,1.27   Vol. 1, pt. 2, pp. 49, 58.

P.244,1.14   Record, p. 182.

P.244,1.20   2 WHITE, A HISTORY OF THE WARFARE OF SCIENCE WITH THEOLOGY 152 (1896); "The Warfare of Science With Theology," 18 *Medico-Legal Jour.* 91 (1900).

P.245,1.31   At 257.

P.246,1.17   At 258. In an earlier book, ANIMAL FARM, he also adverted to the problem of confessions in an authoritarian regime.

P.247,1.25   *N.Y. Times,* Aug. 18, 1955, p. 10, col. 8.

Index